ENDOR

Building off their book, *Renewing You: A Priest, A Psychologist, and a Plan*, Fr. Nicholas and Dr. Roxanne delve into the final hours of Christ's life, sharing with us seven life-giving principles that He shared from the Cross. These same principles provide a lifeline for us as we encounter the dark seasons of our own lives, providing the inspiration and practical steps we need to make it to the other side. Firmly rooted in solid theology and practical psychology, this is a must-read for every Christian.

—Deacon Michael Hyatt, New York Times bestselling author and creator of *The Full Focus Planner*

In a world that keeps getting louder with meaningless chatter, we need voices that stir the soul—voices that inspire us, move us, and point us to God. Father Nick and Dr. Roxanne unpack Jesus' seven statements from the Cross to deepen our love and invigorate our faith as we take them to heart. I wish I'd read this book years ago. It presents the key to unlock a life with more joy, peace, and spiritual maturity.

—Kari Kampakis, bestselling author of *Love Her Well* and host of the *Girl Mom Podcast*

Make no mistake, we will all face difficulty in this life. In *6 Hours, 7 Lessons*, the Louhs shed light on how Christ transcends our darkest moments in this enormously helpful and practical resource, which is rooted and grounded in the words of Christ before He surrenders His life to the Father. So read on and be equipped, edified, and encouraged.

—Hank Hanegraaff, president of the Christian Research Institute, host of the *Bible Answer Man* broadcast and the *Hank Unplugged* podcast, and author of numerous books, including *The Complete Bible Answer Book—Collector's Edition*, Revised & Expanded (2024)

Father Nick and Dr. Roxanne have provided for us in their newest book an insightful and meaningful journey into the last hours spent and last words shared from Jesus during His Crucifixion. You will find this book to be both profoundly reflective and highly applicable as we all strive to grow in our own faith and in our relationships with others.

—Tim Tassopoulos, President and COO, Chick-fil-A

Father Nicholas Louh and Dr. Roxanne Louh's new book marks a triumphant follow-up to their amazing book, *Renewing You*. The Louhs masterfully take the reader through Christ's last words as He was crucified and turn them into an instructional blueprint to help fortify us against the unremitting onslaught of pain, problems, and confusion that happen in life. The scope of this book reflects its authors: thoughtful, detail oriented, insightful, practical, Christ centered, passionate, and brimming with hope.

—ROBERT KRANTZ, actor, producer, and director of *Faith, Hope & Love* and *A Marriage Made in Heaven*

Father Nicholas and Dr. Roxanne Louh's lovely and powerful book , *6 Hours, 7 Lessons: How Christ's Light Transcends Our Darkness,* offers detailed and practical guidance for finding hope, healing, and abundant life through the crucified and resurrected Christ. The authors expertly draw from the deep and ancient well of Orthodox Christian theology and Tradition, together with the best of modern-day psychology and neuroscience. The result is a wise and gentle guide for the most important areas of spiritual life, including forgiveness, loneliness, repentance, and, above all, love. Put this book somewhere close to you and start reading!

—GEORGE STAVROS, Ph.D., executive director, The Danielsen Institute at Boston University

By exploring Christ's last hours on the Cross in *6 hours, 7 Lessons,* the Louhs have once again delivered a book that is captivating, insightful, and full of wisdom. This is not a book to read passively in bed before falling asleep at night. Rather, one should actively engage with it. With Fr. Nicholas and Dr. Roxanne as your guides, you can use this book to work through times of distress and challenge to emerge with closer relationships to Christ and those you love.

—RANDA K. ANDERSON, PH.D., Licensed Clinical Psychologist and president of Orthodox Christian Association of Medicine, Psychology and Religion (OCAMPR)

Father Nicholas and Dr. Roxanne have written yet another wonderfully creative book that weaves together a tapestry of scriptural guidance, life experiences, pastoral wisdom, and Orthodox theology in response to the unavoidable difficult times that accompany daily life. As a theologically grounded yet practically oriented work, this book can serve as both a personal guide and a catechetical reflection on Jesus' ministry and saving message.

—JAMES C. SKEDROS, Michael G. and Anastasia Cantonis Professor of Byzantine Studies at Hellenic College Holy Cross and lecturer on Greek at Harvard Divinity School

6 Hours, 7 Lessons

How Christ's Light
Transcends Our Darkness

Rev. Dr. Nicholas G. Louh

AND

Dr. Roxanne K. Louh

ANCIENT FAITH
PUBLISHING

CHESTERTON, INDIANA

PUBLISHED BY:
Ancient Faith Publishing
A Division of Ancient Faith Ministries
1050 Broadway, Suite 6
Chesterton, IN 46304

Unless otherwise indicated, all Scripture quotations are from the ESV® Bible
(The Holy Bible, English Standard Version®), copyright © 2001 by Cross-
way, a publishing ministry of Good News Publishers. Used by permission. All
rights reserved.

Cover design by Samuel Heble

ISBN: 978-1-955890-58-8

Library of Congress Control Number: 2023951227

Printed in the United States of America

IN LOVE, HONOR, AND APPRECIATION
OF OUR MOTHERS
Violette and Ronnie

TABLE OF CONTENTS

Meet Father Nick and
Dr. Roxanne Louh

THE REVEREND DR. Nicholas Louh was born in Jacksonville, Florida, and currently serves as the senior priest of St. John the Divine Greek Orthodox Church. After graduating from the University of North Florida, Rev. Louh entered Holy Cross Greek Orthodox School of Theology in Boston, Massachusetts. He earned both master of divinity and master of theology degrees, and he earned his doctorate of ministry, with an emphasis in pastoral counseling, from Gordon Conwell Theological Seminary.

Father Nicholas is a devoted pastor, motivational speaker, and compassionate champion for those in need, offering practical tools for applying faith to everyday life. He travels throughout the country, leading retreats and speaking about understanding and living out God's purpose for our lives. Reverend Louh is a council member of the Greek Orthodox Metropolis of Atlanta and serves as the communications chairperson for the Archdiocesan Council of the Greek Orthodox Archdiocese of America. He is also an adjunct professor of world religions at Florida State College at Jacksonville and serves on several local and state boards, including the interfaith organization OneJax and the YMCA.

Dr. Roxanne Louh, a native of Gainesville, is a licensed clinical psychologist in Jacksonville, Florida, where she uses her extensive training in private practice and in public speaking across the country to address a variety of concerns, including the integration of faith and psychology, mood disorders, anxiety disorders, marriage and parenting, eating disorders, and women's issues.

Dr. Louh graduated from the University of Florida with a bachelor of science degree in psychology and a minor in food science and human nutrition. She earned her master of science degree in clinical psychology from the University of Central Florida and both her master's degree and doctorate in clinical psychology from the Florida Institute of Technology. After a residency at Virginia Commonwealth University and the Medical College of Virginia, she worked in outpatient practice in clinical psychology at Baptist Medical Center in Jacksonville and served as the clinical director of psychological services in the Center's treatment program for eating disorders at Wolfson's Children's Hospital. She opened her own private practice in 2006.

Dr. Louh is a member of the American Psychological Association and continues to dedicate much of her time to community-wide presentations, reaching the public through various news media, social media, radio, educational talks, lectures, and blogs. She strongly believes in the prevention of mental health issues through education and awareness.

Together, Fr. Nicholas and Dr. Roxanne cohost a weekly radio show on Ancient Faith Radio, *Live with the Louhs*, on

Tuesday evenings. In addition, they publish daily inspirational messages through email and social media, available through their website at www.TheLouhs.com/Subscribe. Their first book, *Renewing You: A Priest, A Psychologist, and a Plan,* was released in October of 2020. The Louhs live in Jacksonville with their two children, George and Gabriella.

INTRODUCTION

L IFE IS PREDICTABLY unpredictable. We don't know
when suffering will come, but we know we will all suffer. We all experience dark seasons in our life when the
earth gives way beneath our feet and we feel we cannot go
on. Perhaps you have been praying for your child and worry
consumes your heart as you watch events unfold in their
life that you have no control over. Maybe there is strife and
division in your family, and you're exhausted from walking
on eggshells all the time. Maybe a health crisis has totally
blindsided you. Or the bitterness of unresolved hurt keeps
you up at night, burdened with negativity you can't seem to
shake. Christians know we can weather these storms if we are
anchored in Christ, but that does not mean the storms are
not terrifying and overwhelming.

If this speaks to you right now, then we want you to know
that you are not alone. Jesus Christ is not only with you in
the darkness, He has been through His own terrible darkness. He came through it and overcame death itself, and now
He offers us the hope of life eternal in Him. But He also
offers us His presence and guidance for the dark seasons we
will experience along the way. Christ's darkest moment was
His Crucifixion on the Cross, and the Gospels tell us that,
in the course of some six hours, He uttered seven statements.
You can imagine that if, in the darkest moment of His life,
when isolation and anguish consumed Him, He gathered up
the strength to say something to us, then those things must

be of great importance. In fact, those seven statements contain seven principles to live by when we face our own dark seasons. His words reveal lessons of hope, peace, and comfort. When we turn to those words, we find they have the power to bring us into the light of His love and protection no matter what suffering we face.

Christ could have come at any time, but out of His immense love for humanity, He chose to come during one of the most brutal eras in history. On that final Friday of His life, He experienced the pain of betrayal, desertion by His closest friends, and the brutality of death on the Cross. It started the evening before, when He was betrayed by one of His own disciples, Judas, who helped the soldiers arrest Jesus under cover of darkness. That led to late-night trials for crimes He hadn't committed. Then, He faced the savagery of the Roman cat-o'-nine-tails, a whip made of nine cords. At the tip of each was tied broken metal, glass, and rock that would not only bruise and lacerate the skin but rip Christ's body apart. The typical scourging involved whipping the right and left trapezius muscle thirteen times each, separating the shoulder from the neck. Soldiers would then typically whip thirteen more times down the center of the back, for a total of thirty-nine lashes. Numerous times they would use a rod to strike the inner thighs, some of the most sensitive skin on the body.

Then, the Roman soldiers placed a crown of thorns on His head, not only to mock Him but to create intense and excruciating pain in His head, neck, and face. And as if that wasn't enough, they then made Him carry the crude, splintery

125-pound Cross—His own instrument of death—out of the city and up a nearby hill, where they strung Him up by hammering six-inch nails into His wrists and feet. There He would hang while His broken chest collapsed upon His lungs, slowly asphyxiating Him. A small step by His feet would allow Him to push Himself up to get a little more air, scraping His back against the coarse wood, but eventually His strength would give out and He would suffocate to death. Crucifixion was never meant to be a quick death but rather a long, drawn-out form of torture that would horrify all those watching.

But who was watching? While Jesus hung there on the Cross, most of His trusted disciples and followers fled in fear of similar punishment or in horror and grief over what was happening. Earlier in the week, people had lined the streets to welcome Jesus to Jerusalem, proclaiming, "Hosanna," which means "save us," but now they were yelling and spitting, "Crucify Him, crucify Him." Only a small handful of people stayed with Him during the most terrible moment of His life. To say it was a dark season for Christ would be an understatement. Scripture records that even the sky turned dark: "There was darkness over the whole land" (Luke 23:44).

We often share that you can typically tell the value of something to someone by how much they are willing to pay for it. Obviously, death by crucifixion is a high price to pay, and it shows how much Christ values us and wants to save us. The Prophet Isaiah speaks of this in one of the most iconic Bible verses about the Cross when he says, "He was pierced for our transgressions; / he was crushed for our iniquities; /

upon him was the chastisement that brought us peace, / and with his wounds we are healed" (Is. 53:5). Tradition calls the final hours that took place in Christ's life "Good Friday." It was the day that ushered in our freedom—not from a foreign power but from our own sins. It was a day that paved the way to our rebirth from the "old man" to the "new man," freeing us to work toward fulfilling God's purpose for our lives. It was a terrible day for Jesus, but in the end, it was a "good" day for us. It is our contention in this book that Christ also did good for us in His dying breaths. If we can learn from the things He said as He faced His own death, we can receive comfort and grace in our own darkest hours.

Brief mention should be made regarding the recording of Christ's Passion on the Cross amongst the four evangelists. The synoptic Gospels (Matthew, Mark, and Luke) all record the Crucifixion as lasting for six hours (Matt. 27; Mark 15; Luke 23), while the Gospel of John differs in recording the duration of Christ's suffering on the Cross as only three hours. Much debate and discussion has taken place on this issue, and you're welcome to explore that on your own, but for the purposes of this book the duration of time is not important. We're interested in what Christ said while He hung on the Cross.

Now, there is also some debate as to the exact number of statements Jesus shared while He was on the Cross. As St. John writes, "There are also many other things that Jesus did. Were every one of them to be written, I suppose that the world itself could not contain the books that would be written" (John 21:25). And, indeed, intelligent Christians can even disagree about the specific order of the statements. We will follow the order established by Orthodox Tradition. Again, for our purposes, the number of hours or number or order of statements are not as material as what has been recorded and what we can learn from it. We believe that Christ was still teaching us by His life, even in the final hours of His life. With every breath He took, with the pain so unbearable, with His body broken for us and His blood shed for us, the things He believed were worth saying give us wisdom and direction to follow amidst our own difficult moments.

In our first book, *Renewing You: A Priest, A Psychologist, and A Plan*, we outlined eight of the greatest struggles we see people face throughout our ministries. We tried to touch on the major facets of life that could pose challenges to how well we live out our purpose. However, in our travels across the country doing retreats and presentations, we received a fair amount of feedback from people saying, "I really liked your book—I read it twice! But can you speak more on how to deal with the seasons of darkness and despair? How do I get through those seasons? How do I have hope when I'm feeling hopeless? How do I get through when the storms feel unyielding?" Well, we hope that in some small way this book can use Christ's darkest moments to shed light on how we do just that. If you are in a calm between the storms right now, may this book strengthen you and prepare you for the next storm. And if you are going through a dark valley and reach for this book, may it comfort and encourage you.

We wrote this book for all of you who feel these desperate Friday feelings, for the times when you are scared, angry, distressed, overwhelmed, hurt—and wondering where God is in it all. We know Sunday mornings feel like times to be cheerful, hopeful, and worshipful, but the fact is, we do not always feel cheerful, hopeful, or worshipful. Sometimes we come to church on a Sunday morning with Friday evening feelings in our hearts. We want you to know that the disciples themselves felt the same way. They had walked with Jesus, broken bread with Him, and learned at His feet—and still they felt desperate and abandoned by God when Jesus was killed. Not only that, but this book is premised on the idea that Jesus Himself felt these things—and He was on intimate terms with the Father! In other words, there is no darkness so dark that Jesus hasn't also been through it, so deep that He can't carry you through it.

Let's get started!

Father, Forgive Them

And Jesus said, "Father, forgive them, for they know not what they do." —LUKE 23:34

RELATIONSHIPS ARE INCREDIBLY fulfilling, but they can also be incredibly difficult at times. We may sometimes feel as though we have been treated unfairly, vilified by unjust criticism, or stuck in anger over something that betrayed our trust and safety. And while most of us know what being our best self looks like in these difficult moments—that we should lay down our egos in lieu of a soft heart that forgives, avoids blame, lets go of grudges, and leads us with a gentle, healing, merciful, and virtuous disposition—that's not always what our heart prompts us to do. In fact, our joy can be crushed in an instant by someone else's hurtful words, lack of consideration, antagonism, rude tone, offensive behavior, or clear wrongdoing—and in these moments, we feel raw, self-righteous, and angry. Our guard goes up, our tone changes, our friendly demeanor disappears, and we no longer feel able to access our compassion and understanding for the person who hurt us. In these moments, biblical love couldn't seem further out of reach because we get stuck judging, defending, or wanting to fight back to level the playing field or make others know their wrong. You see, when two people's imperfections meet, we see human brokenness illuminated, and our flesh threatens to lead us in ways that hurt our spirit.

As helpful as feelings can be at telling us what we need, they can also misguide us. When anger hijacks our heart, our mind can lean toward negative and judgmental narratives about the person we feel angry at. And unfortunately, once we believe something about a person, we tend to look for those narratives more often, due to our inherent confirmation bias. This tendency makes it easy to vilify people, justify ourselves, and forget our own mistakes. This path leads to one thing: condemnation. Condemnation makes staying angry easy, and staying angry only fuels the condemnation. Now we are part of a vicious cycle of tunnel vision and judgment that robs us of God's peace and the very life-giving perspectives we need in order to forgive.

But if anyone can understand the hurt, betrayal, deception, and injustice that sometimes comes with relationships, it is Christ. Yet in His darkest moment, He says, "Father, forgive them, for they know not what they do." In fact, this is the very first recorded statement Christ makes on the Cross. He chooses to forgive the very people who have betrayed Him, beat Him, mocked Him, spit upon Him, and who are actively executing Him. How can this be? Is this not the God of justice? The God who will judge the living and the dead? And if any human being in history had cause to call down

God's judgment, it was Jesus. Yet in the midst of suffering and dying a painful and prolonged death on the Cross, He chose to act with unparalleled compassion. He did not call down God's wrath or protection; rather, He prayed for God's forgiveness. He chose to prioritize radical forgiveness, modeling for us the most perfect example of undeserved grace, love, and mercy that we could have ever witnessed.

So when we feel most put upon by injustice or by people who don't wish us well or who may have harmed us in some way . . . yes, even in our darkest moments and deepest upsets, Jesus calls us to follow His example. He calls us to forgive.

The Imperative to Forgive

When we're hurt, often the last thing we want to do is forgive. Most of us become more attached to the hurt than to the idea of moving on from the hurt. And even when we think of softening our hearts, most of us struggle to do so because of how we explain the situation to ourselves. For instance, we might think the hurt wasn't accidental—that the person *did* know what they were doing. Or maybe we think, how can we even consider forgiveness if someone physically harmed us or our child or loved one? Not only might we feel forgiveness is out of the question, we might even want them to pay for what they've done.

These are serious concerns, and we will address them in due time. But they don't let us off the hook from following Jesus' first words on the Cross, "Father, forgive them." In order to truly follow these words, we must first understand what forgiveness is and how, exactly, we can learn to give it. When we really understand forgiveness and learn to practice with real people in our lives, we'll discover that it allows us to live into our purpose even in our darkest moments.

Before we go too much farther, let us first assure you that forgiveness does not mean putting yourself in harm's way or ignoring criminal or immoral behavior. It does not mean we let others continue to hurt us. But we are also not saying that forgiveness is easy or natural. No, forgiving people who have hurt you may still be one of the most difficult things you will ever do, especially since sometimes we must forgive a person repeatedly.

A story in Matthew 18 shows us how radically—and how often—Jesus wants us to forgive people. To paraphrase verses 21–22, one time Peter went to Jesus and said, "Rabbi, I hear you talking about forgiveness, about letting people who have offended me off the hook. And I want to do it, but it's tough. I mean, say someone wrongs you, and you forgive them, but then they do it again, and you forgive them again—and then they do it yet again. How long should you let this go on, forgiving over and over again? Seven is a good biblical number—how about seven times?"

Then Jesus said, "I understand it's not easy, but don't stop at seven. Keep forgiving. Forgive seventy times seven times."

If you do the math, Jesus says to forgive 490 times. If someone wronged you once every day, beginning on January 1, you would have to keep forgiving them every day until around April of the following year. Or sixteen times a day for a month. Or every three minutes for twenty-four hours. But

Jesus is not asking us to do math. And if we were to start a ledger and track how many times we forgave someone so that we could stop at 490, we would be missing the point entirely. Jesus tells Peter to forgive and then forgive some more until he loses count. Keeping score is the opposite of forgiveness.

So, must we really forgive? Yes, over and over again.

Again, look at Christ on the Cross. He does not say, "Father, watch closely. See everything they're doing to me. Store up these things so that you may judge them and avenge your Son!" He says, "Forgive them." And in His words to Peter, He suggests that He would do it again and again and again.

Defining Forgiveness

We all have different ideas about what forgiveness is, and this often comes from the way we saw our families act out forgiveness when we were young. We might have grown up in homes where we experienced hurt that was never followed by an apology. Others of us were made to give apologies but never received them. Still others might have been made to both give and accept apologies that didn't feel genuine. And some of us had no example at all because hurts were ignored, not repaired.

The rest of us may have learned that it was important to apologize when we did something wrong and that the appropriate response to an apology was to say "It's okay" or "I forgive you." But as we age, forgiveness becomes increasingly more complicated because the way we understand hurt now is much different than the way we understood it as children.

And the depth of hurt may feel less easily forgivable than the hurt we felt as children.

So what exactly is forgiveness?

A Yearning for Goodness

Forgiveness is an unyielding desire for goodness: the good of others, the good of the world, the good of our souls. Jesus Himself "went about doing good" (Acts 10:38), and while we cannot earn our salvation by doing good, the evidence of a life of faith is a life of doing good as Jesus did. Our yearning for good shouldn't change even when we experience hurt or anger, and the yearning actually makes room for the Holy Spirit to lead us because our yearning for goodness breeds compromise and respect, despite difficult moments. Our yearning for goodness prompts us to accept influence from one another even when we don't completely agree with what's been said. Our yearning for goodness prompts us to overlook faults and to be merciful with others even when it would have been easier to vilify that person in our minds.

Think about your own framework for leading with goodness. We have all been given different spiritual abilities for promoting goodness in this world, whether for peace, patience, words that heal, a joy that is unyielding, a desire for unity, or an empathic heart that can see the person beneath the offense—and yes, even for forgiveness. And God doesn't give us these abilities just for our own benefit. Every spiritual gift He has given us is to draw us closer to Christ and to enable us to share God's grace and love with others. So ultimately, forgiveness is about desiring goodness, despite circumstances, and not letting anything prevent us from the closeness Christ yearns to have with us.

Canceling Debt

Jesus tells a story in Matthew 18:23–34 about a king who wants to settle accounts with his servants. One servant comes in who owes a huge sum of money to the king—the equivalent of about five billion dollars in today's currency. But he can't pay it, so the king says, "Well, the law says you must pay, so you, your wife, and your children will be sold as slaves, and we'll confiscate your property and sell that, too."

The man falls on his knees and pleads with the king, "No, please! Be patient with me. I'll repay it all, I promise!"

And the king is moved to compassion, so he says, "You know what? Forget it. Your debt is canceled."

The man then goes home and finds one of his own servants who owes him the equivalent of about $10,000. That's still a lot of money but much less than the man owed the king. And unlike the mercy the king had just shown to him, he shows no mercy to his own servant; instead, he grabs the servant and demands his money back.

The servant says, "Be patient with me. I'll repay it all, I promise!" But, in response to the man's plea, he has the servant thrown into prison until he can repay his debt.

When the king finds out, he calls the man before him and says, "Shouldn't you have mercy on others, just as I had mercy on you?" Then he tells his soldiers to have the man thrown in prison—because he received what he didn't extend, withheld what he had been given.

In the parable, the servant shows neither a sense of responsibility nor a desire to "pay it forward," but you might think that if you were shown such forgiveness, it would create a powerful obligation to forgive, almost like another form of debt. You might find yourself tormented by what sociologists call the reciprocity norm: the powerful need to reciprocate or respond in kind. The parable shows us that because Christ (the king in the story) has forgiven us, we must, in turn, forgive those who hurt us. The hurts done to us do not create a new form of debt where something is owed to us; rather, they create an opportunity for us to act out the love that Christ has already shown to us. As C. S. Lewis puts it, "To be Christian means to forgive the inexcusable, because God has forgiven the inexcusable in you."[1]

An Internal Process

Forgiveness is not only something we give to someone else but something we do internally that changes us. When someone hurts us, we want that hurt made right, and we can carry that pain for a long time. In an ideal world, the one who wronged us would repent, apologize, and work to make things right. But we don't always get that. So forgiveness

---

1   C. S. Lewis, *The Weight of Glory* (New York: Simon & Schuster, 1996), 135–136.

becomes a process of moving on internally from the injustice, whether or not we get an apology or restoration.

You see, we don't always meet people who are at the same point as we are in our journey of goodness, virtue, and righteousness. Some look out for the collective good, while others live with only their own good in mind. Some are reflective and self-aware, while others are completely unaware of the impact they have on people. Some have a well-developed sense of right from wrong and a strong moral conscience, while others lack integrity. We can't assume that everyone who hurts us is mature spiritually or that they even have the tools to know how to do any better than they are doing.

So forgiving means letting go of demands we place on others to be any different than they are. Not that we won't feel anger, or that we put ourselves in harm's way, but we don't let their struggle dominate us or control how we ourselves choose to move forward. In this way, we turn over our need for justice and restoration to God. Forgiveness means trusting that God brings healing and transformation, that He reveals the truth in His own time but always answers our cry for justice.

A Choice

Forgiveness is a process, but it's also a choice. The process doesn't actually begin until we choose to forgive. It's a deliberate decision that feels difficult and may not always sit quite right with our anger toward the offense but always sits right with our salvation. The choice brings an active and intentional change that takes place in our heart, in our mind, and most importantly, in our soul. Sometimes we attempt to be in charge of changing others by withholding our forgiveness. But the only change that takes place when we do that is the one that connects us to Christ. Remember that when we are wronged, God calls us to trust in Him to bring about change in the offender. It is not our job (Rom. 12:17–21). Our job is to overcome evil with good, clothing ourselves with compassion, kindness, humility, gentleness, and compassion—even when we are feeling hurt (Col. 3:12–17).

I (Dr. Roxanne) recall a time when Fr. Nicholas and I had an opportunity to practice this very kind of choice while on a trip to London. It was our first day there, and it had already been a long day that we tried to stretch even longer so that our daughter could see the famous Harry Potter 9¾ platform in King's Cross Station. Unfortunately, while on our way there, our daughter began complaining of a sore throat. The sore throat quickly morphed into full-on exhaustion and a 104-degree fever. When we arrived at the station, she was too sick to even walk over to the line to get a picture of the attraction she had been awaiting all day. We knew in that moment we needed to get back to the hotel as soon as possible.

We walked to the edge of the street to call an Uber. As we were talking to Uber, three motorcycles came out of nowhere. One crossed in front of us, one directly behind us, and one just behind them both. They came so close that our son had to jump out of the way in order not to be hit. Before I could even register what was happening, I felt my phone snagged right out of my hands by one of the motorcyclists while I was using it. The phone, unfortunately, was in a wallet case, which held all the credit cards and identification we needed on the trip.

As panic set in, we cried out and chased the motorcycles down the street, but we quickly realized there was nothing to be done. A kind man walked up to us just after it happened and allowed us to use his phone to call for help. He shared with us that sadly, this happens often and that we were actually lucky. "Lucky?" we asked.

"Right, normally they whack you if you fight back," he replied. This was certainly an unwelcome reminder of the brokenness of our fallen world, and it was an experience that we will never forget.

And yes, it was natural for us to be upset, to get stuck in questioning how something like this could have happened, and to feel the stress of trying to pick up the pieces. And it would have been easy to get stuck there, feeling angry and righteous, replaying the same thoughts over and over again in our minds, which would fuel our anger but not allow us to reach any new ways of thinking about the situation. Only when we realized that we had a choice were we able to start trying to move on from it. It was a process, but choosing to move beyond unforgiveness and judgment protected what time we had left to enjoy the trip and helped us direct our energy toward picking up the pieces, rather than focusing on what had shattered. As the trip went on, each day we realized how unproductive it would have been to hold on to something we couldn't change. And each day it did get a little easier, as God's healing presence helped us slowly let go of focusing on it.

So ultimately, in any situation, it is our choice that paves the way for the type of relationship we have with the things that happen to us. Choosing to forgive helps us find peace within ourselves, peace with others, and ultimately peace about what happens to us.

Yet, in order to make the choice to forgive, our faith must take the lead over our emotions. And we must remember that without God, that's not possible. So, if you are struggling to make the choice to forgive, lean into prayer by opening up all your thoughts and feelings about the situation to God. Ask Him to guide your heart with a willingness to move on. Pray for the person who has hurt you, for the struggles they have that you know about and for the ones you do not know about. Pray for goodness, mercy, and compassion to lead your thoughts. Remember, when we choose to forgive, God paves the way for our healing by helping our feelings eventually catch up with our decision, because forgiveness is not a feeling we hope to arrive at; it's a decision we arrive at.

The Forgiven Forgive

Forgiveness is woven into our experience of being in relationship with God, and we can see this in the Lord's Prayer as we pray, "and forgive us our trespasses as we forgive those who trespass against us." Interestingly, this is the only prayer among the seven smaller prayers within the Lord's Prayer that establishes contingency or correlation. "As we forgive" can mean one of two things. Either it assumes we are already forgiving others and want God to do likewise, or it suggests that when we forgive, God forgives. Either way, the two notions correlate in how Jesus teaches us to pray. And in fact, a few verses later we hear Him say, "For if you forgive others . . . your heavenly Father will also forgive you, but if you do not forgive others . . . neither will your Father forgive your trespasses" (Matt. 6:14–15).

It shouldn't surprise us that forgiveness also shows up in the Sermon on the Mount. Jesus preaches, "Blessed are the merciful, for they shall receive mercy" (Matt. 5:7) and also, "Judge not, and you will not be judged; condemn not, and you will not be condemned; forgive, and you will be forgiven" (Luke 6:37). In these verses, Jesus is telling us that there is an order to the moral universe. Good leads to good, evil to evil, forgiveness to forgiveness. A similar logic is at work in the commandment to love our neighbors as ourselves. It's not just about being a good person; it's about nurturing the seeds of love, which were meant to spread outward. If we want to experience all the benefits of God's grace, Jesus says we need to play our part in doling them out to others.

This is not to suggest that God's forgiveness literally depends upon us forgiving others. The point is that they go hand in hand. We cannot fully experience God's forgiveness if we do not forgive others.

Dispelling Myths about Forgiveness

Before we go any farther, we want to dispel some common myths about forgiveness. These myths are stories we tell ourselves that influence our actions and attitudes about forgiveness—but they're not true. If we go on believing them, we are getting in our own way and not allowing ourselves to forgive.

It Is Easy

Sometimes we think that because we are good people, forgiveness should come easy to us. But it's often much more difficult than we envision. As C. S. Lewis once put it, "Everyone says forgiveness is a lovely idea, until they have something to forgive."[2] While we are commanded to do so, putting it into practice requires effort, humility, strength, and wisdom. And that's okay. Most of what is good for us doesn't come easy. So rather than beat ourselves up for struggling with forgiveness, we can realize that as humans we are fallen, and that no matter how much we strive toward goodness, inevitably, sin has a way of creeping in. We pray, repent, confess, and the cycle begins again. This is a cycle of renewal, however. So, we can accept that forgiveness is difficult for us, then pray that God will give us the strength, humility, and willingness we need to take the first step. Then we await the work God is yearning to do within our hearts.

---

2 C. S. Lewis, *Mere Christianity* (New York: Macmillan, 1952), 115.

It is worth noting here that while we all have the capacity to forgive, certain people may find it a bit easier because of their personality traits. For instance, traits like agreeableness and empathy tend to be strongly associated with the proclivity to forgive. One could say that for some, these spiritual gifts are inherent to their wiring. If you are one of these people, it may feel easier to extend understanding toward those who have wronged you. So it's easier to let go and move on from some or all of the frustration, disappointment, resentment, or other painful feelings associated with the offense. It's also easier to accept the shortcomings, flaws, and imperfections in others. But if this isn't you, be careful not to think it should be. We all have different gifts, and we are all capable of forgiveness. It's just that some of us will need more tools to help us better practice forgiveness, and we must remember that we get better at anything that we continually practice.

It Minimizes or Forgets the Offense

God does not come to us in our pain and say, "It's okay," or "It didn't really hurt that bad, did it?" or "Look, it isn't that big a deal." Our God is a God of truth, and sometimes the truth is that it's not okay, it shouldn't have happened, it did hurt, and it was a big deal. Forgiveness is not letting go of right and wrong. And we aren't condoning wrongdoing or encouraging you to pretend that something is okay when it's not. Check out Psalms or Lamentations some time if you need a reminder of that. No, forgiveness does not mean removing the offense; it means learning how to move forward despite it.

It Is a Two-Player Game

When we forgive, we often want the person involved to play by the same rules, but that's not always what happens because we are not all at the same point in our spiritual journey. That's okay. When we can work things out with the other person, that can be a very good thing, but reconciliation does not always accompany forgiveness. Reconciliation is a two-player game, and forgiveness often makes it possible, but that is not always the result. Forgiveness can happen whether a relationship is repaired or not—so it doesn't necessarily need to involve the other person.

The 1983 film *WarGames* is a great illustration of this. In the movie, Matthew Broderick plays a kid who hacks into NORAD's computers and accidentally convinces a supercomputer to activate the US's nuclear arsenal. This leads to a global crisis that could turn into World War III, but the computer has taken over, so there's nothing the people at NORAD can do. As the critical moment approaches, when the world could end in nuclear war, the computer runs simulations of the possible outcomes of firing the missiles, and then it shuts everything down. No one understands why, but then the computer says, "Strange game. . . . The only winning move is not to play."

So when we are faced with needing to forgive someone, instead of arguing about who did what and ruminating over who is at fault and who is responsible for apologizing, sometimes the best move we can make is to stop playing the game. We don't want to make someone else's apology the condition we wait on to extend our forgiveness. This only holds us hostage to the level of spiritual maturity of the person who hurt us. We don't have to wait for anyone else to make a move in order for us to pursue what we know is right. After all, we have no control over the people who hurt us—their response, their mindset, their spiritual health, their repentance, or their intentions. So we cannot tie our well-being to theirs. Instead, we can keep a healthy boundary by saying, "I can pursue good even when someone else doesn't."

It Is about What's "Fair"

Our sense of justice runs deep, and we often want justice in cases of wrongdoing. But forgiveness is not about justice or about what we deserve. Forgiveness is about offering mercy and grace that is far greater than what is deserved. Remember, the forgiven forgive. If our forgiveness depended on what was fair, then we would need to go back to Jesus and pay for our sins before we ever accepted His forgiveness. Was there anything "fair" about the Son of God, who was Himself perfect, suffering for our imperfections? Forgiveness is not about giving someone what they deserve; it's about giving someone what they need. The truth is, those who hurt others need someone who breaks the cycle, not someone who participates in it by reinforcing it.

It Is about Agreeing with the Other Person

When we forgive someone, it doesn't mean we agree with their behavior. It just means we aren't willing to let their struggle become our struggle. The truth is, most behavior has deeper roots that extend far beyond the moment we were affected by it. And when we seek forgiveness, we choose to let compassion drive our willingness to examine those roots— or what they might mean about someone—rather than getting stuck in judgment about who someone is because of what they have done. At the end of the day, we can understand why something happened and have compassion on the person but still not agree with the way they acted toward us. If we make agreement a condition for our forgiveness, we're getting back into that two-player game scenario, and we want to avoid that. We don't have to agree that an action was justifiable or acceptable in order to forgive someone for it.

It Should Save a Toxic Relationship

Again, forgiveness is not about reconciliation. When we forgive someone, we have no obligation to let them back into our lives or to put ourselves in situations where they can repeatedly hurt us. We don't have to compromise healthy boundaries in order to move on from the pain of an unhealthy relationship. Letting go of the bitterness that resides in our hearts does not require us to abandon our self-respect.

Many Christians get confused on this point. Because Christ modeled sacrifice, sometimes we think we too must sacrifice by staying in an unhealthy or toxic relationship.

But the Bible urges strongly against this, saying that these types of unhealthy behaviors in others will ultimately have an unhealthy influence on us. Saint Paul says, "Do not be deceived: 'Bad company ruins good morals'" (I Cor. 15:33), and God calls us to flee from people who seek to compromise us spiritually, as we "test the spirits to see whether they are from God" (I John 4:1). The Bible also tells us to flee from anyone who calls him or herself a believer but is sexually immoral, greedy, an idolater or reviler, a drunkard, or a swindler (I Cor. 5:11). God even cautions us to be wary of those who are hot-tempered and easily angered, "lest you learn his ways / and entangle yourself in a snare" (Prov. 22:25).

It Is a One-Time Thing

Some transgressions really are so small that we immediately move on from them and forget them completely. But other times we experience hurts that influence us for a very long time. So we mustn't think of forgiveness as something we do once and then the hurt magically disappears. In fact, similar circumstances can bring up the hurt all over again, even when we think we've moved on. Sometimes we must walk back through the motions of forgiveness again and again.

It Is an Act of Willpower

If we believe we must will ourselves to forgive others, then we believe we must have the internal resources and strength necessary to do all of the work of forgiveness on our own. And if we believe this, then forgiveness will be impossible. But as we saw earlier, forgiveness comes first from God, and it is by His grace that we are able to forgive. Human willpower is a finite resource. We tend to run out of it, especially in trying circumstances. But God's power is limitless.

And yet, this doesn't mean we are passive in the process. Our will and God's power work together. This is a wonderful mystery, the synergy between our effort and God's work. While we know that we can do nothing without God, we also know that God gave us free will and chooses to use us to accomplish His purpose. Paul describes this cooperation when he writes, "For this I toil, struggling with all his energy that he powerfully works within me" (Col. 1:29). So don't worry that you have to find the strength to forgive on your own. Ask God, and you will receive the strength you need.

Why We Forgive

If we think about faith as a set of rules to abide by, we misunderstand the role it is supposed to play in our lives. You see, forgiveness is a command, but it's also a means of bettering ourselves, bettering our relationship with God, bettering our relationships with those around us, and bettering our ability to be vessels of God's goodness in this world. Thus, it can be a sanctifying process that helps us work alongside God to grow more into the image of Christ. Forgiveness helps us "work out [our] own salvation" (Phil. 2:12) and "trains" us to be godly (1 Tim. 4:7). In a sense, it can act as a catalyst to spur on our own spiritual growth in ways that transform a theoretical knowledge of faith into a deeper, more profound, and perfected experience of our faith.

To envision this, think of life like a cross. The vertical dimension represents our spiritual connection to God, and the horizontal represents our relationship with the physical world. This image helps us see that it's all connected. Our relationship with Christ shapes the relationship we have with the outside world. And how we relate to our world affects the relationship we have with Christ. When we forgive, we strengthen that vertical dimension by drawing closer to Christ. And drawing nearer to Christ makes it easier to forgive. When we forgive, we ultimately learn how to depend more on God and let our relationship with Christ define our relationship with others.

Right Relationship to Ourselves

The devil makes small sins seem smaller in our eyes, for otherwise he can't lead us to greater evil. —ST. MARK THE ASCETIC[3]

If we commit to living a life in Christ, we must also work to block out all that seeks to distract us from living that life. Refusing to forgive and instead holding on to hurt and anger is one of those distractions. It can leave us harboring the kind

---

3   "On The Spiritual Law: Two Hundred Texts," in *The Philokalia: The Complete Text*, compiled by St. Nikodimos of the Holy Mountain and St. Makarios of Corinth, trans. and eds. GEH Palmer, Phillip Sherrard, and Kallistos Ware, vol. I (London: Faber and Faber, 1979), 116.

of negativity that darkens our hearts and affects our relationship with ourselves as it begins to erode the joy, peace, and goodness we experience when we live more in the fullness of the Holy Spirit.

We must keep in mind that angry feelings can bleed into other areas of our life and affect our emotional and spiritual well-being. Angry feelings we haven't healed from change our ability to be fully present and our proclivity to operate from a place of goodness, even in situations that have nothing to do with the original hurt. Although we like to think of ourselves as mostly reasonable, open to logic, unbiased, and sensible, the truth is, unresolved emotions like hurt and anger can completely distort our logic in any situation that triggers our recollection of previous upsets.

And because our emotions shape our thoughts and our thoughts keep shaping our emotions, we can easily get stuck in a vicious cycle of upset that replays what happened within a narrative of judgment, blame, and self-righteousness. Additionally, research into the psychology of forgiveness has discovered that when we hold onto bitterness, it makes us tense and anxious, and we become preoccupied with the offender. It can also lead to toxic anger that builds up and causes us to overreact and misdirect our anger. This then results in negative consequences that we have to manage.[4]

---

4   Robert D. Enright and Richard P. Fitzgibbons, *Forgiveness Therapy: An Empirical Guide for Resolving Anger and Restoring Hope* (Washington, DC: American Psychological Association, 2015), 19.

Where does that leave us spiritually? Far from the ability to give and receive love freely.

It's worth mentioning here that emotions themselves are not right or wrong. They are real reactions to what happens to us, a way our body gives us information about the world. For instance, anger is almost always trying to protect us or someone else, and that's why it surfaces in situations of injustice. When we feel it on our own behalf, it often means that someone did not respect our values, our sense of what's right, or that they crossed an important boundary. It's often anger that gives us the courage to stand up for ourselves or create boundaries with someone who is not treating us well. Other times it protects us against the experience of more vulnerable emotions like grief or sadness that can leave us feeling helpless and out of control. Either way, all emotions have meaning. But how we interpret our emotions, and what we decide they mean about a person or a situation—that is what can be right or wrong. This is where we need to pause, slow down and reflect, and find constructive and healthy ways of dealing with what we feel so our feelings don't leave us standing self-righteously, yet unable to stand in right relationship to God.

We live in right relationship to ourselves when we make room for our feelings without letting them consume us or lead us without discernment. We don't have to be beholden to whatever we're feeling, but we do have to create enough space between what we feel and what we choose to do with it so that we realign our emotions within a greater framework of our faith and our values. So, healing from upset doesn't mean the damage never existed. It just means the damage no longer controls us in ways that could derail our spirit. Forgiveness allows us to write new chapters in our lives from a place of peace, well-being, and goodness. It allows us to live as our true selves. And as the research shows, forgiveness also helps reduce anxiety and depression, restores our ability to see the positive, improves our self-esteem, makes us more resilient to stress, and can reduce our physical health problems.[5]

Right Relationship to Others

Forgiveness helps us restore a right relationship to other people because when we hold onto bitterness, it colors not only how we see the person who hurt us but also how we relate to everyone else in our lives. Saint Paul beckons us, "If possible, so far as it depends on you, live peaceably with all" (Rom. 12:18), but we cannot be at peace with anyone when we hold bitterness toward them.

There is a great spirit of division in our world today, and the devil loves it because the more we fight among ourselves, the less good we're able to do in the world. In this spirit of division, our grievances toward others can create a lifetime of conflict, severed relationships, and wounds with no means of healing—all of which ultimately derail our spirit in relation

---

5   See Enright and Fitzgibbons. Also Loren Toussaint, Alyssa C.D. Cheadle, and Amy D. Owen, "Forgive to Live: Forgiveness, Health, and Longevity," *Journal of Behavioral Medicine* 35, no. 4 (June 2011): 375–86.

to everything else. Perhaps this is what Jesus meant when He told His disciples, "Every kingdom divided against itself is laid waste, and no city or house divided against itself will stand" (Matt. 12:25). But we worship a God who unites, who tears down walls, and who calls us to be "eager to maintain the unity of the Spirit in the bond of peace" (Eph. 4:3). When we forgive, we free ourselves up to live at peace with others, thereby following Christ's calling to keep the unity of the Spirit through the bond of peace.

We need to remember that God has written His name on each of us, and that makes each of the seven billion-plus people on this planet valuable. When we forgive others, we honor the value God has assigned to them and do what we can to live in right relation to those God has placed along our path. We must keep in mind that we don't always know why God has placed certain people in our life. But we do know that relationships provide opportunities for growth, for learning perspective, and for learning how to develop a more merciful, benevolent, selfless, and loving heart.

Forgiveness also benefits our relationships because it can help bring others to Christ through us by redirecting the temptations that keep us from living out I Corinthians 13:4–7: to be patient and kind; to not be envious or boastful; to not insist on our own way; to not be irritable or resentful; and to not rejoice at the wrongdoing of others. As we let go of bitterness, judgment, and self-righteousness, we see more clearly what is needed in any situation—where to step in, what to overlook, how to help where someone else struggles, and how to use what God has given us to restore one another gently back to His design or to provide the reflection others need to grow themselves. Remember it is because God first loved us in our most imperfect and unworthy condition that we must remember to love others in their own imperfect and unworthy condition.

Right Relationship to God

So while forgiveness helps us live in right relationship to ourselves and others, it also helps us remain in right relationship to God because we can't very well succumb to ill will toward someone and serve God at the same time. Keep in mind St. Paul's prayer for us that we not only grow in love but that our love "may abound more and more, with knowledge and all discernment, so that [we] may approve what is excellent, and so be pure and blameless for the day of Christ, filled with the fruit of righteousness that comes through Jesus Christ, to the glory and praise of God" (Phil. 1:9–11). This means that as we learn more about God's love for us, we also grow in our knowledge of how to love others in ways that aren't self-serving but God-serving.

Being God-serving means following God's teachings and commandments and letting our choices be motivated by our relationship with Him over our relationship with anything else. Living with this kind of spiritual integrity means living with an undivided heart that seeks what is right by God, even if it doesn't always feel right by our feelings.

So when someone has not honored their commitment to living righteously, we serve God by seeing that situation as an opportunity to grow into the fullness of Christ. It is this commitment that helps us navigate our lives with spiritual integrity, so that no matter what happens to us on the outside, our reactions match who we claim to be on the inside. Yet, too often our choice to forgive rests on whether we believe a situation or a person deserves it. It's based on wanting to forgive when it *feels right* as opposed to because it *is right*. Imagine that a business you love erroneously gives you too much change in return for payment. It just feels right to give it back. But imagine that same thing happened at a business that hasn't treated you well. Would you give it back, or would you think, "Serves them right! They owe me that"?

You see, it's easy to do the right thing when it feels right, but it becomes a moral choice to do the right thing even when it doesn't feel right. And living righteously before God means aligning even our thoughts about others with how God would want us to think about them because, as the Bible reminds us, God discerns our thoughts from afar: "Even before a word is on my tongue, / behold, O LORD, you know it altogether" (Ps. 139:4).

When do you find it hardest to live in right relationship to God? Do you find it hard to forgive someone in your heart, even though on the outside you are going through the motions of a polite response? Do you find it hard to think merciful thoughts toward those who have hurt you? Or how about when someone doesn't seem like they deserve grace? Do you get caught up in what's fair? Again, living in right relationship to God means choosing what *is right*, not what *feels right*. When Jesus came into this world, we didn't deserve the forgiveness

He granted us through having endured the Cross. But God gave us this opportunity anyway out of His immense love for us. Through the Cross, we are all invited to restore a right relationship with Christ, but when we choose to withhold our forgiveness from others, we reject that invitation.

Remember, forgiveness is not an option—it is a command. "As God's chosen ones," says St. Paul, bear "with one another and, if one has a complaint against another, [forgive] each other; as the Lord has forgiven you, so you also must forgive" (Col. 3:12–13). Forgiveness goes hand in hand with belonging to God; we are called to forgive if we want to live in right relationship with Him. "Do we refuse to forgive?" asks St. Tikhon of Zadonsk. "God, too, will refuse to forgive us. As we treat our neighbors, so also does God treat us."[6] We see again this principle of reciprocity and synergy at work. We share in the grace of God when we work to show grace to others.

How to Forgive

We have covered a lot of ground in our discussion of forgiveness. We know that Christ models it for us and commands it of us. And we know that in practicing it, we live in right relationship with God, ourselves, and others. We also know that the Bible connects our forgiveness of others to

---

6   St. Tikhon of Zadonsk, *Journey to Heaven: Counsels on the Particular Duties of Every Christian* (Jordanville, NY: Holy Trinity Monastery, 1994).

God's forgiveness of us. And we know that the myths we sometimes believe about forgiveness often keep us from forgiving. At this point in the chapter you might be thinking, "Now what? I still feel hurt and angry. How do I *actually forgive* someone?"

First, remember that the work of forgiveness can be very difficult and can take a long time. And deciding to pursue repair and reconciliation is a choice we have to make through reflection and trusted guidance, but it is one that doesn't necessarily accompany forgiveness. The bulk of the work involved in forgiveness is something that happens within us, not necessarily between us, and only with God's grace. So now let's look at the steps involved in moving from hurt and anger to forgiveness.

Process Your Pain

Forgiveness isn't necessarily something that happens just because we want it to. When we're hurt, we need to first do some work to process what has occurred.

I. **Reflect on the pain.** When we react defensively to our hurt, it can cloud our understanding of what's actually happened and why we're upset. For instance, instead of seeking understanding, we can get so bogged down in the play-by-play of what happened—replaying every word that was said and wanting to defend every unfair accusation that followed—that we sometimes lose sight of understanding ourselves and the root cause of our initial upset. Therefore, to keep from reacting defensively, remember that your hurt and anger are there to teach you about what mattered to you in the situation. Try explaining the situation by describing your feelings about what happened rather than describing the person who hurt you. When we stay focused on understanding ourselves instead of describing the person who hurt us, we protect ourselves from getting stuck in critical narratives that don't help us grow.

Even when we attempt to reflect in a non-defensive way, we can't assume the story we tell ourselves when we are hurt or angry is objective truth, but it is still a helpful window into better understanding our deeper values. So as you process your hurt and anger, try to remain open enough to it to become aware of how and why you see things the way you do. As you reflect, consider these questions: What wrongdoing do you feel occurred? What was lost as a result? Do you feel it's a pattern in this relationship? If you aren't sure, look at the facts, not the emotion: What is the evidence of *intentional* hurt/wrongdoing? Is this a situation where you could give the benefit of the doubt? What kind of heart does this person normally possess in other situations? Is this a pattern that warrants creating a new boundary? Does what happened betray a core value of yours?

Consider unpacking the situation in this way: "When this happened, I felt (name an emotion) _____ and (name an emotion) _____."

"I got angry because I took it to mean (describe how you saw the situation, what you thought about it) _____." "It upset me so much because I deeply yearn for (name the value beneath your anger) _____." "In the future, I would hope that (what you need moving forward) _____." As you unpack your hurt, really consider the deeper reason behind your strong feelings.

2. **Reflect on yourself.** In humility, ask what role you might have played in the situation. Was there anything going on for you at the time that could have made the situation worse? Anything that might have made you more sensitive to what happened? Could the event have triggered some vulnerable spot for you from your own past? Does it feel like a familiar feeling you've experienced before, even with other people? Was there already a critical, judgmental, or negative thought process about that person in your mind? Could that have set you up to be looking for offense, or to take something personally that wasn't meant to be personal, or to be less likely to give the benefit of the doubt? This isn't about blaming ourselves but about carefully considering who we were in the situation that upset us. If there was nothing that set you up for it, consider leveling the playing field for a moment by seeking humility—have you also said or done things before that you maybe shouldn't have or that ended up being hurtful to someone in some way?

As you process your pain, remember that anger is a natural human emotion. God created us to have emotions, but He does not want us to be imprisoned by them. So when anger hits, strive to remain in charge by responding to it in a way that feels productive, life-giving, and Spirit led. Let your emotions be a cause for pause, not a directive on how to treat people. Be curious about the deeper meaning of it all. What deeper convictions, values, or needs lie beneath your anger?

Choose to Forgive

We have said that forgiveness is a process and a journey—an active exercise of our heart, our mind, and our soul. But if we ever expect to forgive, we must first decide that we want to. This is an important place to begin because forgiveness isn't always intuitive—meaning, it doesn't always sit well with our egos (though it sits well with our salvation), and the myths we fall prey to about forgiveness often undermine our decision to begin the journey. So if you are struggling to choose the road of forgiveness, remind yourself of the following:

- **Unforgiveness won't solve anything.** It doesn't make people understand their wrong, pay for their wrong, or turn away from their wrong. It does, however, make *you* pay for their wrong as you nurture bitterness and division within your soul.
- **Forgiveness is not about giving people what they deserve.** It is about giving to others what God has already given to us.

- **You can't forgive on your own.** Invite God into your choice: "Lord, I want to forgive. Help my unforgiveness." Pray for His voice to fill your spirit with more merciful thoughts that help you see the wrong as a deeper part of someone else's brokenness. If it feels hard to hear His voice, read Scripture, but pray beforehand: "Lord, speak to me. Open my heart to Your word, even if I've been too angry to listen." Pray for His courage and strength: "Lord Jesus Christ, Son of God, strengthen me; I don't feel strong." Pray for humility: "Help me to seek your Spirit of goodness."

Finally, remember that you cannot be in right relationship to God if you do not seek to live in right relationship to others. So if you find it hard to forgive them, forgive for Him.

Seek Humility

To truly forgive, we must seek humility. This step and the next are about leveling the playing field, so to speak, so we don't go into forgiveness with so much one-sided judgment.

When we think about something that upsets us, most of the time it is our upset that starts speaking, not our humility. As the upset speaks, our anger strengthens, and we find ourselves validating our own anger without questioning it, remaining on Team Us against the other person. As we attach more strongly to our position, tunnel vision sets in, and all we can see is someone's flaws. As we replay the same angry, self-righteous message over and over again, we forget that we too are imperfect.

Instead, in humility, consider whether you too struggle with a persistent sin of your own, since no matter how much we strive to do our best, sin inevitably creeps in because we are all fallen in some way. This is the lot for us all: sin, confess, repent, recommit, repeat. Even St. Paul, who wrote most of the New Testament, called himself the chief of sinners. And he wasn't talking about his life before his epiphany of Christ—he was talking about his deepening awareness of his own imperfections the closer he drew to Jesus.

And yes, there will be some wrongs done to us that are far beyond what we have done to others. When this happens, we may say, "Yes, I am imperfect, I am guilty of hurting others, but I have never done anything so horrible as what that person did to me." Finding humility will be a greater challenge in this case; and in such cases, we will require more grace to get there. But the Cross covers all manner of sins.

Remember the story in John chapter 8 of the woman caught in adultery? The men who had seized her were angry that she had been immoral, and they wanted Jesus to pronounce judgment and have her put to death according to the Law of Moses. But Jesus says something like, "Okay, you're so eager to hold her accountable for her sins? Let's do it, but let's be consistent. If you are free of sin, you get to throw the first stone." As we know, none of them were willing to claim they were without sin, even in the height of their self-righteous zeal.

What about you? Could you have thrown the first stone?

Jesus didn't condone the woman's behavior, but neither did He condemn her. He chose to love her when she needed an ally. This story should stop us in our tracks when we are bitter and angry. Even when someone is in the wrong, Jesus may take their side if that's where His love is needed. We don't want to let our anger turn into a self-righteousness that puts us on the other side of God's love. If we are to "judge not," we must learn to be humble even when we are in a position to judge.

And then, the most profound source of humility is the Cross. There we see an innocent Man suffering the consequences of our own sins, showing us His great love when we did nothing to deserve it. Even if someone does the worst thing imaginable, Jesus could forgive them, and if He could forgive them, who are we to say someone should not be forgiven? In truth, we will never have to forgive someone more than God forgave us.

Choose to Learn

Try using the situation that upset you to focus on your own growth. Perhaps the situation gave birth to a new conviction that you yearn to do something good in this world. Perhaps the situation became an opportunity to show mercy, have humility, replace judgment with empathy, choose not to criticize, draw closer to God, and yes, to extend forgiveness. With this we ask God to cleanse our hearts and enlighten us through the difficulty, praying, "Teach me, Lord. What can I learn here? What are You using this for?"

Remember, too, that a mind that is open and seeks to grow is also a mind that realizes how little it knows. And a heart that humbly "asks," "seeks," and "knocks" at the door of God's wisdom in persistent prayer realizes how much it needs God (Matt. 7:7–8). It's easy to forget that we don't have all the answers and that there is still so much we don't yet understand about ourselves, others, our situations, and our world at large. But in truth, we don't always know where our own growth is needed. We don't always know how our upsets may be helping us, acting as a sanctifying process within us. But if we pursue wisdom in all things, we find humility. And if we pursue humility, we find more wisdom. It's a beautiful cycle of spiritual growth that begins with a willingness to let something grow us, not embitter us. So no matter our affliction, if we let God's wisdom penetrate our soul, it can change us in ways we could never have prompted on our own. So when you are hurt, keep an open, sincere, and humble heart, and let everything grow you, convict you, and change you for good.

Humanize Those Who Hurt You

Remember also that we are all weak, are very easily overcome by passions, and therefore be meek and indulgent to those who sin against you, knowing that you yourself often suffer from the same infirmity as your brother. —St. JOHN OF KRONSTADT[7]

---

7   Ivan Ilyich Sergiev, *My Life in Christ: The Spiritual Journals of St. John of Kronstadt*, 2nd ed., ed. Nicholas Kotar, trans. E. E. Goulaeff

Until we recognize our own failures—our own sin—it is very hard to look upon another's shortcomings with any level of grace. Yet we must. Doing so humanizes other people because we can acknowledge that we struggle and sin just like they do.

Realizing that people often act out of ignorance also helps us humanize them. On the Cross, Jesus could have given any number of reasons why He wanted His Father to forgive, but He went with the empathic one: "Father . . . they know not what they do" (Luke 23:34). He assumed that the people hurting Him were not acting out of blatant evil but at least in part out of ignorance. Even good hearts can fall prey to poor methods of navigating feelings and to motivations they may not thoroughly understand or have good tools for managing. After all, everyone struggles with something. And we must still have empathy even for those with truly hardened hearts, for St. Paul tells us: "They are darkened in their understanding, alienated from the life of God because of the ignorance that is in them, due to their hardness of heart. They have become callous and have given themselves up to sensuality, greedy to practice every kind of impurity" (Eph. 4:18–19).

When we humanize people, we see the person beneath the offense. We try to identify with the universal nature of brokenness, and we keep in mind that life isn't exactly fair. Not everyone has had the same opportunities or been granted the same blessings or experienced the same level of support. Not

---

(Jordanville, NY: The Printshop of St. Job of Pochaev, 2021), 112.

everyone was raised to know love. In fact, some people have known only hate. Some of us were born into wonderfully loving families, while others had families that left much to be desired. Some were born with difficult dispositions they never learned how to manage, while others seem to have been born with an unceasing joy that can't be dampened. Some of us have the patience of Job, yet others struggle with waiting for a red light to turn green. Some of us are easygoing, agreeable in nature, and have never met someone we couldn't get along with, but others seem bothered and offended by most everything. We all have different challenges that have affected our spiritual maturity, and in order to humanize and forgive others, we need to have empathy for their challenges and enduring vulnerabilities.

Scientists have found that successfully imagining forgiving someone activates increased activity in the neural circuits responsible for empathy and the regulation of affect through cognition.[8] In other words, we explain the situation to ourselves in a way that helps us alter the way we feel. This is why empathy is a key feature of forgiveness and an integral part of the process. So if you are struggling to humanize and forgive someone, try being curious about their story. This involves not only looking inward at your pain but outward at the pain of others. After all, something has brought them to this point. Consider what could be driving their hurtful

---

8   Emiliano Ricciardi et al., "How the Brain Heals Emotional Wounds: The Functional Neuroanatomy of Forgiveness," *Frontiers in Human Neuroscience* 7 (December 9, 2013).

behavior by asking yourself questions like: Can you see any reason why their ideas and behavior might differ so much from your own? What values do they seem to prioritize or deem important? Why? Can you tell if their empathy and compassion were ever nurtured or developed by the important people in their life? Do they seem willing to accommodate and cooperate with others, or were they only taught to one-up and compete with others? Do they suffer psychologically from things that have nothing to do with you? Can you see good in them?

While we may not have all the answers, these questions help open our minds to the story behind the behavior. And as we navigate our hurt with empathy, we learn that most people don't hurt us primarily out of evil or to cause harm, but rather because their stories are different from our own. Since every behavior has a lifetime behind it, there will always be vulnerabilities we don't understand. But that doesn't mean we shouldn't try. Humanizing people is a step toward breaking the cycle of hurt and restoring goodness.

Let's be clear, though, that seeking to understand a behavior is not about making an excuse for that behavior. It's just what helps us realize that the story *before* the hurt often explains a big part of the *current* hurt. In this way, we create healthy boundaries spiritually. We don't allow someone else's vulnerability to become our vulnerability by reacting to it, becoming embittered by it, or letting it change us into somebody we were never meant to be. This doesn't mean we are minimizing the offense in any way or choosing not to draw appropriate boundaries where they are warranted. Rather, it's what helps us draw more effective boundaries, not hurtful ones, so we don't take on struggles that are not our own.

Let It Go

> *For freedom Christ has set us free; stand firm therefore, and do not submit again to a yoke of slavery.* —GALATIANS 5:1

If there is a moment when we can finally say we have forgiven someone, it would be the moment when we have finally let it go. What does this mean? It means bitterness no longer dominates our soul or influences how we think about or treat the person who hurt us. It means we have placed everything that happened in God's hands, and we trust Him to bring about change and reflection in the heart of the offender. It means we have recognized that it's not our job to change people, make them see their wrong, or punish their crime. It means we are more willing to overcome evil with good, heeding the words of St. Paul:

> Beloved, never avenge yourselves, but leave it to the wrath of God, for it is written, "Vengeance is mine, I will repay, says the Lord." To the contrary, "if your enemy is hungry, feed him; if he is thirsty, give him something to drink." . . . Do not be overcome by evil, but overcome evil with good. (Rom. 12:19–21)

Letting go means we are willing to replace our anger and hurt with God's presence because there is no peace that can come close to the peace we feel when we learn to lean more on Him than we do on ourselves. As we lean into God, we also learn to surrender the desire to change the other person that our anger might be insisting on. Remember, we cannot change others. Only God can do that. Letting go helps us stop insisting on our own way and lays fertile ground for something new to be born—for God to bring about the change He wills, not the change we will. As we let go, we remember that it's God who brings understanding and softens hardened hearts, not us. And it's God who helps us think about our hurt in ways that heal and who guides us with the kind of goodwill we need to find rest amidst all the brokenness.

But to truly let go and experience this freedom, we need good boundaries to contain the things of our flesh that threaten to re-afflict our spirit. That means recognizing bitter, judgmental, and unhealthy thoughts that only reignite the flame of negativity. These are thoughts that do not move us in any helpful direction. They are thoughts that, when unknowingly followed, can urge us toward things that separate us from God. Recognizing these thoughts is an important step in learning to let go, so that rather than being imprisoned by hurt, we can learn to break free.

Be the Light They Need

> For God, who said, "Let light shine out of darkness," has shone in our hearts to give the light of the knowledge of the glory of God in the face of Jesus Christ. —2 CORINTHIANS 4:6

When we struggle to forgive, we must remember that it truly is our love that brings others to know Christ's love. It is not our preaching, not our correcting, not our judging, and certainly not our wrath. We can all be vessels of God's goodness, and He calls us to let His light shine with transparency—both in us and through us—so that others may ask, "Who is this God you worship?"

You see, we must never forget that everyone we meet has had a different experience with learning who God is. Some have come to doubt His existence; others have come to know Him only as someone to fear or as something that is far from them because of their past mistakes. But our God is a loving God who shows mercy and compassion, and who does not condemn but yearns to save. We worship a God who wipes the slate clean when we turn our hearts to Him. And yet, no one will come to know our loving God if we don't learn how to reflect His goodness in a way that transcends brokenness. We can't underestimate our influence on others. We can't forget that we can be a positive part of someone's story, a fork in their road, a light that helps draw them in the right direction. And at the very minimum, we strive not to be the obstacle that blocks their path to light.

Through the way we live, we can turn others toward goodness by our goodness. We need only to manifest His spirit of love, humility, and mercy so that we become demonstrators of our faith, not only proclaimers of our faith. In this way, we fulfill the law according to Scripture, which demands us to love our neighbor without partiality and to let "mercy triumph over judgment" (James 2:13). So let us lay aside every judgment, every complicated approach to control, and watch as God works through us to bring healing, comfort, and renewal to us, simply by being a vessel of His goodness.

When we strive to let no enemy work within us, we will stop seeing so many enemies outside of us.

Pray for Them

> To the extent that you pray with all your soul for the person who slanders you, God will make the truth known to those who have been scandalized by the slander. —St. MAXIMUS THE CONFESSOR[9]

While most of us know we should pray for those who hurt us, this can be difficult to do from an authentic place if we haven't first laid down our egos in lieu of a soft and open heart. When we pray, God restores us to goodness in ways that open our hearts to being better able to sincerely pray from a place of goodwill and pure intention. After all, praying may be the primary good we can do not only for ourselves but for the person who has hurt us. Saint Maximus counsels us: "If your brother does not wish to live peaceably with you, nevertheless guard yourself against hatred, praying for him sincerely and not abusing him to anybody."[10]

Jesus tells us not only to love our enemies but to bless those who curse us (Luke 6:27–28), and He also says, "You have heard that it was said, 'You shall love your neighbor and

---

9   "Four Hundred Texts on Love," in *The Philokalia: The Complete Text*, compiled by St. Nikodimos of the Holy Mountain and St. Makarios of Corinth, trans. and eds. GEH Palmer, Phillip Sherrard, and Kallistos Ware, vol. 2 (London: Faber and Faber, 1981), III.

10 *Philokalia*, vol. 2, 104.

hate your enemy.' But I say to you, Love your enemies and pray for those who persecute you" (Matt. 5:43–44). And St. Paul tells the Romans to "bless those who persecute you; bless and do not curse them" (Rom. 12:14). So what better way to bless others who have hurt us than to pray for them? When we get hurt, we aren't necessarily called to give people what they deserve; we are called to give them what they need. We know also that if someone is caught in sin, we who live by the Spirit are called to restore that person gently— not to belittle them, judge them, or condemn them—but to restore them gently by our grace (Gal. 6:1). What better way to restore someone gently than by praying for them?

Ultimately, we pray for others because this life was never meant to be just about us; we do not exist for ourselves but to share God's grace and love. And there has never been a person who didn't matter to God. Even people who hurt us matter to God. In fact, as we noted earlier, those who hurt us are often manifesting hurt that is already in their hearts. So the hurting need our prayers—perhaps more than most. In choosing to pray for those who hurt us, our values in Christ become more important than our anger, and we become more willing to fight for goodness than the devil is willing to fighting for division. And keep in mind that even if praying does not change someone else, we can rest assured that it most certainly changes us.

Have Goodwill Toward Them

Lastly, we remember our instruction not only to leave wrath to God (Rom. 12:19) but rather, as St. Peter says, to "not repay evil for evil . . . but on the contrary, bless, for to this you were called, that you may obtain a blessing" (1 Pet. 3:9). When others act in ways that hurt and disappoint us, it's tempting to forget our boundaries and internalize the offense in ways that change us for the worse. So if we want to operate out of a place of goodness, this isn't the time to separate from our faith but to draw more upon it. To live in right relationship with God, we have to guard what we allow to enter our hearts.

When we approach hurt with goodwill, our thoughts are more contained by wisdom, we pray more, we borrow God's compassion even if we can't feel it, we use humility to remember we too have shortcomings, and we remain discerning over what we allow to take root within us. In this way, goodwill keeps us from internalizing the offense in ways that make us mirror it. When we keep goodness in our heart, it's good not only for us but for the offender, because our goodness can inspire others to reflect and potentially reset, rather than remain hurtful and justified in their ways. We want to act as a mirror of accountability, not in ways that allow the offender to justify their ways.

So the next time you feel hurt by someone's choice, be the change you wish to see and decide to keep goodwill toward them. See the person beneath the mistake: take a moment to consider their past, their abilities, what might have set them up to respond poorly. Remember, most people are likely doing the best they can with what they know and what's in their hearts. Also make sure to choose your words wisely if you share the situation with others. It's easy to lose our goodwill when we start sharing about our anger, because we tend to describe the person who hurt us rather than how what happened affected us. When we share, we must also keep in mind that not every audience listens with a heart that yearns to benefit the work of the Holy Spirit within us. So be discerning who you share your hurt with, being careful to find supportive people who help you respond in ways that honor God. And avoid speaking about your hurt from a place of judgment, criticism, or bitterness, and instead just describe your feelings about what happened. As you strive to keep goodwill, pray for God's mercy to wash over you, the person, and the situation while you wait in hope and anticipation of the healing and greater good that only He can bring.

Conclusion

Christ's words of forgiveness may be the most difficult of the words He spoke on the Cross. Perhaps that is why they were the first—and this is why we must also keep forgiveness first and foremost in our own hearts. Forgiveness *is* difficult, but it is the key to our life in Christ.

The Apostle Paul wrote, "And you, who were dead in your trespasses and the uncircumcision of your flesh, God made alive together with him, having forgiven us all our trespasses, by canceling the record of debt that stood against us with its legal demands. This he set aside, nailing it to the cross" (Col. 2:13–14). You and I are that man, unable to erase our sins on our own, yet relieved of the burden of them by that beautiful Man, Our Savior, who, even as we, His children, took His life from Him, cried, "Father forgive them, for they know not what they do."

FOR DISCUSSION: THE THREE RS—
REST, REFLECT, AND RESPOND

1. What grievances are you holding onto right now that have been hard to forgive?

2. What feelings and thoughts come up in your mind as you read about the "imperative to forgive"?

3. How did the family you grew up in define forgiveness? How did they handle conflict?

4. Does forgiveness feel exceptionally difficult for you or like less of a struggle?

5. What positive qualities or spiritual abilities for promoting goodness do you seem to possess? What comes naturally to you? i.e., Are you a natural at wanting to heal differences? Do you still seem to see the good in others, even amidst your upset? Are you guided more by unity than division? Are you more understanding than judging? Do you seem more drawn toward seeing the silver lining, even in trying situations? Are you drawn toward compassionate and merciful perspectives because empathy feels natural? Which of these natural gifts do you use when it comes to trying to forgive?

6. How might your need for justice or restoration have kept you holding onto anger? How has that anger affected your life?

7. What myths of forgiveness do you most identify with? That if you forgive, you're minimizing what happened? That if you forgive, you're letting the person get away with their behavior? That it would seem like you're just agreeing with what happened? That it would mean you need to save the relationship?

8. How has holding onto anger affected your relationship with God? Yourself? Other people?

9. Do you feel you have truly processed your hurt? Understood why it's there? Is it a pattern in this relationship? How does this person tend to behave in other situations? Do you think your hurt warrants a boundary? If so, what might that look like? What role, if any, do you feel you played in the situation? Was there already a critical, judgmental, or negative narrative about that person in your mind?

10. How can humility help you when you get angry at someone else?

11. How can you use what you are upset about to grow in some way?

CHAPTER 1: *Father, Forgive Them*

12. Can you see the person beneath the offense? How could you humanize them? Though you can't rewrite their childhood or their unique disposition, how might their own struggles have led up to the moment that angered you?

13. Do you struggle with unhealthy thoughts that keep re-afflicting your spirit? Have you replaced the pain with God's presence?

14. Knowing that people are often fighting battles we don't always see, how could you be the light they need? How could you pray for them? Keep goodwill toward them?

PRAYER

O Heavenly Father, as we have completed our reading of your first recorded statement challenging us to also forgive others, let these words not just be words on a page but words that are engraved on our hearts. For we offer this prayer to You, seeking to become, as St. Paul says, "crucified with Christ. . . . [so that] it is no longer I who live, but Christ who lives in me" (Gal. 2:20). We yearn to die to our old self, having been imprisoned by unforgiveness, and to begin a new life, thinking and doing your will of peace, love, compassion, empathy, and grace toward others. Therefore, we humbly ask You to empower us with Your strength so that when we face the darkness of betrayal, hurt, desertion, and insults, we can look to the light of Your love, compassion, and grace revealed to us on the Cross and extend it toward others. Reveal to us when our minds and hearts feel closed in ways that keep us from enjoying the gift of today because we are living in the hurt of yesterday. Help us to remember that none of us are without sin, but it was You, who through the shedding of Your blood, tore up the record of our own sins and destroyed the power of death so that, by Your example, we could learn to be merciful toward the mistakes of others. As we move on to the next page of this book, strengthen us to turn the page on hurt and pain so that we can begin a new chapter, yearning to fulfill the dreams You have for our lives. We pray this in the name of the Father, Son, and Holy Spirit. Amen.

CHAPTER 2

With Me in Paradise

One of the criminals who were hanged railed at him, saying, "Are you not the Christ? Save yourself and us!" But the other rebuked him, saying, "Do you not fear God, since you are under the same sentence of condemnation? And we indeed justly, for we are receiving the due reward of our deeds; but this man has done nothing wrong." And he said, "Jesus, remember me when you come into your kingdom." And he said to him, "Truly, I say to you, today you will be with me in paradise." —LUKE 23:39–43

IF WE UNPACK this Scripture passage, we hear one of the most touching stories in the Bible, a story that gives us hope. It is a story that not only challenges us to take ownership of our mistakes and to constantly grow toward the person Christ has created us to be, but it also assures us that when we turn to Christ, in the process we will be met with the immeasurable and indescribable love of our Savior.

Here, we see Jesus hung on the Cross, unjustly crucified alongside two criminals. We hear the first criminal, who does not appear to believe in Jesus' spiritual authority, hurl insults at Him, saying, "Aren't you the Messiah? Save yourself and us!" Rather than truly asking Jesus to save him, the first thief is lashing out in anger in his final moments. He shows no ownership for his own crime nor compassion for Jesus' innocence. On the other hand, we hear the second criminal rebuke the first, saying, "We are punished justly, for we are getting what our deeds deserve. But this man has done nothing wrong." His humility and genuine reverence for Christ moved him to repentance. And even though he knew he was undeserving, he simply turned to Christ and asked Christ to remember him in His Kingdom.

In this moment, we see a remarkable demonstration of Christ's love and unfailing mercy as He offers up what little energy He had to show us a heart, mind, and will bent toward humankind. In the midst of his own excruciating pain and immense suffering, and out of His profound love for humankind, Christ used one of His last remaining breaths to give this criminal (and, really, all of us) His reassurance that when we turn to Him, He is there to receive us and offer us the hope of salvation.

When Jesus rewards the "penitent thief," He shows us that, even in our mistakes, He is for us, not against us. Christ's response reminds us that nothing can separate us from God if we are honest with ourselves, and if we are willing, amidst our sins, to acknowledge our strongholds—sinful habits that we can't overcome on our own—and to build upon a foundation of genuine reverence for who God is. Yet, how often do we still find ourselves knowingly or unknowingly feeling separated from God amidst our sins?

Our Struggle with the Mirror

Examine yourselves, to see whether you are in the faith. Test yourselves. Or do you not realize this about yourselves, that Jesus Christ is in you?—unless indeed you fail to meet the test! —2 CORINTHIANS 13:5

It is not simply sin itself that creates barriers between us and God. Our *reactions to sin* often build the barriers we have created even higher. The penitent thief shows us the way to remove those barriers, through his willingness to own his mistakes and his deep reverence and trust in Christ as his Redeemer.

Unfortunately, because it's common to avoid anything that makes us uncomfortable, we often unknowingly avoid the type of self-reflection that helps us openly and honestly examine ourselves in the light of Christ. This makes it hard to confront the things that separate us from God. Perhaps this is why the Bible refers to the enemy as the voice of the accuser and the author of deception, because he can, and often does, deceive us into either not seeing our mistakes or convincing us that our mistakes define our value. It is the enemy who establishes all-or-nothing standards that cause us to berate ourselves when we fall short, leaving us feeling condemned and ashamed as we try to confront sin. Ironically, it's also the enemy who fans the flame of sin in our lives by keeping us distracted and blind to temptation. Who has not experienced what Paul describes in Romans 7:15–20?

> For I do not understand my own actions. For I do not do what I want, but I do the very thing I hate.

Now if I do what I do not want, I agree with the law, that it is good. So now it is no longer I who do it, but sin that dwells within me. For I know that nothing good dwells in me, that is, in my flesh. For I have the desire to do what is right, but not the ability to carry it out. For I do not do the good I want, but the evil I do not want is what I keep on doing. Now if I do what I do not want, it is no longer I who do it, but sin that dwells within me.

Though our difficulties can present opportunities to reflect and renew our faith in ways that draw us nearer to Christ, sometimes we feel we lack the strength to embrace these opportunities. Consequently, we get emotionally and spiritually locked into harmful habits and attitudes that hold us back from fulfilling God's greater purpose for our lives. To break down these barriers, we must remember, as Christ reassures us, that there is no one who lives and does not sin. Only Jesus "knew no sin" (2 Cor. 5:21). All the rest of us "have sinned and fall short of the glory of God" (Rom. 3:23), and we are all still learning how to live more closely in His image. We fall, we learn, we get back up, and we do it all over again. Thankfully, God is interested in our hearts, not our faults.

We reflect on ourselves only in order to bring it all back in humility to God as we recognize our need for His grace, love, and mercy. We trust that the Holy Spirit will expose our faults and strengthen us in all places where we struggle, so that we may grow and remain on His path for our lives. When we reflect before God in prayer, we can pray the Troparion from Great Lent found in the Compline service, which could almost be an extrapolation of the penitent thief's words: "I have sinned, O Savior, have mercy on me. Awaken my mind and turn me back; Accept me in repentance and take pity on me as I cry: I have sinned against you, save me; I have done evil, have mercy on me."

Why Vision Matters in the Reflection

Where there is no prophetic vision the people cast off restraint, but blessed is he who keeps the law. —PROVERBS 29:18

If we ever expect to contend with our mistakes in healthier ways, we must maintain a spiritual vision that protects us against doubt, despair, and condemnation. A blind man once asked the Desert Father St. Anthony the Great, "Can there be anything worse than losing your eyesight?" "Yes," replied St. Anthony, "losing your vision."[11] The word for vision in Greek is ὅραμα (*hóramah*), and it means "that which is seen" or "a sight divinely granted."[12] In English, one of the definitions of the word *vision* is "the ability to think about or plan

---

11 Christopher Dullen, *A Little Book of Faith* (Bloomington, IN: Trafford Publishing, 2014), 37.

12 *Bible Study Tools*, s.v. "Horama," accessed September 19, 2023, https://www.biblestudytools.com/lexicons/greek/kjv/horama .html#:~:text=hor'%2Dam%2Dah,in%20a%20sleep%2C%20a %20vision.

the future with imagination and wisdom."[13] Having godly vision, then, means letting what we imagine or see in our future be divinely established and based in God's wisdom. When we have this kind of vision, we affirm who God says we are and can better attend to the guidance of His Holy Spirit. It allows us to keep surrendering our life to God and pursuing His purpose within us, even when our will fails us. It also means continuing to remember and being willing to use our gifts, even in light of our weaknesses. When we maintain this kind of vision, we keep the Holy Spirit close to us. We believe and trust in the great things God has planned for us, and we continue to pray for these things even when we falter.

Inherent in this kind of vision is a trust that God can use our circumstances to grow us in more ways than we dare to dream and that our life will contain chapters better than we can see or imagine. Ironically, having this kind of vision actually strengthens the neural connections we need in order to live that vision. As magnetic resonance imaging (MRI) shows, when people simply imagine themselves doing something—say, competing in a tennis match—the specific areas of their brains necessary for actually performing that action light up, indicating neural activity. Could it be that this is what Romans 12:2 means when it describes

---

13 *Oxford Learner's Dictionary*, s.v. "Vision," accessed September 19, 2023, https://www.oxfordlearnersdictionaries.com/us/definition /american_english/vision#:~:text=%5Buncountable%5D %20the%20ability%20to%20think,politician%2C%20but %20he%20lacks%20vision.

the "renewing of our minds"? That as we envision ourselves living out the values Christ set forth, we actually begin to strengthen the neural pathways in our brains that are necessary to do so?

Does your vision renew your mind and give you hope, despite your mistakes? Does your vision engender the type of purposeful action that helps you to choose the next right thing? Or, does your vision leave you defined by your past? Condemned? Unable to change direction? If the latter is true, know that you are not alone. The world is ever with us, repeatedly telling us who we are, what we can become, and what should define our worth. The voices of dissuasion and disintegration are many, and the struggles we face in this world can cloud our vision and wear us down over time, making us lose sight of all we were meant to become. Because it requires effort and persistence to renew our calling amidst our battles, keeping a godly vision helps bring us back to our calling so that our strongholds do not dictate the course of our lives.

If you struggle to believe in this kind of vision, remember God's assurance that He can use everything we experience— both positive and negative—for our good, growing us in ways we need in order for Him to write the next chapter in the book of our life. This is the moment when we make the promise of Romans 8:28 manifest in our hearts: that in all things we experience, God uses them for our good. Our struggles are merely pruning us for things we don't yet know or fully understand. So our vision shouldn't be defined by what has happened *to* us but by what God is using it for *within* us.

Strongholds Explained

Any area of our life that plagues us and separates us from God is called a *stronghold*. A stronghold is a metaphor or shorthand description of sinful habits of thought, word, and deed that become places in our life that we can't overcome by our own spiritual effort. It could be an innate part of our disposition, an unhealthy thinking style, or a strong temper; it could also be a persistent temptation that hijacks our priorities and consumes our focus, or even an unhealthy habit that no longer serves us well, that we've developed as a result of past experiences. Even something as innocuous as self-pity can become a stronghold if it doesn't allow us to grow in ways we may need to grow. Sometimes we know what our strongholds are, and other times we may only know that there's something that creates distance between us and God.

Either way, strongholds all share something in common: they hold us captive by convincing us that we are in some way trapped by them. We can see this illustrated by a technique that circuses used to use to train elephants to remain under their control. While the elephant was still a baby, trainers would chain it to a stake in the ground. The baby might try to walk off, but it would soon learn that was uncomfortable. It would hurt to pull against the chain, so it was best to wait for the trainer to come and untie it. As the elephant grew, the circus could replace the chain with a simple rope—a rope that the elephant could easily snap. But because the elephant believed that the bond was too strong and that it would be useless to tug against it, it remained captive. We'd all like to think we're more intelligent than an elephant, but the truth is that the human mind often lets breakable bonds hold it back when in fact we are well equipped to overcome so much of what we allow to control us and to separate us from God.

How Can We Detect Our Strongholds?

How do you know if you're stuck in a stronghold? Well, the first indicator is that strongholds separate us from God. The second indicator is that they radiate destruction. Father Nick sometimes asks people in confession to hold up their hands in the shape of a triangle. The tip of that triangle is supposed to represent what we prioritize most in our life. The base is everything else that matters. Whatever is at the tip of our triangle serves as the guiding force for our decisions, the types of thoughts we follow, and our unconscious reactions. It shapes our life. When God is that guiding force, we find His peace, goodness, grace, compassion, and wisdom flowing into every area of our life. But when that guiding force is a stronghold, every domain of our life is affected by its destruction until it dominates our soul.

How can you detect a stronghold? Some common indicators are:

- **They distract us.** Strongholds distract us from anything life-giving because they hijack our focus, perceptions, reactions, and relationships. They operate in the background of our minds, no matter what we are doing. For instance, an overly critical nature can distract us from being present in life's precious moments, unconsciously redirecting our focus toward things that keep us from feeling grateful, accepting, and kind. Or a persistent temptation that we know isn't healthy for our lives may keep unconsciously forcing us to make choices we wish we wouldn't make. Strongholds have an intrusive, almost automatic and reflexive propensity to circumvent our attention and motivation. And instead of being able to pursue the kind of life God intends for us, we feel controlled by their power.

- **They consume us.** Our strongholds can become so much a part of the way we navigate life that we can't tell the difference between them and ourselves. Their voice becomes our voice. Their priorities become our priorities. Their focus becomes our focus, so much so that we forget what truly matters to us and what God would say truly matters.

- **They derail our purpose.** We can become so beholden to our strongholds that we begin to lose sight of our greater purpose. Rather than living the life God intended for us, we live the life our stronghold dictates for us.

- **They target our desires.** The Book of James makes it clear that temptation does not necessarily afflict us out of the blue but can sometimes originate out of our own desires: "But each person is tempted when he is lured and enticed by his own desire. Then desire when it has conceived gives birth to sin" (James 1:14–15). So we can sometimes detect our strongholds by attending to things we deeply yearn for. The devil then energizes those desires and uses them to energize sin. For instance, the desire to be recognized can give birth to pride or envy. The desire to be accepted or loved can lead us to compromise boundaries for what's healthy in a relationship.

Our Reactions to Our Strongholds

I think that if God forgives us we must forgive ourselves. Otherwise it is almost like setting up ourselves as a higher tribunal than Him. —C. S. LEWIS[14]

We must be careful that our reactions to our strongholds don't build even higher walls between us and God than our sin has already created. For instance, pride can prompt blame and defensiveness. Anxiety can prompt avoidance. And judgment can prompt self-disparagement. These responses all block the self-reflection, understanding, and curiosity we need in order to grow through repentance.

---

14 *The Collected Letters of C. S. Lewis: Narnia, Cambridge, and Joy, 1950–1963,* ed. Walter Hooper, vol. 3 (New York: HarperOne, 2007), 109.

Guilt

One of the most common reactions to our strongholds is unproductive guilt. This kind of guilt keeps us looking back at what we cannot change. It's a voice that condemns and belittles, convincing us that we do not deserve love, goodness, mercy, peace, and freedom. It dims our light.

But guilt is a funny thing. Because God has given us a built-in moral compass, our conscience, we know that some guilt can be helpful. Helpful guilt alerts us when we have strayed and urges us to make an adjustment to get back on track because something we've done doesn't sit right with our soul. This type of guilt changes our direction away from things that are separating us from God. It also prompts us to return to faith and seek forgiveness rather than create suffering. Helpful guilt never dims our light but rather shines light on things the Holy Spirit yearns for us to attend to. So this kind of guilt actually draws us closer to God instead of pushing us farther away. Unproductive guilt does not grow us or renew our calling; rather, it traps us in intrusive thoughts of our past that no longer serve us but only leave us feeling condemned and ashamed.

To test what kind of guilt is guiding you, ask yourself whether your guilt makes you recoil from God, like Adam and Eve after they ate the fruit, or turn toward God, like the Apostle Peter rushing toward the risen Christ after having denied Him. If you have asked for forgiveness and corrected your wrongdoing but still feel mired in guilt, then you are being held more strongly by your mistakes than by God.

Pride

Pride is like the flip side of guilt, though it has a similar effect. Rather than feeling downcast about our mistakes, pride causes us to be defensive and to double down in defiant support of our behavior. We might even revert to throwing stones at mistakes other people make, to level the playing field and deflect attention away from our own mistakes.

Pride is a reaction to the vulnerability of true self-awareness as it relates to things that feel hard to acknowledge. The truth is, it's hard to admit our mistakes and own up to things we deeply struggle with. Most of us don't want to be confronted with our brokenness because it leaves us exposed, insecure, and uncomfortable. It's easier to insist that something isn't really a problem or that our behavior is a result of someone else's behavior. It's the "I wouldn't criticize you all the time if you would fix the things I'm asking of you" mindset. So if pride is a struggle for you, look out for downplaying your mistakes, making excuses for why they happen, or turning the tables to assign blame elsewhere. Blame, deflection, and minimization are all the fruits of pride.

Ultimately, pride keeps us more focused on clearing our own name than on glorifying God's name. And although some part of us will know we're doing this, the other part of us will believe the defense and can stay angry at those who may try to bring it up or remain convinced that our struggles are someone else's fault.

Denial

For now we see in a mirror dimly, but then face to face.
Now I know in part; then I shall know fully, even as I have
been fully known. —1 CORINTHIANS 13:12

Another kind of pride denies there is any problem at all. We're familiar with this in cases where change may seem more difficult to address, such as in the case of addiction, betrayal, or deceit. In these situations, pride keeps us from confronting changes we may not be ready or willing to confront, even though it's usually evident just how much our behavior is destroying not only our life, but the lives of those we love. For this kind of pride, admitting that we are enslaved to something feels so damaging and overwhelming that we do almost anything to avoid acknowledging it. But this kind of defensiveness only blinds us to the truth, and we continue to avoid self-reflection, responsibility, and growth. In the end, what we're really avoiding is freedom, because denial keeps us enslaved to sin. As St. Peter wrote, "For whatever overcomes a person, to that he is enslaved" (2 Pet. 2:19). Denial keeps us from confronting the very thing that is controlling us. So in a sense we become slaves, mastered by our own sinful desires.

Helplessness

Sometimes we recognize a stronghold in our life but avoid doing anything to overcome it because it seems too difficult and we feel helpless in the face of it. This can happen if others have taught us to see our limitations rather than our potential. It can also happen if we were criticized, shamed, or made to feel anxious about our mistakes, rather than having been given permission to reflect on them and space to learn from them. It can even happen if we haven't had to deal with many failures or setbacks throughout our life—and now, as a result, we're not used to having to address problems or fix our mistakes.

Despair

At the extreme end of our reactions to our strongholds is despair. Despair is the fruit of hopelessness, and it happens when we have completely lost our vision. We despair, not because we are afraid to see our failures but because when we see them, we are afraid things will never change. It can result from trying and failing so many times to improve something in our lives that eventually, we lose all hope. Despair is one of the most negative and destructive of human emotions because it manifests not only in our thoughts but in our emotions, behaviors, and biology.[15] Its insidious power can leave us feeling forgotten and wondering if maybe we're the one exception to every one of God's promises.

---

15 Lilly Shanahan et al., "Does Despair Really Kill? A Roadmap for an Evidence-Based Answer," *American Journal of Public Health* 109, no. 6 (June 2019): 854–858.

Self-Condemnation

When we react to our sins with self-condemnation, that may feel virtuous or pious, but we can unknowingly give the enemy a foothold in our lives because we begin listening to a voice that is not from God. Think about how Jesus reacted to sin. He didn't condone it, but He also didn't condemn the sinner. More often than not, we hear His overwhelming mercy, love, and undeserved grace toward the sinner and a reminder of truth when it comes to the sin itself. It's truth and grace all at the same time. Getting caught up in self-condemnation can be dangerous for our souls because by blaming and reproaching ourselves we actually create additional wounds that leave us more destabilized.

We must remember that change is led more by grace than reproach. When we give ourselves grace, we lay fertile ground for something new to be born. We bring water out of a desert, allowing God to work in us and through us. Our grace enables us to experience God's grace. We will never change anything positive by withholding compassion, mercy, gentleness, and grace from ourselves; we will only prevent ourselves from experiencing God's compassion, mercy, gentleness, and grace.

Tears

*I will be merciful toward their iniquities, / and I will
remember their sins no more.* —HEBREWS 8:12

When the weight of our heart immobilizes our best efforts
to deal effectively with our feelings, this shouldn't surprise
us. We read in one of the Bible's shortest verses that "Jesus
wept" (John 11:35). These two brief words profoundly illus-
trate how Jesus experienced the same depth of emotion we
do. His tears are a loving reminder that it's okay to cry, to
feel the weight of the world, to recognize change is difficult,
and to pass through seasons of regret and uncertainty. Tears
remind us that the human body was built to endure the difficulties of this life. In fact, our tears are a built-in release
valve for emotion we can't express any other way, because
overwhelming feelings can, and often do, make it hard to
open our hearts and confront what's there. But as tears fall,
the body can release some of the intensity that is blocking
our ability to grow.

So don't despair when the pain is beyond words. In such
moments, we know that the Holy Spirit intercedes for us and
speaks for us when we have no idea what to say. Saint Paul
tells us that "the Spirit helps us in our weakness." We do
not know what we ought to pray for, but "the Spirit himself
intercedes for us with groanings too deep for words" (Rom.
8:26). God also promises that He will be "a shield about
us," "the lifter of our heads," and will "answer us from His
holy hill" (Ps. 3:3–4). So no matter how tough the season
you're facing, don't be afraid of your tears, and "pray without

ceasing" (I Thess. 5:17). Trust that God hears you, loves you, and will answer the worries of your heart because "the Lord is near to the brokenhearted / and saves the crushed in spirit" (Ps. 34:18).

What Lies beneath Our Strongholds

The Bible says, "Be sober-minded; be watchful. Your adversary the devil prowls around like a roaring lion, seeking someone to devour" (I Pet. 5:8). We mustn't forget that we face a spiritual enemy, and we shouldn't underestimate his subtlety. We give the enemy a foothold in our life when we don't attempt to turn away from our sins or when we react to them in ways that make us more vulnerable to sin.

Saint John Chrysostom speaks to our struggles with the enemy when he writes about the Jesus Prayer:

> [The] entire struggle of the devil is to separate and distract the mind from God, and to mislead man into worldly pleasures. And the entire struggle of the soul is to see that the mind is not separated from God. . . . It is therefore necessary that we securely bridle and guide the mind, and reprove every thought and every activity through the name of our Lord Jesus Christ, who takes away the sin of the world.[16]

---

16 *St. John Chrysostom and the Jesus Prayer*, trans. Maximos Constas and Peter A. Chamberas (Columbia, MO: Newrome Press, 2019), 27, 29.

And one of the ways the devil separates us from God is by convincing us that he doesn't exist, because we will not fight against something we don't think is there. He does this by distracting us from focusing on our life and from focusing on God. This disconnection makes it hard for us to recognize when a change of direction is needed, which is how he gains the ability to direct our lives. You see, although the enemy has power, we are the ones who give him the authority to execute that power in our lives. And sadly, while many of us feel awake in this life, we are asleep in our faith, unaware of the darkness that subtly operates in the background of our lives. The sobering truth is that we cannot bear fruit unless we regularly confront *with discernment* the areas of our lives where sin is winning the battle over our soul. We must remain watchful and awake to notice when we are about to follow anything that is not fueled by the Spirit, because we can't *conquer* what we aren't seeing.

This must be why we hear in the Kontakion of Compline during the first week of Great Lent: "My soul, O my soul, rise up! Why are you sleeping? The end draws near and soon you shall be troubled. Watch, then, that Christ your God may spare you, for He is everywhere present and fills all things."

When we feel under attack from the enemy, what can we do? We can call out to Christ, using the Jesus Prayer: "Lord Jesus Christ, Son of God, have mercy upon me, a sinner." You see, "we have an advocate with the Father, Jesus Christ the righteous" (1 John 2:1), and we know that through the

Holy Spirit, He is always at work within us and always on our side. And the teaching of the Orthodox Church reminds us that even the mere mention of Jesus' name has the power to renew a right spirit within us and forcefully repel our enemies, no matter what the enemy is using against us to wage war. Remember, it was the power of Jesus' name, paired with the disciples' faith, that made the demons subject to the disciples: "Therefore God has highly exalted him and bestowed on him the name that is above every name, so that at the name of Jesus every knee should bow, in heaven and on earth and under the earth" (Phil. 2:9–11).

As we resist the enemy, we make room for the Holy Spirit to thrive within our hearts and for God's Word to be a lamp to our feet. We discover a joy that is unparalleled by any circumstantial joy we find in this life. We also begin to experience an inner peace that cannot be contrived by even the greatest gift of Sabbath rest. And as we strengthen our walk of faith in our own daily habits of faith, it becomes easier to identify anything attempting to lead us that's not God's voice. In this way, we help to immobilize the work of the enemy by God's grace as we become deeply committed to living the life He intended for us.

Breaking Free of Our Strongholds

When we turn to God in humility and repentance, we're not only turning away from our destructive strongholds, we are turning toward something life-giving. As St. John Climacus reminds us, "To repent is not to look downwards at our own shortcomings but upwards at God's love, it is not to look backwards with self-reproach but forward with trustfulness, it is to see not what I have failed to be, but what by the grace of God I have yet to become."[17] When we keep our eyes and our hearts fixed on God in the midst of our strongholds, we learn to be more dependent on Him. And as His glory is revealed, we begin to experience what it means to trust in His promises and in the work of His hands.

We must also never forget that God's power to direct our lives is affected by our freewill decisions—by what we fuel, what we choose to let overtake us, and what we allow to simmer in our hearts. That is why we play a role in battling sin. It is upon us to help battle by asking God to shine the light of His Holy Spirit into our hearts when we are thinking in ways we wish we wouldn't, because darkness cannot thrive in light. And we must remember that relying on God's power does not mean we can be passive in the journey of life. In Ephesians 6:10–20, St. Paul insists that in order to win spiritual battles within us, we need to take responsibility for our life and "be strong in the Lord." This is why we hear St. Paul use phrases like "put on," "stand firm," "take up," and "keep alert." These are all active commands that remind us of the importance of our role in battling darkness and choosing to bring light into that darkness by drawing upon God's wisdom, asking the Holy Spirit to renew a right spirit within us.

---

17 William J. Abraham, Jason E. Vickers, and Natalie B. Van Kirk, *Canonical Theism: A Proposal for Theology and the Church* (Grand Rapids, MI: Eerdmans Publishing Company, 2008), 189.

So when the enemy tries to attack our life, we must learn to see it as nothing more than a temptation threatening to take root and that we have a choice not to give the enemy power by watering those seeds.

Perseverance

It's important to remember that breaking free of our strongholds isn't a one-and-done situation; it requires consistent effort. Most people who eventually succeed at something difficult have often failed several times in earlier attempts. The defining difference between those who succeed at a difficult task and those who fail is that those who succeed have demonstrated the humility and patience to persevere. In fact, it's often not the most gifted people who succeed in life but the most determined: the ones who are willing to learn valuable lessons from their failure, dust themselves off, and make another attempt with renewed focus, a different strategy, and an unfailing commitment to succeeding. Overcoming our strongholds requires us to fight with perseverance, as if everything depends on us, and believe in the work of the Holy Spirit, as if everything depends on God. In the waiting, we can remember the words of King David in response to his own continued opposition: "So our eyes look to the LORD our God, / till he has mercy upon us. . . . Have mercy upon us, O LORD, have mercy upon us" (Ps. 123:2–4).

How do we not lose hope during our own metamorphosis? By remembering that God yearns to use our life for good, to honor and to serve Him. And that He knows our hopes and dreams and is always in control. For, as Psalm 139:4 says, "Even before a word is on my tongue, / behold, O LORD, you know it altogether." So even when we can't see how things could possibly come together in light of our struggles, we must remember that "faith is the assurance of things hoped for, the conviction of things not seen" (Heb. 11:1).

Where to Start

God never asks us to change direction without giving us direction, so you can begin to challenge your strongholds with these five steps:

1. **Name it.** This is my battle. (Ps. 32:5; Prov. 28:13; 1 John 1:9)
2. **Own it.** This is my part in the battle. (Ps. 51:3; James 4:8)
3. **Let humility help you through it.** This is why I'm not surprised by my battle. (Rom. 3:23)
4. **Understand it.** This is why I struggle in this battle. (1 Cor. 10:13)
5. **Know why it matters.** This is why I fight the battle. (Rom. 8:13; Gal. 5:19–21)

NAME IT

The first step is to name our struggle. This means putting words on whatever it is that separates us from God or doesn't allow us to serve Him fully. When we name things, they begin to lose their grip on us. Thankfully, there are several seasons throughout the ecclesiastical year where the

Church creates opportunities for us to participate in honest self-reflection. Great Lent is a natural time for this since it is a time to reflect and renew our focus on where we've been and where we wish to go. Think about your own life. What behaviors or thought patterns keep separating you from God? Perhaps you could identify them from one of these common categories below:

- Unhealthy Conflict Patterns (due to reactivity, aggression, or passive aggression)
- Addiction
- Impatience
- Gossip
- Lack of Integrity (doing things in secret)
- Self-Centeredness
- Pride
- Seeking Glory and Recognition
- Wanting Power
- Seeking Status and Reputation
- Wanting Acceptance
- Greed

These are all external strongholds. There are also internal strongholds like:

- Apathy
- Self-Loathing
- Resentment
- Chronic Negativity (that assumes the worst in others)

- Control
- Worry
- Self-Doubt
- Envy
- Hopelessness and Despair

Naming our strongholds requires first becoming aware of them. Think about what creates stress in your life. What keeps you up at night? What causes repeated conflict between you and the important people in your life? What feels hard to say out loud? What do you think about but never say? What do you do but keep secret from others? What do you struggle to forgive in yourself? What blocks you from using your life to serve God? Often, the situations that create the most angst in our life are the ones that illuminate areas where we need to grow, and they point to potential strongholds.

The Bible also gives us certain filters to help us discern our specific strongholds. For example, Romans 8:5 says, "For those who live according to the flesh set their minds on the things of the flesh, but those who live according to the Spirit set their minds on the things of the Spirit." Saint Paul goes on to describe more specifically the desires of the flesh that are opposed to the Spirit. They are "sexual immorality, impurity, sensuality, idolatry, sorcery, enmity, strife, jealousy, fits of anger, rivalries, dissensions, divisions, envy, drunkenness, orgies, and things like these" (Gal. 5:19–21).

So consider which of these urges may be at work within you, causing you to act or think in ways that actively oppose the Spirit. Keep in mind that idolatry could be anything we place above God. Our identities and values can become disproportionately molded by what the world says is important—things like reputation, image/appearance, success, wealth, and social status. If we are not careful, we make gods of these things, as St. Cyprian wrote: "Whatever man prefers to God, that he makes a god to himself."[18] We sometimes make gods out of these other earthly sources of identity. But we can't serve two masters. We have to choose for ourselves, in the midst of temptation, whom we will serve (Josh. 24:15).

Saint Paul also reminds us that "the fruit of the Spirit is love, joy, peace, patience, kindness, goodness, faithfulness, gentleness, self-control" (Gal. 5:22–23). We know that when the Holy Spirit is empowered within us, our thoughts and actions are more likely to be rooted in these fruits of the Spirit. But when our strongholds are empowered, the opposite is true. So to help yourself discover your strongholds, consider what situations keep you from feeling loving or kind. What moments steal your joy? When are you robbed of patience? When do you feel a lack of goodness or faithfulness driving you? Where might you need to be gentler? Where do you lack self-control? Whatever is working against these things is likely a stronghold for you.

---

18 Rosemarie Scott, *Clean of Heart: Overcoming Habitual Sins Against Purity* (North Charleston, SC: CreateSpace Independent Publishing Platform, 2015), 26.

When we are discerning enough to see our own faults, we give ourselves an opportunity to name them and turn away from them. This is why discernment has been called the crown of the virtues. When we are observant, keen in understanding, and self-aware, we begin to recognize our greatest opportunities to embrace the gentle guidance God provides to help us live more closely in His image.

Own It

Once we name our stronghold, we must work to change it. You see, we can name something and still never address changing it because of how we define that struggle to ourselves. For instance, if we name our struggle but put the responsibility or blame on someone or something else (as in "I do this because he/she does that"), then the responsibility for changing it always rests on something or someone else. Rather, when others act in ways that upset us, owning our role in that struggle means knowing we are still called to operate out of a place of light. It's recognizing that our commitment to act according to goodness is what paves the way for light to transcend our difficult moments. Without knowing our part in something, we can unknowingly fuel darkness.

To own something is not about blame per se, but about acknowledging that we have some responsibility in the struggle we face and realizing we have a choice in how we respond to our difficulties. When we acknowledge our part in something, it empowers us to be able to improve upon it. For instance, to say, "I play a role in permitting my insecurity and self-doubt to keep me from using my gifts in ways that serve God" or "I play a role in allowing my critical nature to keep hurting the people I care about" means we take some level of responsibility, no matter the origin.

If we do this in prayer or with a spiritual leader, it can be quite life-giving. Shining the light of truth on our hearts shows not only our own weakness—where, again, Christ's power is made perfect (2 Cor. 12:9)—but also the weakness of our stronghold.

A good way to own our part in our struggle is to consider the things that bother us and ask, "What could I do or have done differently to make this situation better?" You may also need to ask related questions like:

- What's *my* role in this situation? What do I see in myself when this temptation hits?
- How do my reactions to the situation fuel my struggle or make the situation worse?
- Do I hear blame when I tell myself the story of my struggle?
- What am I saying to myself that could be giving me permission not to see my part in this? Does it sound like God's voice? The enemy's voice? My own voice?
- How does this struggle at the tip of my triangle affect other areas of my life?

Through self-reflection, the wisdom that is present in all things will help us grow and will illuminate our own path to righteousness.

LET HUMILITY HELP YOU THROUGH IT

To truly see our strongholds, we must be open to wisdom, and to be open to wisdom, we must also be open to humility. Humility does not mean feeling bad about ourselves. It just means realizing that we are all still learning how to live more like Christ, as evidenced by St. Paul's reminder that we "all have sinned and fall short of the glory of God" (Rom. 3:23). Humility gives us the foundation we need to live out our purpose, to grow more and more into the likeness of God by opening our hearts to grace. And while the process of learning to live more like Christ is the result of the work of the Holy Spirit, our openness to doing that work is paramount because God does not force us to live in communion with Him—He gives us the freedom to choose to live in communion with Him. Humility, then, helps us receive the grace God yearns to give us.

Keep in mind that if we struggle with humility, it may not necessarily be because of pride. It could be due to things like perfectionism driven by insecurity, which keeps us defensive about our own shortcomings. If this is you, try to remember that our confidence was never supposed to be in ourselves but in what God can do within us. And our flaws don't define us, or change whose we are; we are all sons and daughters of Christ whom He loves and has created for good works. Our flaws don't change what God can use us for or what He can accomplish through our lives. So we name our strongholds not to feel worse about ourselves but to be realistic about what we're up against and to open ourselves up to working on what separates us from God.

UNDERSTAND IT

Once we've identified our stronghold and owned our role in it, with humility as our foundation, now it's time to make sense of why it's there. Because in order to change the "what" in our life, we must understand the "why" that keeps us going back to it. For instance, if we struggle with living life frantic, exhausted, overloaded, and overwhelmed, we may not succumb to the healthiest of behaviors to keep us going, or we may find ourselves dealing with a stronghold of negativity, irritability, or reactivity. Or if we live life without properly learning how to manage our insecurities, we may find ourselves dealing with a stronghold of self-pity or envy. To better understand your stronghold, try to track it, get curious about it, and study what drives it. Try pausing the next time you find yourself struggling and practice nonjudgmentally noticing what's going on. You might ask yourself:

- What need is this stronghold serving in my life?
- Is there something it gives me that seems to matter to me more than God?
- Could it be a hardwired part of my personality?
- Did I see this in the people around me when I was growing up?
- If I had to tell my story of how this came to be, what would I say?
- Who am I pleasing by doing this?
- What blocks me from doing the right thing?
- How does it help or hurt my journey toward Christ?

- What do I usually feel right before I engage it? What's typically going on for me?
- How have other people conquered this issue, and what can I learn from them?
- What tools might I need to overcome this?

As we learn more about our stronghold, we'll start to see ways to overcome it, because when we seek understanding in the light of Christ, we gain it. We hear this in the prayer of the Trisagion Hymn: "You have created man according to Your image and likeness and adorned him with all the gifts of Your grace. You give wisdom and understanding to the one who asks, and You overlook not the sinner, but have set repentance as the way of salvation." So it's important to pray for wisdom and understanding, and to refuse any unhealthy reactions that block that understanding and threaten to tear us down rather than draw us to grow toward Christ. Keep in mind, God doesn't want us to focus only on what we've done but on who He is calling us to become.

Why It Matters

Just because we don't acknowledge spiritual warfare doesn't mean it's not there. The enemy doesn't come in a red cape and big horns. Rather, he is often in the details—the subtle things we find ourselves seeing as acceptable. He's in the detachment we feel about things that should matter to us and the people God has placed in our lives. He's in the priority we place on material things and in the hurry we feel that doesn't allow us to truly stop and see the people

God has put along our path. He's in the temptation to be driven more by money than by changing people's lives, and he's in the way we allow life to get so far out of balance that we struggle to feel the peace and goodness of the Holy Spirit. He's in all the things that distract us from living for God.

That is why the Bible warns us that the enemy yearns "to steal and kill and destroy" us (John 10:10) and why we are called to stay alert. Because despite our best intentions, it's quite easy to succumb to temptation, to bow down to the wrong values, and to find ourselves putting something on this earth ahead of God. Although we were made in the image of God, we are very much imperfect in our humanity. We are free to set our minds on the things the Holy Spirit desires—to actively pursue what is upright, good, virtuous, and pleasing to God. Or, we are free to be driven by the flesh, by habits and attitudes that oppose the spiritual life and lead us away from God.

So, the gift of a new life is not magical; it requires our willingness to live in ways that honor God by creating the right conditions for grace to abound within us. When we strive, the Holy Spirit helps us thrive.

If you don't think temptation is at work within you, threatening to take charge over your life, try dealing with difficult people and not getting defensive or combative, especially when you feel questioned, talked down to, or otherwise not supported. Try praying for ten minutes straight and notice how quickly your mind begins to wander. Try showing respect and curiosity with a pure heart when someone is

upset or criticizing you. Try committing to daily Bible reading, and watch how quickly other tasks threaten to replace
it. Try allowing an interruption from someone in need, even
when you are in a hurry. Try being patient when you are
tired, or loving when you are angry, or try to honor Christ
when you feel unjustly persecuted.

The truth is, it's hard to choose well, and we are all still
learning how, by God's grace, to conquer the sinful passions
that arise when we surrender to the temptations of the flesh.
This is why St. Paul calls us to act with intention, to:

- Live as "Children of light" (Eph. 5:8–10), which
  means we must remain vigilant of our motivations,
  striving to live wisely according to what God says
  matters most, because "the days are evil" (5:16).
- "Be imitators of God" (Eph. 5:1), "walk in love"
  (v. 2), and "take no part in the unfruitful works of
  darkness" (v. 11).
- "Walk by the spirit" so we do not "gratify the desires
  of the flesh," which are "against the Spirit" and "are
  opposed to each other" (Gal. 5:16–18). The flesh
  here refers to our carelessness, and our human nature
  in its present weak and imperfect condition, which is
  what manifests itself in sin.
- "Not be conformed to this world, but be transformed
  by the renewal of your mind, that by testing you may
  discern what is the will of God, what is good and
  acceptable and perfect" (Rom. 12:2).

Notice these are all verbs—commands and calls to action. Because to be passive in addressing our struggles does not allow us to do our part in separating from darkness. And we must strive to live in such a way that allows God to work in our lives, accepting that both our effort to live wisely, and our full dependence on God to produce the result of our efforts, can and should exist simultaneously. It is only in this way that we find peace, transformation, and rest for our souls.

CHANGING DIRECTION

The very first sermon Christ preaches is "Repent, for the kingdom of heaven is at hand" (Matt. 3:2). Repenting, or changing direction, means changing how we live in the world today and choosing to live more for the Lord. We've been paving the way for repentance by reflecting on our stronghold, naming the area of our life where we keep getting stuck, owning our part in it, and coming to an understanding of why it's there. The next step is to repent of continuing to put that stronghold between us and God. That means we make an active decision to stop allowing our stronghold to control our lives.

Repentance does this for us by helping us reflect and reorder our priorities. Because there's a name for our strongholds that we haven't used yet: *idolatry*. Anything we give power to above God is an idol. So in this step we're saying, "God, you are first in my life, and I'm going to reject anything that tries to come before you." It's no accident that the first commandment is "You shall have no other gods before me" (Ex. 20:3). Because anything we prioritize in this life will have power over our life. So repentance is literally about interrupting our unhealthy cycles of behavior or thought at any point:

- **Before the behavior or thought occurs:** Anticipate the thought or behavior, repent, and reroute to something that better reflects your faith.
- **After the behavior or thought has begun:** Catch yourself as you slip, then repent and reroute at any point. It's never too late to do the next right thing.
- **After you find yourself doing it again:** Confess, repent, then go back to name it, own it, and work to understand it. Replace condemnation with curiosity to continue to gain understanding. Decide on a plan to reroute next time. How will you approach it next time, to give God glory instead?

After you have interrupted the thought or behavior you are trying to break free from, it can be helpful to pray Psalm 51, the great psalm of repentance.

It can also help you to remember that in your repentance, you are not alone in your struggles. The Bible provides us with numerous examples of people who struggled.

- Esau gave up his birthright for stew (Gen. 25:29–34).
- Ananias and Sapphira wrecked their lives for money (Acts 5:1–11).
- Judas betrayed Jesus for coins (Matt. 26:14–16).

- Pilate fell to peer pressure (Mark 15:15).
- Samson lost his anointing because he was lustful and had a problem with women (Judg. 16:4–21).
- King David had affairs (2 Sam. 11:1—12:25).
- Joseph's brothers were jealous—seeking to be masters, they became enslaved (Gen. 37:1–11).
- Joseph faced temptation when Potiphar's wife attempted to seduce him (Gen. 39:6–12).

FASTING

Participating in spiritual disciplines such as fasting can also help us vanquish our strongholds. The Church has developed spiritual disciplines for a reason. These are the tools we have found useful over the centuries for encountering God. While fasting may be a culturally popular activity for health reasons, we mustn't underestimate its usefulness for us spiritually.

As we look at how fasting affects us physically, we begin to see great parallels for how it helps us spiritually. When the body fasts, it does not have access to its preferred source of fuel. This forces the cells to resort to other means of producing energy. Interestingly, the body begins a natural process of producing its own sugar. Fasting forces cells to rely on processes that are not usually stimulated when a steady stream of fuel exists from external forces. By putting the body under mild stress, fasting forces our cells to learn how to rely on other processes to sustain life that already exist within us, but the adaptation itself actually makes them stronger and more resilient. Research has shown fasting boosts mental clarity and cognitive performance, preserves learning and memory, slows disease processes in the brain, benefits us in the battle against disease, and rids our bodies of toxins and damaged cells and replaces them with new healthy ones.[19]

Spiritually when we fast, we practice dying to our flesh and our passions. We let go of earthly things that normally fuel us, and we force our bodies to adapt and rely on a source of replenishment that already exists within us. Fasting teaches us to rely on another source to sustain us. As we do so, we gain mental clarity and find freedom as the desires and impulses of the body are brought more under the harness of self-control. We essentially teach the body to submit to the soul and learn to depend more on God in every circumstance. This spiritual realignment disciplines our fleshly nature to stay in its proper place.

Fasting is not an end in itself, nor does it make us more perfect on its own; rather, it is a tool to help our spirit strengthen for spiritual warfare. The prophet Isaiah reminds us that fasting serves to loosen the bonds of sin and empowers our spirit to bring about good works within us:

---

19 See Roger Collier, "Intermittent Fasting: The Science of Going Without," *Canadian Medical Association Journal* 185, no. 9 (June 11, 2013): E363–4 and Rafael de Cabo and Mark P. Mattson, "Effects of Intermittent Fasting on Health, Aging, and Disease," *The New England Journal of Medicine* (December 26, 2019): 2541–2551.

Is not this the fast that I choose: / to loose the bonds of wickedness, / to undo the straps of the yoke, / to let the oppressed go free, / and to break every yoke? / Is it not . . . to hide yourself from your own flesh? / Then shall your light break forth like the dawn, / and your healing shall spring up speedily; / your righteousness shall go before you; / the glory of the LORD shall be your rear guard. (Is. 58:6–8)

As we fast to conquer our struggles, we must also pray for God to enable us by the power of His Holy Spirit so that we can acquire the virtues we need and grow in wisdom and character.

So now there is a large body of evidence that supports the benefits of fasting, but we know that great people of faith in the Bible have modeled this practice for years as a means of growing closer to God. We hear about Moses, who fasted for at least two recorded forty-day periods before he received the Commandments, and Christ, who also fasted forty days and nights before starting His public ministry. We also hear about David, Elijah, Daniel, Paul, and countless others who all fasted as a tool to grow closer to God—for repentance, for protection, and for answers to prayer.[20]

PRAYER

In order to conquer our strongholds, we must also pray unceasingly! Prayer puts us in communication with God, not

---

20 See Ex. 34:28; Deut. 9:18–19; 2 Sam. 12:15–20; I Kin. 19:8; Dan. 9:3, 10:2–3; Matt. 4:2; 2 Cor. 11:27.

to remind Him of our presence, but to remind us of His. As we open up our concerns, questions, struggles, and needs to God with vulnerability and transparency, we open our hearts to His Holy Spirit, and even when we come to God and don't know what to say or how to say it, the Holy Spirit intercedes and speaks for us. Through prayer we acknowledge our humility before God and our need for Him, and we remember that we were never meant to battle alone. When we battle our strongholds by falling to our knees with our hands outstretched, we remember that faith is our shield and God's love is our armor. In prayer, we trust that through the grace of the Holy Spirit, God gives us what we need to overcome any struggle that affects our salvation.

Prayer has two sides: the words we speak to God and the words we receive by listening to Him. Often, solitude is important so that we can listen in the silence that follows prayer. Reading our Bible can help, too, to replace the voice of this world with the voice of the One who loves us, designed us, and promises good things for us. To help you hear the voice of God as you read the Bible, before reading it, pray what the priest prays before we hear the Holy Gospel in the Divine Liturgy: "Shine in our hearts, O Master Who loves mankind, the pure light of your divine knowledge, and open the eyes of our mind that we may comprehend the proclamations of Your Gospels. Instill in us also reverence for Your blessed commandments, so that, having trampled down all carnal desires, we may lead a spiritual life, both thinking and doing all those things that are pleasing to You." While listening in silence to God's voice, we suggest again praying the Troparion that echoes the words of the penitent thief so well: "I have sinned, O Savior, have mercy on me. Awaken my mind and turn me back; accept me in repentance and take pity on me as I cry: I have sinned against you, save me; I have done evil, have mercy on me."

GRACE

Thankfully, we were never meant to overcome our weaknesses alone. The Apostle Paul reminds us about the strength of God's grace in weakness: "But he said to me, 'My grace is sufficient for you, for my power is made perfect in weakness.' Therefore I will boast all the more gladly of my weaknesses, so that the power of Christ may rest upon me" (2 Cor. 12:9).

As we work to free ourselves from our strongholds and embrace the vulnerability of our weaknesses, we make room to experience the gift of God's grace. In all our mistakes, God grants us His grace because none of us are immune to sin. He knows our secrets, our failures, our brokenness, and all the things our weary hearts struggle to hold on to because of moments of regret. Yet, God doesn't want us to carry our burdens alone and reminds us, "Come to me, all who labor and are heavy laden, and I will give you rest. Take my yoke upon you, and learn from me, for I am gentle and lowly in heart, and you will find rest for your souls. For my yoke is easy, and my burden is light" (Matt. 11:28–30).

When self-compassion and humility accompany our repentance, we lay fertile ground for God's grace to work within us. Self-compassion is a means of confronting our inadequacies with a merciful rather than judgmental inner voice. It stops us from global attacks on our character and instead allows us to confront our struggles with loving-kindness rather than harsh criticism and condemnation. Self-compassion is protective to our soul because, rather than getting caught up in the currents of unnecessary secondary emotion that can cause our spirit to drift into dark places, we can instead focus on growth as we learn to assess our shortcomings with a pure heart in ways that breed goodness and the transformation God seeks for our life. It is His grace that calms our spirits and breathes new life into our troubles. It is His grace that stops the emotions that flood us as we struggle with our strongholds and helps them begin to dissipate, and it is His grace that helps us become more receptive to the work He wills within us. And we will need to open ourselves to grace over and over, as our Faith teaches us that the spiritual journey involves constant falling and getting back up again in an environment of grace and hope.

If we are accepting God's grace as sufficient, we are also remembering to avoid all of those reactions that only create more shame and despair, and distract us from real problem-solving and keep us stuck in negative emotions and a vicious cycle of continued struggle. Accept grace and commit to being a gentle guide to yourself. And do what you can to maintain an internal voice that reflects God's loving voice of compassion, knowing that God would never lead us in ways that are unloving because "all the paths of the LORD are steadfast love" (Ps. 25:10).

Moving On

> *So we do not lose heart. Though our outer self is wasting away, our inner self is being renewed day by day.* —2 CORINTHIANS 4:16

Do not despair if all of this feels difficult. God is on our side, and He has a plan for us to bear much fruit for His Kingdom. We set ourselves up to grow when we reflect on our values in relation to our impulses and choices, learn from them, and then reset and try again tomorrow. We must keep in mind that we don't have to do any of this on our own. The goal of remembering God's grace is not to find ourselves sinless but to look at our real-life struggles, mistakes, and regrets through the lens of Christ's love and assurance. In this way our spiritual life unfolds as a journey, rather than as a stumbling block that keeps us far from Christ.

And to truly break down our barriers, we must remember that there is no one who lives and does not sin. Only Jesus "knew no sin" (2 Cor. 5:21). Thankfully, God is interested in our hearts, not our faults. And thankfully, His grace is there to meet us in our weaknesses.

And although we often make choices in our lives that we wish we could go back and change, we cannot evaluate our choices in the *past* with knowledge and wisdom we have realized in the *present*. Why? Because that would mean we would be judging ourselves for not having the very wisdom we gained as a result of having had those experiences! So keep in mind, although we live our lives looking forward, we are often only able to make sense of things when we look backward. Life is a constant evolution of learning and growing in Christ. And God can't write a new chapter in our life if we keep living in the guilt of old chapters. Through Christ, we can turn the page. The whole point of finding freedom through repentance is to turn our focus toward the future God has planned for us, rather than being held up by the sin our enemy has planned for us.

We all have within us deeply rooted weaknesses, passions, and defects. This cannot all be cut out with one sharp motion but requires patience, persistence, care, and attention. The path leading to perfection is long. Pray to God so that He will strengthen you. Patiently accept your falls and, having stood up, immediately run to God, not remaining in that place where you have fallen. Do not despair if you keep falling into your old sins. Many of them are strong because they have received the force of habit. Only with the passage of time and with fervor will they be conquered. Don't let anything deprive you of hope.

For Discussion: The Three Rs—
Rest, Reflect, and Respond

1. What stronghold affects your life most? What feels hard to acknowledge within yourself?

2. How do you talk to yourself about this struggle? How do you normally react to thinking about it?

3. How does it affect your vision? What vision do you think God still has for your life?

4. What do you see as your gifts, even in light of your struggles?

5. What destruction does your stronghold radiate throughout your life? How does it distract you? Consume you? Affect God's purpose within you?

6. Which reaction to your strongholds threatens to separate you even further from God? Guilt? Pride? Denial? Helplessness? Despair? Self-condemnation?

7. Name what creates stress in your life. What keeps you up at night? What causes repeated conflict between you and the important people in your life? What do you think about or do that you would rather keep secret from others? What within you keeps you from bearing the fruit of the Holy Spirit?

8. Own what you take responsibility for in perpetuating the struggle you fight. What could you be doing differently to improve your response to this struggle? What values and priorities are maintaining it?

9. Understand your stronghold. What and why is it there? What need is it serving in your life? What do you fear if you let go of it? What biblical story feels similar? What can you learn from that story?

10. What is on your throne of your life?

11. What active decision can you make today to stop doing whatever it is you struggle with? Have you sought forgiveness? What active change can you make today that could change the direction of your life?

12. How can you better anticipate acting on your stronghold and reroute ahead of time?

13. How can you better catch yourself if you have fallen into it, and reroute in real time?

14. How can you better understand your fall, and what can you learn from it to help you better be able to reroute next time?

15. How are you using prayer and fasting to help you with your stronghold?

16. How does your stronghold help you depend more on God?

17. Is there a stronghold you have not let yourself move on from, even though you have overcome it?

18. How could you better contain your thinking about it within the walls of the virtues set forth for us: mercy, empathy, compassion, and nonjudgment?

PRAYER: FROM THE SERVICE OF HOLY COMPLINE

As you confront your strongholds, return to this prayer as often as it is helpful:

Prayer to our Lord Jesus Christ

And grant to us, Master, as we depart for sleep, rest of body and soul, and preserve us from the gloomy slumber of sin, and from every dark and nocturnal pleasure. Arrest the drives of passion; extinguish the burning arrows of the evil one which insidiously fly in our direction; suppress the rebellions of our flesh, and calm our every earthly and material thought. And grant to us, O God, alert mind, prudent thinking, sober heart, light sleep free of any satanic fantasy. Awaken us at the time of prayer rooted in Your commandments and having unbroken within us the remembrance of Your ordinances. Grant that we may sing

Your glory through the night by praising and blessing and glorifying Your most honorable and majestic name, of the Father and of the Son and of the Holy Spirit, now and ever, and to the ages of ages. Amen.

CHAPTER 3

Woman, Behold, Your Son

Standing by the cross of Jesus were his mother and his mother's sister, Mary the wife of Clopas, and Mary Magdalene. When Jesus saw his mother and the disciple whom he loved standing nearby, he said to his mother, "Woman, behold, your son!" Then he said to the disciple, "Behold, your mother!" And from that hour the disciple took her to his own home. —JOHN 19:25–27

WE ALL EXPERIENCE times in our lives when we feel like we are in a cycle of one bad day after another— or worse, when we start to feel like the ground beneath us is crumbling and we are scared, broken, angry, or worried. When we go through these difficult days, it is natural to feel overwhelmed by the pain of our circumstances because they impact us not only emotionally but spiritually and physically. During these times, we can feel very alone. It can be helpful to realize that even the Theotokos, the Mother of God, felt as we sometimes do. We can hear her sadness summed up beautifully with the words of the hymnographer when we pray during the Orthodox Church's Holy Week service:

> The Virgin Mother, seeing her own Lamb led to the slaughter, followed wailing with the other, and cried

[to her son], "Where are you going, my child? Why do you travel along so fast? Would there perhaps be another wedding in Cana, and you hurry there, to turn from them water into wine? Can I not come with You, my Child? Or delay with You? Speak to me a word; You, who are the Word. Pass me not by in silence, You, who kept me pure. For You are my Son and my God."[21]

To make matters worse, Joseph, the foster father of Christ, had already died, since he was not present at the Crucifixion—and this would have further amplified the loneliness and despair the Blessed Mother felt.

But in His third statement from the Cross, Jesus offered hope and comfort to His mother—as well as to us. Despite the excruciating pain Jesus must have been enduring, His focus was not on His pain but rather on providing comfort. He was not so consumed with the agony of the Cross that He forgot the healing power of connection. These words remind us all that even in our darkest days we can find comfort in the connection we were meant to have with the people God has put in our lives. We were not meant to walk through our struggles alone.

---

21 *Greek Orthodox Holy Week and Easter Services: New English Translation*, comp. and trans. George L. Papadeas (Daytona Beach, FL: Patmos Press, 2016), 250.

Our Need for Connection

While most of us intuitively understand that we need connection, and most of us would choose to have strong, intimate relationships over being alone, too many of us struggle
with feeling alone. In fact, at any given time, roughly sixty
million Americans acknowledge loneliness as a major source
of unhappiness and feel that no one in their life "really knows
them well."[22] But what is loneliness, exactly? Loneliness as a
condition has been described as a "discrepancy between an
individual's preferred and actual social relations."[23] This discrepancy between the connections we want to have, and the
ones we actually have, leads to the negative experience of feeling alone or the distress of feeling socially isolated even when
among family or friends.

With loneliness, then, it's possible to experience feeling a
lack of connection, whether we are alone or surrounded by
others. And the truth is, no one is immune from loneliness.
It can strike all of us at any age and at any season of life.
Whether we have become a new mom, moved to a new community, transitioned to working from home, have become

---

22 "The Loneliness Epidemic Persists: A Post-Pandemic Look
   at the State of Loneliness among U.S. Adults," The Cigna
   Group Newsroom, accessed February 25, 2023, https://
   newsroom.thecignagroup.com/loneliness-epidemic-persists-post
   -pandemic-look
23 Julianne Holt-Lunstad et al., "Loneliness and Social Isolation as
   Risk Factors for Mortality: A Meta-Analytic Review," *Perspectives
   on Psychological Science* 10, no. 2 (March 2015): 227–237.

homebound due to a chronic health condition, have lost a loved one, or just don't feel a sense of true connection with the people around us, many life situations can leave us susceptible to loneliness, where we experience a lack of belonging, not just a lack of people.

Loneliness manifests in situations like these because God created us to live in community and to experience the life-giving power of connection. Throughout human history, we've actually adapted based on this need. Whether it came to meeting our basic needs for food, water, and shelter or protecting ourselves from physical threats, our very survival as a species has depended on our ability to connect to one another! Studies have demonstrated that our need to connect is hardwired into our survival. For example, in studying how stress, loneliness, and social isolation affect the brain and mind, neuroscientist Livia Tomova found that loneliness triggers the same neural activity in the brain as what we see when people are hungry and looking for food. So essentially, loneliness can cause cravings for companionship that are as strong as hunger or thirst.[24]

Studies have also suggested that when we feel loneliness from rejection, brain regions tied to feelings of uncertainty, rumination, and stress light up on functional magnetic resonance imaging (fMRI).[25] Another study found that when people were told to think about rejection or were reminded of

---

24 Stephanie Cacioppo et al., "A Quantitative Meta-Analysis of Functional Imaging Studies of Social Rejection," *Scientific Reports* 3, no. 2027 (2013).

25 Cacioppo, et al.

having been rejected by a relationship ending, their thoughts provoked the same activity in brain regions as when people experienced physical pain.[26] This is why rejection hurts so much, because neurologically speaking, it's literally painful. Feeling lonely can also have bearings on what we pay attention to. Researchers have found that the brain activates more in response to negative stimuli than to positive triggers when we feel lonely.[27] So, when we feel lonely, we are more likely to attend to things that make us feel cynical or hurt by others and to withdraw from relationships we feel have hurt us, which creates a "self-reinforcing loop." Loneliness can make us feel stressed, distant, uncertain, and prone to overthinking, and it can damage our sense of well-being and our relationships.

Perhaps unsurprisingly, studies also show that people with close friends fare better than those without. For starters, people with strong relationships are a full fifty times less likely to experience premature death.[28] They are also more likely to feel happy about their lives and to be in good

---

26 Ethan Kross et al., "Social Rejection Shares Somatosensory Representations with Physical Pain," *Proceedings of the National Academy of Sciences of the United States of America* 108, no. 15 (March 2011): 6270–5.

27 Julianne Holt-Lunstad, Timothy B. Smith, and J. Bradley Layton, "Social Relationships and Mortality Risk: A Meta-analytic Review," *PLOS Medicine* 7, no. 7 (July 2010): e1000316.

28 Javier Yanguas, Sacramento Pinazo-Henandis, and Fransisco José Tarazona-Santabalbina, "The Complexity of Loneliness," *Acta Biomedica* 89, no. 2 (June 2018): 302–314.

health.[29] Additionally, a 2015 meta-analysis detailed scores of benefits of relationships, from longevity to positive effects on body mass index, diabetes, cancer, cognitive decline, and numerous psychological measures.[30] These studies show us, but we also instinctively know, that the presence of rich, deep, joy-producing, life-changing, and meaningful connection is essential to our emotional, physical, and spiritual well-being.

Interestingly, we can even see our built-in wiring for connection in how we react to other people's emotions. Whether pain, sorrow, joy, or surprise, emotions can actually be passed from one person to another. How? Because we have discovered something within human beings called *mirror neurons.* These brain cells fire the same way whether we experience an emotion ourselves or whether we see others experiencing that emotion. For example, when we see someone else's sadness, our mirror neurons fire in response, allowing us to experience their sadness as well, which lends itself to our experience of empathy.[31]

29 Debra Umberson and Jennifer Karas Montez, "Social Relationships and Health: A Flashpoint for Health Policy," *Journal of Health and Social Behavior* vol 51, suppl. (2010): S54–66.

30 Jessica Martino, Jennifer Pegg, Elizabeth Pegg Frates, "The Connection Prescription: Using the Power of Social Interactions and the Deep Desire for Connectedness to Empower Health and Wellness," *American Journal of Lifestyle Medicine* 11, no. 6 (2015): 466–475.

31 Lea Winerman, "The Mind's Mirror," *The American Psychological Association* 36, no. 9 (October 2005): 48, https://www.apa.org/monitor/oct05/mirror.

Isn't that remarkable? We are literally built to mimic each other in ways that build emotional connection. It's why we synchronize facial expressions, vocalizations, postures, and behaviors with those of others. And this happens involuntarily, which means we are responding all the time to what happens to people around us.

So as we are seeing, connection is of utmost importance for our lives in so many ways! And it's also a necessity for our spiritual lives. Consider for a moment:

> Whether it's the simple gesture of the one person who takes notice of you and genuinely smiles;
> or the stranger who offers up a random compliment in the midst of your terrible day;
> or the person whose genuine care says "I'm with you" in the midst of a dark season;
> or the person who says nothing at all but whose reassuring and unwavering presence feels safe and dependable;
> or the person whose compassion makes you feel less alone because they aren't afraid to enter into whatever emotional space you are in;
> or the person who listens without passing judgment;
> or the person whose lighthearted and joyful disposition lightens whatever load you are holding because you are able to borrow their spirit of joy just long enough to come up for air when life feels heavy . . .

It's the comforting words and presence of others that help us experience God's healing comfort. After all, isn't it through others that we often feel His presence and hear the words He wants us to hear?

Scriptures about Connection

While we have seen clear evidence that we were built for connection in the flesh, does Scripture have anything to say about the spiritual benefits for us? Let's journey back to the beginning of creation. We know that when God first created human beings, He saw that it was "not good that the man should be alone" (Gen. 2:18), so He made Eve. We also know that God makes new life possible when a husband and a wife are joined together. And that when the spirit of a person and the Spirit of God come together in Holy Baptism, a new birth takes place, and that when the disciples came together on the day of Pentecost, there was an outpouring of the Holy Spirit, exemplifying the words in the Book of Matthew that where two or more are gathered in His name, God is present (Matt. 18:20). We hear King Solomon echo this idea when he says, "Two are better than one, because they have a good reward for their toil. For if they fall, one will lift up his fellow" (Eccl. 4:9–10). He expounds on this by saying that "though a man might prevail against one who is alone, two will withstand him—a threefold cord is not quickly broken" (4:12). This is why the enemy works so hard to divide and isolate us. He splits marriages, friendships, countries, communities, and churches.

Scripture also talks about the spiritual benefits of connection in terms of the Church community. The writer of

Hebrews tells us to "not [neglect] to meet together, as is the habit of some," but to "[encourage] one another, and all the more as you see the Day drawing near" (10:25). And Peter says, "As each has received a gift, use it to serve one another, as good stewards of God's varied grace" (I Pet. 4:10).

And truthfully God, by essence, is relational. He yearns for a relationship with us and yearns for us to have relationships with each other. He tells us that the two most important commandments are to love Him and love others. He reminds us that apart from Him we can do nothing and that we should "abide" in Him because we cannot bear fruit unless we remain connected to Him (John 15:4). Even the act of Creation itself was an expression of God's love for us and His desire to connect with us, and it now offers limitless opportunities for us to share His love with each other.

So part of what it means to be made in God's image is to have a capacity and proclivity for relationship and connection. In essence, we all have a relational identity because of our being made in the image of the eternal, heavenly communion of love that is the divine relation of Persons, Father, Son, and Holy Spirit. And the Holy Spirit longs to be powerfully at work in every encounter we have when we connect to others.

Obstacles to Receiving Connection

If we were built for connection, why do many of us struggle so much to feel connected? The truth is, there are all sorts of obstacles, internal and external, to feeling connected.

Isolation

Many of us feel isolated, like we literally have no one with whom we truly connect. This feeling is a very different experience than what we experience in solitude. Solitude is when we choose to be alone for the purpose of prayer, stillness, or self-reflection. Solitude can be renewing and recharging in many ways; it nurtures our inner peace and offers a break from external demands. It is also a choice that can always be unmade, that we can move in and out of with ease. That is, we can choose to rejoin community.

Isolation, by contrast, we do not choose. Isolation is an experience of profound disconnection. Where in solitude we might commune with God and Scripture and hear ourselves think, in isolation we often feel stuck in our heads, and ours is the only voice we hear. It can leave us discouraged and alone, unsure of how to find our way back to connection, life, and belonging.

Fear of Becoming a Burden to Others

Sometimes we convince ourselves that we'll be a burden to others if we try to connect during a time when we don't feel great joy. But you see, in our darkest hours, though we may not have the capacity to love, that doesn't mean others don't still get something out of being able to love us. So what if we didn't always look at connection through our own lens? What if it wasn't about the love we were supposed to give, but the love others were meant to give to us? When we open ourselves up to receive love, we serve the purpose of allowing others to use their intended gifts for God's glory. When God stirs the hearts of those who love, they experience something intangible—they become more conformed to the image of Christ. Thus, in a sense, our willingness to be loved is part of a very important equation for salvation. When we make the unilateral decision that our problems are burdens, we actually prevent others from receiving that intangible gift because we prevent light and love from flowing freely through others and out into the world.

And remember, God built us for connection. In fact, Paul refers to us as all being part of one body that takes care of one another, as the Body of Christ (I Cor. 12:12–27). That means that sometimes we give love, and sometimes we are meant to be on the receiving end of it. Indeed, without both giving and receiving, there can be no connection! In working together as members of one body, all necessary parts of the equation are needed to bring the light of Christ into this world, helping mature the Body of Christ. So let us "pursue love, and earnestly desire the spiritual gifts" (I Cor. 14:I) so that encouragement, comfort, strength, and light may pour forth into this world through the weight of what we bear.

Fear of Becoming Vulnerable

Real connection requires vulnerability, yet we all feel social pressure to uphold an image that "all is well," "life is great," and "we have it all together." It's hard to put imperfection out into the world. But the truth is, as human beings, one of our greatest commonalities is that *we don't have it all together.* "We all stumble in many ways" (James 3:2). There was only one Person who lived and was perfect; the rest of us are working out our salvation day by day, struggling along the way. Our weakness lives alongside our strengths. But our imperfections make us human and are a beautiful reminder that we need God's grace, mercy, and love.

We may think we're "being strong" or "positive" by smiling and acting like everything is fine, but truth be told, our masks aren't about projecting strength as much as they are about hiding fear—the fear of being judged for what we lack, the fear of being exposed by our mistakes, or the fear of just not being enough in some way. In other words, we live in fear of judgment. When we fear judgment, we lose sight of the fact that there is only one Person we are called to please. His perception of us should be the one that matters because as we please Him, so also do we please others. And we please Him when, in our weakness, we learn to lean on one another in ways that reveal His light. Truthfully, the world doesn't need another highlight reel that masks the normalcy of everyday struggle. The world needs people who are willing to break the cycle of projecting perfection through authenticity, honesty, and transparency.

And the good news is that, while, yes, some people do judge, *more people love.* It's only human to care about how others perceive us, but we should not overvalue perception at the expense of receiving the life-giving love, support, and discernment we need. Rather, when we root our connections in vulnerability, we realize that God is with us in every untold story, in every weakness, and in every mess we have made, and the people along our path become expressions of His presence when we become willing to share our story.

Fear That Our Struggles Are Worse than the Struggles of Others

One common barrier to vulnerability is the belief that our imperfections are so much worse than the imperfections of others. But none of us is better or worse than another; our flaws are just different. Some of us have had more advantages starting out in the race of life; others of us, more challenges. The type of guidance we have been given, the amount of love we have received, the things we have been taught about empathy and compassion, and the dispositions we've been given all serve to create our unique experience in this life. Those experiences shape our struggles and our successes. So although our flaws may seem more apparent to us, we must keep a framework of remembering that we were all cut from the same fabric, just sewn into different clothes.

So, be humble and compassionate with yourself. If you find yourself worrying about comparisons, try leaning into self-reflection for a moment. What am I really afraid of? We all have stories that live beneath our smiles as we manage our experiences and our unique challenges.

So the next time you think about projecting perfection, be willing to be real instead. Be willing to be the example of honesty and transparency the world needs, rather than the one who exacerbates the problem of projecting perfection.

Try being someone who breaks the cycle of social media depictions with truth, rather than a snapshot in time of our best moments. In this way, we start to invoke the voice of support that God's light can bring us in our truth.

Fear That We're Bad Christians

Does revealing our struggles somehow expose us as lacking in faith? If we feel unhappy, depressed, grieved, or stuck in shock or sorrow, does it mean we don't have a strong faith or aren't doing all the things we're supposed to be doing? It's hard to connect with someone if we feel inferior about our deepest convictions.

Again, this is self-deception. Who among us hasn't had moments of despair, moments when they felt defeated or regretful about a choice they wish they hadn't made? Faith is not the absence of struggle but the belief that God can use that struggle to make us into something better. God uses so many moments to teach us, convict us, get our attention, and direct our path in light of what we need in order to grow according to His will. Believing we're bad Christians because of our struggles would mean we haven't yet realized that life is a spiritual journey where everything we experience serves to help us grow in true self-knowledge, be conformed more into the image of Christ, and to eventually learn to see ourselves the way God sees us.

So whatever your sufferings in the moment, try not to see them as a deficit in faith but as part of your own spiritual journey. Let your self-knowledge be guided by a spirit of wisdom and bound by discernment and the love God has for you.

Types of Connection

Connection comes in many forms. That is why no two relationships are exactly alike, and it is also why no one relationship can fulfill all our needs. That is why we have friends, families, and the church as a community; each gives us something a little different. The Bible never tells us to find one relationship and pour everything into it; rather, the model in the Bible is always community. When you seek connection, consider what kind of connection you need.

Physical Care

The most basic kind of connection we need is those who physically care for us. Think of how we hand newborns to their mother as soon as we can after they are born. Think about how attachment forms through those who care for us in dependable ways we learn we can trust. The safety of knowing we can count on someone soothes our cries and provides comfort to our soul. This basic need doesn't change just because we become independent adults; it just looks different. As adults, we still need to know we can depend on someone. That might be the person who offers to do our shopping, take our children out for the afternoon, or take something off our plate because they can see it's overflowing. It could be the person who pays attention to the things we are experiencing and reminds us they're there to help because they have already anticipated our need for their help and support.

The Bible acknowledges our need for physical care and gives us some examples of how we may care for one another. For example, Exodus tells a story about the Israelites being attacked by Amalek while they wandered the desert. Moses stood on a hill overlooking the battle, and as long as he held his staff over his head, the Israelites gained ground. But when he put his hands down, Amalek began to prevail. So as Moses got tired, Aaron and Hur rolled a rock over for him to sit on, and then they each held up one of his arms so that the Israelites would overcome their enemy. Even Moses, who stood up to Pharoah, parted the Red Sea, and made water flow from a rock . . . even he needed support in order to endure the struggle (Ex. 17:11–13).

While we often read things like this metaphorically, sometimes it's useful to look at the literal meaning, which in this case is an admonition to be there to literally help each other up. We see this example even with Jesus in the story of Simon of Cyrene, when Simon steps in to take the Cross from Christ's shoulders (Luke 23:26). When we are exposed or vulnerable, we simply need people who have our back and who can help us bear a burden we are struggling to handle alone.

Encouragement and Comfort

When life feels like it has been turned upside down, and our minds can't seem to settle down and we can't make sense of anything, it's amazing what changes when we allow our-selves to be loved, comforted, and encouraged. In moments like these, we all need to know that someone is on our team, by our side, standing in our corner and cheering us on. We yearn to be seen, to have the best parts of us encouraged, to be accepted without pretense, and to be valued for who we are, not only for what we do. When others see our goodness, it breaks apart the lies we tell ourselves and reminds us of our value. Whether it's a familiar voice of comfort when every-thing else feels stressful, or the person who gives us strength that we don't feel we have. Or the person who provides a soft place to land when everything beneath us feels like it's crum-bling. Or the person whose voice makes it safe to feel again when our pain has left us numb. There's healing power in comfort and encouragement!

Guidance and Wisdom

No one after lighting a lamp covers it with a jar or puts it under a bed, but puts it on a stand, so that those who enter may see the light. —LUKE 8:16

I do not cease to give thanks for you, remembering you in my prayers, that the God of our Lord Jesus Christ, the Father of glory, may give you the Spirit of wisdom and of revelation in the knowledge of him. —EPHESIANS 1:17

We also need life-giving connections to remind us of God's wisdom. We all have so much to learn about ourselves in this life, and we are all still growing in true self-knowledge, into seeing ourselves the way God sees us. Because most of us don't have to have everything figured out right now, it helps when we surround ourselves with people who reflect the light of Christ. They make our struggles easier, not because they are preaching to us but because of how they live their lives. When light is the foundation of our support, it feels nonjudgmental, offers us compassion, gives us hope without being invalidating, does not fuel the negative, and does not celebrate when our struggles seem to defeat us.

When it comes to the support we seek, we must remember that there is a difference between knowledge and wisdom. Knowledge is everything the world feeds us in our struggles. It comes at us from every direction. It may be filled with dead ends or empty promises, moving targets we keep chasing to feel better but that don't bring real inner peace. At its worst, it's the voice of the enemy in disguise, and so it divides, condemns, judges, shames, discourages, confuses, frightens, torments, and overwhelms us. It seeks vengeance, sees everything as a competition, and feeds our pride and ego.

Wisdom, however, is information bound by Christ. It's a reminder of God's voice, when all we can hear is our own. In contrast to the enemy's voice, God's voice calms, comforts, convicts, encourages, enlightens, leads, reassures, and stills us. His is the voice of peace, mercy, and love. When we find this kind of support in others, it's life giving. When others possess God's voice, their support often reveals truth without judgment and kindness that reminds us of God's goodness. These individuals are centering and grounding in a crisis, peace seeking and accepting in conflict, compassionate in moments of guilt, and hopeful and trusting when it comes to difficult seasons. Wisdom is the fruit of a spirit that is close to God; it is intrinsically hopeful. And because of that hope, we can find comfort in the wise one's presence—and the strength to get back on our own path to light.

Making Room

Another form of connection we need is someone who knows how to make space for us emotionally so that we can share what's on our hearts without being told how we need to feel or what we need to do to solve our problems. This is the person who stops what they are doing and gives us their full attention, listening intently by investing their whole heart into simply trying to understand our experience. As Carl Rogers put it, "I can testify that when you are in psychological distress and someone really hears you without passing judgment on you, without trying to take responsibility for you, and without trying to mold you, it feels . . . good!" He goes on, "It relaxes the tension in me. It has permitted me to bring out the frightening feelings, the guilts, the despair, the confusions that have been a part of my experience. When I have been listened to and when I have been heard, I am able to reperceive my world in a new way and to go on."[32]

What we need most in our struggles is to know that we are not alone, that someone else gets what we're going through. We just want to feel heard, seen, felt, and understood, rather than be talked out of our feelings. Yet because it's uncomfortable to experience someone's struggle without relieving it,

---

32 C. R. Rogers, *A Way of Being* (Boston: Houghton Mifflin, 1995), 12.

many well-intentioned individuals who want to help wind up trying to talk us out of what we feel, urging us to see things more "reasonably," to "look on the bright side," or not to worry because "it's all going to be okay." Without realizing it, when people use these kinds of words, they try to bring us out of the emotional space we are in rather than meeting us where we are.

Spiritual Connection

Finally, brothers, whatever is true, whatever is honorable, whatever is just, whatever is pure, whatever is lovely, whatever is commendable, if there is any excellence, if there is anything worthy of praise, think about these things. What you have learned and received and heard and seen in me—practice these things, and the God of peace will be with you. —PHILIPPIANS 4:8–9

Finally, we need spiritual connection, and the image of the Cross itself symbolizes this. It has two beams: one represents our relationship with God, and the other represents our relationship with others. Our vertical relationship with God shapes the horizontal relationship we are capable of having with others. When we start with Him, we are better able to connect with others in life-giving ways. Sure, two are better than one, but we must also remember that only a cord of three cannot be broken (Eccl. 4:12). So, although we need the loving care of people God has placed in our lives to pray for us and minister to us, we also know that the ultimate source of care for our spirit comes from God. And the healing power of connection we receive from others is greatly affected by our own connection to Christ.

And though connecting to God may be the thing we need most, sometimes it's the last thing we think of. According to Maslow's hierarchy of needs, this makes sense. We tend to pursue more primitive needs before seeking to fulfill higher-level needs. But we also know that in times of stress the enemy works harder, and because of that we need the Holy Spirit to renew us, to lead us, and to strengthen us, especially if our more basic needs have not been met.

Caring for our spirit means creating time and space for prayer, quiet time, and reading our Bibles. We can't be in a relationship with someone we aren't talking to or learning about. It wouldn't work in our social relationships, and it doesn't work in our relationship with God. If we are not connected first to Him, then we can't expect to bear the fruits of His Holy Spirit in our struggles.

Our spirit connection is paramount because it's hard to reflect wisdom in our connections when it isn't already in our hearts. And we can't rely solely on going to church on Sundays; we need a daily habit of faith. Even just fifteen minutes a day can make a difference! We talk about the Rule of 15 in our previous book, *Renewing You*. Using the Rule of 15 can help us create a daily habit of connecting with God by engaging in:

- 5 minutes of prayer
- 5 minutes of reading our Bible
- 5 minutes of a daily devotional or any kind of faith-based reading

We like to say that if prayer is our means of talking to God, reading our Bible is how we listen for His response. If you find yourself too busy, work it into what you already do! Try listening to your Bible on a long commute. Try listening to Christian music when you turn on the radio. Try tuning into a podcast as you go to sleep at night. Try praying before you even get out of bed. Use the natural pauses throughout your day for moments of stillness and prayer—red lights and grocery lines are perfect opportunities!

ENCLOSING THE BIBLE IN OUR HEARTS

Unfortunately, many of us Christians do not read the Bible as we should. We revere the Bible, but we don't actually read it, and this is one of the reasons why many of our laity are often so spiritually weak. Amongst the greater body of Christians, the Barna Group found in a recent survey that only between 12 and 16 percent of Christians read their Bible daily.[33] And if we try to rely only on hearing the Bible in church on Sundays, in many Christian churches the service covers only a very small percentage of the Bible.

Yet St. Paul tells us that the Holy Scriptures give us the wisdom that leads to salvation and that it is also useful in a variety of ways: for teaching, exposing the truth, correcting our faults, and giving guidance and instruction for how to live rightly (2 Tim. 3:15–16). In some ways,

---

33 "State of the Bible 2021: Five Key Findings," Barna, May 19, 2021, https://www.barna.com/research/sotb-2021/.

reading our Bible is like looking in a mirror with a very bright light. That light reveals how we are thinking about our life and our circumstances, and what we need to clean up. As Psalm 119 says, "The unfolding of [God's] words gives light" (v. 130).

The Bible, after all, is not merely a series of letters on a page. Saint Paul demonstrated this when he praised the church in Thessalonica because they received his teaching not as the words of men but as the Word of God (1 Thess. 2:13). The word *received* in Greek is the same word we would use to describe welcoming a guest into our home. To receive Scripture this way is like welcoming God Himself into our home. To help us do so, before we read, we can pray this prayer of St. John Chrysostom that is found in the Divine Liturgy right before the priest proclaims the gospel:

> Shine within our hearts, loving Master, the pure light of Your divine knowledge, and open the eyes of our minds that we may comprehend the message of Your Gospel. Instill in us, also, reverence for Your blessed commandments, so that having conquered sinful desires, we may pursue a spiritual life, thinking and doing all those things that are pleasing to You. For You, Christ our God, are the light of our souls and bodies, and to You we give glory together with Your Father who is without beginning and Your all holy, good, and life-giving Spirit, now and forever and to the ages of ages. Amen.

You see, we can't manufacture the fruits of the Holy Spirit; we have to draw closer to Christ if we want to manifest them in ways that yield light in our relationships. Remaining connected to Him is what helps us approach connection with a pure, open, and trusting heart that is attuned to the good in others. In this way, our relationships become the source of comfort and encouragement we need most in the midst of difficulty, and we grow spiritually in ways that help us receive the healing power of connection in the midst of our struggles.

How to Find Connection

Connection is wonderful and serves us on many levels, but how do we find it? Especially since, as we observed at the beginning of this chapter, we are most likely to avoid connection in just those times when we most need it. Nobody is saying this will be easy—especially if you are struggling with isolation and loneliness right now. There is a popular expression that states, "The best time to plant a tree is twenty years ago, and the second-best time is today." The same goes for connection. Ideally, we cultivate connection when we have the energy and capacity to do so, so that it will be there for us when we do not. But the next best thing is to take any small step right now. In other words, there is an inevitable need for self-advocacy here. So don't wait. Make a phone call. Text someone. Write an email.

If you feel convinced that you need connection and you are aware that you need to take action to find it, you may still wonder where to start. Begin by taking another look at who God has put in your life. Who do you see on a daily basis? Weekly? Who do you encounter at work, in your neighborhood, in your church community? Who are the people in your family? Who always says hello or smiles from across a room? Who remembers what's happening in your life?

Think about your broader community and who might be a good candidate for you to develop a closer connection with. Who has been kind to you? With whom do you get along really well? Who would you like to know better? We all want and need connection, but we don't always think to ask for it. Inviting someone out for a coffee or lunch could be the start of a beautiful friendship.

Beyond companionship, consider who is trustworthy and could be a source of support. Who has been a reliable person in your life? Who has come through for you in the past? You can also flip the question around and think of who has asked you for help. That person may be open to a deeper relationship.

You can't expect a new relationship to go from enjoying a coffee together to carrying one another's burdens overnight. There's no minimum time it takes; each relationship has to find its own pace and its own depth. But you may be surprised how positively people respond to developing a relationship with you.

Whether we want to have a friend we can rely on or whether we feel a profound need for connection right now, we can't get the connection we need if we only think about it. We must make time for it and show people we're open to it.

Finding Connection by Overcoming Internal Barriers

We spoke earlier about our emotional barriers to connection, but we face some dispositional barriers as well. Because we aren't all created the same, our disposition matters when it comes to forming relationships. If we don't spend time learning about ourselves, we can unintentionally miss out on finding ways to connect that feel natural, rather than intrusive, and renewing, rather than exhausting. The following are some potential dispositional barriers that may keep us from connecting:

INTROVERSION/EXTROVERSION

While extroverts are often described as talkative and outgoing because they derive their energy from engaging with their environment and can feed off the responses of the people and events around them, introverts are much the opposite. They can find too much outside stimulation like noise, commotion, or large groups of people exhausting because it drains their energy. They are also more likely to be described as reserved because they prefer time for contemplation and to think things through in their mind before they share them. And while extroverts can get stressed by going too long without connection, introverts can get stressed by the wrong type of connection.

So if you tend to be more on the introverted side, that means you were built for *depth* of connection, not *lack* of connection. You might need to try being slightly more open to meeting new people and to chance conversations. It may start with a willingness to look up, make eye contact, smile, or go out of your way to say something when you otherwise wouldn't. Keep in mind that in order to connect you may need to be more mindful about deliberately making your inner world available to others, and to be purposeful about sharing what's on your heart, rather than just listening and observing others in your social environments. And while friendliness may be easier for extroverts than introverts, we all still require support, emotional intimacy, disclosure, positive regard, and reliable connection.

We also can't convince ourselves that social media will suffice. Social media platforms often emphasize numbers over real human connection: we tend to focus more on the likes and follows we have than on the connections themselves. In fact, social media can create the exact opposite qualities we need for healthy relationships because online relationships are distant, sometimes disingenuous, and often impersonal. Social media connections can feel like empty calories when what we really need is a more satisfying, balanced meal.

Listening vs. Sharing

Do you tend to be more of a listener than a talker? While listening is powerful because it enables other people to feel seen, heard, and understood as they disentangle their thoughts, if listening is not balanced by sharing, it can affect the connections we are capable of making. Plus, research shows self-disclosure plays a key role in forming relationships, building connections, and helping us feel a sense of support. People also acknowledge liking others more who disclose to them, and people disclose more to someone they like.[34]

So for those of us who are good listeners by nature, we may have a tendency to keep our inner world to ourselves and not give others the opportunity to really support us or know us. So if you are feeling alone but people are reaching out to try to support you, try being more willing to open the door and let them in. Be deliberate about leading conversations with topics you're convicted or genuinely curious about so that self-disclosure feels more natural. If you struggle with a fear of being judged, try to avoid giving short responses that close conversations. Instead, allow others to know you just a bit more by offering open and honest reactions. If you do ask questions, ask them about topics you can relate to so that meaningful reactions and your own related stories might follow. If you struggle with opening up, try sharing a childhood memory, a life-changing experience, a book that shaped you, a vivid dream, a funny moment, a compliment that meant a lot to you, a worry you can't seem to shake, or a hope for the future.

TASK-ORIENTED VS. PEOPLE-ORIENTED

If you tend to be task-oriented rather than people-oriented, you may have to work a little harder to let togetherness be

---

34 Kathryn Greene, Valerian J. Derlega, and Alicia Mathews, "Self-Disclosure in Personal Relationships," in *The Cambridge Handbook of Personal Relationships*, eds. Anita L. Vangelisti and Daniel Perlman (Cambridge: Cambridge University Press, 2006), 409–427.

your only purpose when you are with someone. You can start by practicing just being present—that is, not obsessing over everything going on in your head but just letting yourself be in the moment. Sometimes in our busy lives, we can get so caught up in our work or in our own needs that even if we do have free time, we focus on our work, our own goals, or the things we want to get done, rather than take advantage of available moments to truly connect with each other. Our no-nonsense, pragmatic, hardworking personalities that make us successful in our careers can sabotage our ability to pause and listen to others in our personal lives.

When someone we care about starts asking about our day or sharing about their long day, we must sometimes resist thoughts like "I don't have time," "I'm too tired," or "I still have so much work to do." It's important to respond with sensitivity. In these moments, we must try making ourselves fully present by tuning in and listening in a way that mirrors emotions, shows interest, and reflects openness. In this way, we open ourselves up to receiving connection that may have been surrounding us all along but that we didn't pause long enough to realize.

FEELING "TOO EMOTIONAL"

Are you someone who tends to keep everything inside because you just feel too emotional and that your own feelings aren't reasonable? Or maybe you believe others won't understand? Sometimes we judge ourselves and can overthink our reactions, but that doesn't change our need for connection; in fact, sometimes it means we need it even more. But if we aren't at a point where we can genuinely open up about our own struggles, we can try connecting around someone else's. Just getting outside of our own head for a bit by hearing someone else's story may help us gain perspective in our own. In the best case, the intimacy will build the type of trust that helps us invite others into our inner world to love us right where we are.

There are countless other dispositions that can present internal barriers to connection. Consider yourself for a moment. What stops you from connecting? Maybe you are someone who waits for others to reach out, rather than going after connection yourself. Maybe you are someone who has always felt you could do everything on your own and that you don't need people. Whatever it is, consider your internal barriers to connection, pray about them, and take one step toward connection.

Offering Connection

> *Finally, all of you, have unity of mind, sympathy, brotherly love,*
> *a tender heart, and a humble mind.* —1 PETER 3:8

> *Whoever brings blessing will be enriched, / and one who*
> *waters will himself be watered.* —PROVERBS 11:25

We wanted to take a little time at the end of this chapter to speak to the other side of connection: offering connection. If people in the midst of difficulty need to accept and seek connection, how much more should those of us in good times take action to offer it where it's needed most?

The other day we experienced a moment just like this. A child at a sporting event lost control and hurt another child on the field so badly that stitches were required. Though many onlookers were present, few acknowledged it. Most just walked by as if unmoved by what they had seen. It made us think for a moment, "Did they not know what to say? Did they think, 'Not my problem'?" It felt upsetting and isolating. Watching as if we were on the outside ourselves, we began to wonder, where has empathy gone? Have we forgotten to consider other people's perspectives and show kindness? The "what if it were me" moment?

There was one person, however, who chose not to be a bystander. Her presence and meaningful silence said everything the parents needed to feel. She acknowledged in a few words what she had observed, expressed her support, validated their reactions, and then remained present in meaningful silence. Her body language continued to speak long after her words. Though simple, her support in our experience spoke volumes of comfort at a time when we needed it most.

This situation made us think about how many of us at one time or another have made the choice to avoid someone else's discomfort, have chosen to "walk right on by," either because the situation made us uncomfortable or because we didn't know what to say. Or, perhaps we walk by because the situation wasn't happening to us and didn't affect our lives. Yet isn't compassion a fundamental ingredient to the

Christian life, whether it's choosing to speak up when something is wrong, caring about something even if it doesn't affect us, standing by someone who has been mistreated, extending our hand of comfort, our words of encouragement, or most of all, our care and compassion? Even meaningful silence can be enough to show our concern for others when we don't have the words. But we don't always think about the impact we are called to have in the lives of others. We sometimes let our discomfort dictate our connection. And so often it is the unintentional hurts, the overlooked moments, that can leave just as great of a mark on someone's life as the intentional ones. And the mere absence of empathy in situations where compassion is needed can be damaging in and of itself.

If you feel like you've struggled with being a bystander too often, there are several skills you can practice to become better at spreading light and offering connection.

Consider Your Impact on Them

To become better at offering connection, we must think about how our presence affects others. Do you tend to bring light or more darkness to others? Do you bring comfort or more stress? Do you ease pain or unintentionally worsen it? Do you bestow encouragement or listen just to be in the know? Do you help others move toward solutions to their problems, or do you heap blame upon them instead? We can all be vessels of light, but only when we take possession of the light that is within us. Christ gives us this opportunity every day, by way of His Holy Spirit. When we connect to His Holy Spirit within, we tend to be more life-giving to those around us. Try giving a compliment in the midst of someone else's bad day, and watch as they light up. The little bit of light we shine will always be capable of breaking through darkness in some way.

Our presence truly has the power to change the direction of someone's day. If we are willing to direct others toward the light by our light, we will always leave others better off than we found them. Strive to become a positive part of someone's story, a light that draws them in the right direction. Or at the very minimum, do not be another obstacle that blocks their path to light, life, and goodness.

See Them

So often we only skim the surface of people's lives. We say hello, we might even ask, "How are you?" but we don't expect to hear the real answer. We expect to hear, "Great, how are you?" rather than an exposing of the heart. Yet what lies in people's hearts is often the very thing that needs to be revealed, comforted, connected to, and supported. It's what we don't always share that often reveals our most beautiful vulnerabilities: deeper values, worries, convictions, and things that weigh heavily on our hearts.

Seeing people might mean taking notice of the long sigh or the frustration on someone's face after a long day, then acknowledging it and stepping into it with curiosity and compassion. And when we greet someone with "How was your week?" we help others feel seen when we ask it in a way that says we're truly interested in the answer, rather than just offering a social nicety. That might mean we follow up on their response with curiosity, asking "What made it so busy?" or "What made it so rough?"

In order to truly carry each other's burdens, we need to tap into the deeper experiences of others through sincere caring. We need to "not love in word or talk but in deed and in truth" (1 John 3:18). As we see the need, we can better follow the heart and let the convictions that God has placed upon our heart breed the kindness He has already made manifest in our soul by the grace of His Holy Spirit.

Listen to Them

> Let the wise hear and increase in learning, / and the one who understands obtain guidance. —PROVERBS 1:5

> A fool takes no pleasure in understanding, / but only in expressing his opinion. —PROVERBS 18:2

Our impulse when we encounter discomfort in others is to do something to make the discomfort go away. We may say something to make it better or find a way to change the subject or get out of the conversation altogether. But when someone is hurting, they need to feel understood, heard, and supported; they don't want to feel invalidated, ignored, or told to feel differently than they do. So instead of ignoring discomfort or trying to make it better, we can offer connection by being willing to step into it, taking the time to truly listen with an open heart to what's being shared. Keep in mind, most people can tell when we are asking a question to truly know the answer or when we are just asking to be polite. They know when we are distracted. They know when something else matters more than what they are sharing. They know when we are listening just enough to respond or listening to truly understand their perspectives. It is this kind of active listening that gives people the permission they need to open up, because they can sense we are making room for the fullness and validity of their experience. Active listening is one of the purest and rarest forms of generosity.

There's more to say on active listening, but the basic skills can be described briefly:

- **Control your impulses.** Your in-the-moment reactions, whether interest, disinterest, discomfort, etc., may cause you to interrupt and try to take control. Avoid this.
- **Listen without judgment.** Don't get distracted by what the person shares. Monitor your own opinions and listen to understand, rather than listening to respond.
- **Let go of other goals.** Be willing to put away your work, put down your phone, and let go of other tasks or goals. Prioritize the person who needs you in that pocket of committed time.
- **Mirror emotions.** This is about tuning in to the emotional state of whomever is speaking and reflecting

it back in our demeanor, our words, and our non-verbal expressions to communicate understanding. Remember, we were actually built to synchronize facial expressions, vocalizations, and nonverbal behaviors with those around us.

- **Ask questions that demonstrate interest.** Let your questions deepen the conversation or lead you to better understand what the person is saying. Encourage them to expound by saying, "Tell me more about that" or, "And then what happened?"
- **Suspend the need to agree.** You don't have to agree with someone to offer support; you just have to try to understand their experience.
- **Follow up.** Pay attention to what they share and check back in later. If there was something they were looking forward to or were anxious about, ask them how it went.

Look for an opportunity to practice these skills, then prepare yourself to be present. Try asking someone how this last week has *felt* or what seems heavy on their heart, then listen to what they share. Look for opportunities to ask questions or show support.

Show Empathy for Them

Empathy depends on compassion. And compassion depends on empathy. Before empathy can take place, we have to first see others and sense that they are feeling an emotion. And then, we have to care. The quality of how we respond in moments of need depends upon both our ability to sincerely care about others and our ability to see situations from their vantage point. It is our sensitive concern to that perspective that helps us engage in ways that display compassion.

It's asking, "What does this really feel like for them?" rather than focusing on what it would feel like for us. Or thinking, "How do they see things?" rather than thinking about how we would see things. And considering, "What might they need in light of their experience?" not what we would need in light of ours. Empathy allows us to walk into someone's story and be able to meet them right where they are and communicate that understanding, so that what transpires becomes a witness of Christ's love. It allows us to follow Jesus' command to "love the Lord your God with all your heart and with all your soul and with all your mind. This is the great and first commandment. And a second is like it: You shall love your neighbor as yourself" (Matt. 22:37–39).

It's important to note that because people's stories are not always written over their wounds, empathy can be blocked by judgment. For instance, the negativity we routinely see in someone could be a product of chronic unhappiness that surfaces as complaints and pessimism. Or a resistant and stubborn soul could also just be someone plagued by fear that keeps their lighter side heavy laden with burden and worry. Or perhaps that jealous or competitive person was really just tormented by feelings of inadequacy. And perhaps the self-centered person had an upbringing that required them to fight for what they got, creating a me-first mentality, or perhaps they never learned to see the needs of others because no one ever recognized the needs within them.

We must remember that because not all wounds are visible, we need empathy to help us override judgment and help us consider other explanations for the more difficult behaviors we come across. Empathy lets our faith lead when we're faced with hard exteriors in people fighting battles just beneath the surface that we know little about.

Be Present with Them

Being present with someone means putting aside all other concerns and making what's happening in that moment with that person the most important thing to you. It means letting everything on your to-do list fade into the background as you draw yourself into the physical and emotional presence of someone else. So choose to simply exist in the presence of another, without any other distraction. Make that person your only priority in that moment. Close your laptop, put down your phone, and turn away from whatever task you are doing and let the opportunity to connect be realized. The truth is, emotional connection only happens when we allow ourselves to fully enter into and experience the same moments together with someone else. People are changed by our presence. And while they may not necessarily remember what we say, they will always remember the way our presence made them feel, especially in their darkest times.

Pray for and with Them

Our God is a God of comfort. He comforts us in all our troubles and comes alongside us through the gift of the Holy Spirit (John 14:26), so we offer comfort to others when we pray with them and for them. Scripture reminds us to love others the way God loves us and to walk with others in their pain. To pray for others—sincerely pray for them—not just say that we will. To share in intimate closeness with them as their pain tugs at our hearts and urges us to bring comfort and love. This is transformational not only for others but also for us. God designed us to give love, to shoulder each other's burdens, and to share all that He has given us. When we do so, we feel a closeness to the Holy Spirit within us. And when God answers the sincere prayers we offer on behalf of others, He is glorified, our own faith deepens, and our testimony expands.

We should also have a strong prayer life so that we stay connected to God ourselves. When we are connected to God, we become emotionally safe people for others to connect with. We become more reliable, more trustworthy with people's vulnerability, more able to carry another's burdens. And we're not as caught up in our own stuff, so we have more to give to others.

Practice Connection

Connection is not an act or an obligation; it is a reflection of our own connectivity to God. It is the evidence of the Holy Spirit leading our hearts. So the next time you see hurt, approach it. The next time you hear hurt, make time to listen. And when you respond to hurt, speak to the heart, not to the head—this isn't the time to help someone be more reasonable about their situation or teach them how to see it more positively. No, be willing to simply step into the room of someone's emotional experience and connect in whatever way you can. Just do so with humility, remembering we never know all there is to know about someone else's experience. We are just there to try to understand and make it safe enough for someone to feel whatever it is they feel, in whatever space they are in, and to help them feel less alone in their burden. As St. Paul says, "Rejoice with those who rejoice, weep with those who weep" (Rom. 12:15).

With gentle, warm, and sincere persistence, we gradually make our way into people's hearts—and let them into ours. Whether you genuinely stop in to check on someone you already know, or take the time to say more than a hello to a neighbor in a way that reminds them they matter, or take a moment to truly connect with someone in the midst of struggle, be intentional about making a difference in the life of someone who needs it.

When Jesus spoke to John and Mary at the foot of the Cross, He showed His care for them by giving them to one another—both as someone to take care of them and someone *they could take care of*. There is no difficulty so great that connection cannot help you across. Just take a step, any step, and watch as the presence of the Holy Spirit works through the power of connection to bring healing, comfort, and direction.

For Discussion: The Three Rs— Rest, Reflect, and Respond

1. Have you experienced a season of loneliness? How did it affect you?

2. When was the last time someone's presence made you feel less alone?

3. What voice inside of you sometimes stops you from receiving connection or reaching out to others?

4. What obstacle keeps you from receiving connection? Isolation? Fear of being a burden? Fear of being vulnerable? Fear of judgment?

5. In the midst of difficulty, what kind of physical support is most helpful to you? Who could you reach out to or rely on within your community for this type of support?

6. What kind of emotional support do you need most when you are struggling? Do you need someone who provides comfort, makes it safe to feel, encourages you, helps you problem solve, helps you take a step forward, gives you strength, or who just listens? Who might you reach out to or rely on within your community for this type of support?

7. What reminds you of God's wisdom? What kind of wisdom do you normally need a reminder of? To be gentle in anger? To have hope in worry? To trust in God's promises in defeat? To see the good in others? To surrender control? To let go of shame? To put away pride?

8. What does your connection to God look like in daily life?

9. What Scripture might you need to enclose in your heart to open you up more to receiving the healing power of connection?

10. Take another look at the people God has put in your life. Who do you see on a daily basis? Weekly? Whom do you encounter at work, in your neighborhood, in your church community? Who are the people in your family? Who always says hello or smiles from across a room? Who remembers what's happening in your life? Who might be a good candidate for you to develop a closer connection with? Who has been kind to you? With whom do you get along really well? Who reaches out to know you better?

11. Which internal barriers might be blocking you from connection that is renewing? Do you tend to be more introverted? Do you tend to be more of a listener

than a sharer? Are you more task oriented than people oriented?

12. When it comes to offering connection to others, what's your impact on them?

13. What is one thing you could start doing to help you notice the needs of others more?

14. What listening skill might help you connect more with others?

15. How could empathy help you with feeling compassion? Does empathy feel natural to you? Why or why not?

16. How present do you feel you are with others? Do you often stop what you are doing and give them your undivided attention? Or do you frequently multitask in the midst of connection? What is one thing you could do to be more present?

PRAYER

O Lord Our God, the Savior of our world, You loved us so much that even in the midst of Your unbearable pain You lovingly shared with us the importance of connecting during our pain. It was You who knew the despair and loneliness that Your mother and beloved disciple John would experience, and You shared with them the need not to journey through that pain alone. It was You who reminded us of the importance of having connection in our crises, when You allowed Simon of Cyrene to carry Your Cross.

Lord, as I face the crosses of my own life, help me not to withdraw in my pain but to reach out. Allow my heart to be open to seeking help in my struggle. Help me not to fall into the darkness of loneliness and despair but to lean on the people that You have placed in my life to help carry my crosses. Finally, give me the eyes to see those who are also struggling to carry their crosses, and empower me with Your words, guidance, comfort, and strength to be a Simon and help carry their burdens and fulfill Your will for my life. In Your holy name, we pray. Amen.

My God, My God, Why Have You Forsaken Me?

*And about the ninth hour Jesus cried out with a loud voice, saying,
"Eli, Eli, lama sabachthani?" that is,* "My God, my God,
why have you forsaken me?" —MATTHEW 27:46

IN OUR LIVES, it is not a matter of if, but when, we will experience a dark season. We may lose a loved one, learn of a cancer diagnosis, worry about a child who has gone off course, or feel the hurt of human betrayal in a relationship. In such times, it is easy to feel isolation and loneliness. We may wonder if anyone understands what we are going through. Worse, we can wonder where God is through it all.

If you have ever felt those lonely, dark days, then the fourth statement Christ makes on the Cross is for you. In this moment, Christ experienced extreme anguish and pain as the weight of His body made it increasingly difficult to breathe. As He suffered this extreme anguish, He looked around and saw none of His disciples, with the exception of the Apostle John and the myrrh-bearing women. No longer did the people wave palm branches over Him and hail Him as king, as they had earlier that week. Instead, they had turned on Him, waving their fists and shouting, "Crucify him, crucify him!" No longer did they embrace Him, declaring that they would never depart from Him. They rejected Him, abandoned Him.

We hear the hymnographer on Holy Thursday encapsulate the feelings of Christ on the Cross when he writes:

> O my people, what have I done to you,
>> how have I upset you?
>> I gave sight to your blind;
>> I cleansed your lepers;
>> I raised the man who lay paralyzed on his bed.
> O my people, what have I done to you,
>> and how have you repaid me?
>> Instead of manna, you fed Me gall;
>> instead of water, you gave Me vinegar;
>> instead of loving Me, you nailed Me to the Cross.

And it is in this moment that Christ utters words that reveal dark depths of human emotion: *"Eli, Eli, lama sabachthani?"* which translated from the Hebrew means, "My God, My God, why have you forsaken me?" (Matt. 27:46; Ps. 22:1).

Jesus knows what it means to suffer. He was both fully God and fully human without separation, so He could identify with every human emotion we experience. In this particular moment, even as Jesus fulfills the prophecies when He repeats the beginning of Psalm 22, we can also see, as in many examples throughout the Bible, that He identifies with human suffering. He experienced it, and He did so in one of the worst ways imaginable—through the undignified torture and crucifixion of a criminal.

Even before His Crucifixion, Jesus felt deep anguish over what He knew He had to endure in order for us to live truly free. We read that He literally cried out to His Father: "Abba, Father, all things are possible for you. Remove this cup from me. Yet not what I will, but what you will" (Mark 14:36). The Bible says that Jesus' anguish was so great that He sweated "drops of blood" (Luke 22:44). And we even hear Isaiah prophesy that Christ would be "a man of sorrows and acquainted with grief" (Is. 53:3). So, the Bible is certainly not quiet about suffering.

Sometimes in our own pain, we can feel as though God has forgotten us, and Jesus identified with our humanity on the Cross when He cried out to God. This happens because in some ways, life can feel like an obstacle course. There are twists and turns we don't expect and difficult moments we can't make sense of. We can find ourselves contending with dark and heavy feelings we just can't shake. In this space, the temptation to question God's presence in our lives is born. We can begin to wonder, "Why am I experiencing this suffering? Why has God forgotten me? Why am I facing this situation? Why is there so much suffering in this life?"

Yet, at the same time, we are taught as Christians not to be surprised by this kind of distress (see, for example, 1 Pet. 4:12). In fact, we are told to regard suffering as a normal part of this life. Whatever befalls us—whether disappointment, grief, disease, natural disaster, or any other kind of tragedy— we are not immune just because we are faithful. And we will not receive closure in every situation: some things will not be explained or understood on this side of life. And no matter how much we attempt to control our lives by our own will or by the protective measures of modern science, we can still find ourselves contending with things we don't understand and wish weren't happening.

We know that God is a safehouse for the battered, closest to the brokenhearted, a sanctuary during difficult times. Even in shifting tides, He is who He has always been. The moment we arrive in His presence, we find rest—and when we rest in His presence, we realize He was with us through it all, ever present, standing both behind us and in front of us all at the same time. When we struggle to bear the pain that living brings, we must be careful that we don't let it rob us of the life in Christ that our faith brings. This is when faith means not cheerfulness or confidence but trust in the God whose Son also felt our anguish.

Forsaken Figures in the Bible

While we see that Jesus Himself experienced human suffering, the Bible is also not quiet about the struggles that major heroes of our faith had with seasons of depression, loneliness, and sadness. We hear David throughout the Psalms writing of his anguish, loneliness, fear, and guilt as he battled despair. We hear about Job, who suffered through tremendous loss, affliction, devastation, and physical illness. Though Job maintained his faithfulness to God throughout his life, he struggled deeply, having literally lost everything. At one point, he cried out, "I loathe my life; / I will give free utterance to my complaint; / I will speak in the bitterness of my soul" (Job 10:1). We also hear about Elijah, whose story Fr. Nicholas loves to tell. Elijah struggled greatly with depression, but notice that it happened after some great spiritual victories. For example, in one story, during a time when the people of Israel were worshipping an idol named Baal, Elijah defeated the prophets of Baal and Asherah (1 Kin. 18). There were 850 pagan prophets against one man of God, and Elijah built a sacrifice before the Lord God and soaked it with water. God came down from heaven and consumed not only the sacrifice but the water itself, and then all the prophets of Baal and Asherah were put to the sword.

In the next story, Elijah goes from this great spiritual high to praying for rain to come after three years of drought— and then the rain comes! These are great victories. You would think that right after these, Elijah would have a party to celebrate all that God had done. But no! Here is what happens next:

> Ahab told Jezebel all that Elijah had done, and how he had killed all the prophets with the sword. Then Jezebel sent a messenger to Elijah, saying, "So may the gods do to me and more also, if I do not make your life as the life of one of them by this time tomorrow." Then he was afraid, and he arose and ran for his life and came to Beersheba, which belongs to Judah, and left his servant there.

> But he himself went a day's journey into the wilderness and came and sat down under a broom tree. And he asked that he might die, saying, "It is enough; now, O LORD, take away my life, for I am no better than my fathers." (I Kin. 19:1–4)

Then Elijah fell asleep, and an angel woke him up, provided him with food and water, and encouraged him to take nourishment. Here Elijah felt hopeless, alone, and afraid. He wanted to die. He wanted to sleep and had to be encouraged to get up and nourish himself. Sounds a lot like depression. And we see it in Elijah: a prophet, a biblical hero, a person of faith.

You would think that a man who could handle a three-year drought and stand up in front of 850 prophets of Baal and Asherah could handle a threat. But this message from Jezebel freaked him out so much that he ran. And when he came to Beersheba, the place where he had made an oath to serve God, he said, "I don't think I can do this." He had heard the voice of God and witnessed miracles, yet with one simple threat from Jezebel, he prayed that he might die. He was in a season of depression, sadness, and despair—and we love how the Bible tells us that it is okay. For there, in the midst of all of it, Elijah was rescued by God, and the story goes on to tell us about how Elijah went out and transformed people's lives.

Another example Fr. Nicholas likes to talk about is the Prophet Jeremiah (Jer. 15:17–18; 20:7–8). Jeremiah suffered rejection by the people he loved and reached out to. And although he displayed great faith, we also see his honesty as he wrestled with despair and a sense of failure. Jeremiah, as Fr. Nicholas puts it, not only wrote the Book of Jeremiah but also another book *dedicated* to depression, called Lamentations, as if he is saying, "Let me give you a whole book about how sad I am. Gloom and despair and agony." And in the book, he says things like this: "My soul is bereft of peace; / I have forgotten what happiness is; / so I say, 'My endurance has perished; / so has my hope from the LORD.' Remember my affliction and my wanderings, / the wormwood and the gall! / My soul continually remembers it / and is bowed down within me" (Lam. 3:17–20).

Have you ever felt like this? As if you have completely lost your peace and nothing in your life is working out? And even when you have asked God to help, you feel that He is not helping? And all you feel is your affliction and your pain? *This is Jeremiah. A prophet. A person of faith.*

As we look into the New Testament, even the great Apostle Paul, who would write much of the New Testament, says this: "For we do not want you to be unaware, brothers, of the affliction we experienced in Asia. For we were so utterly burdened beyond our strength that we despaired of life itself" (2 Cor. 1:8). Essentially, he was saying, "Even though it looks like I have it all together, actually I have had troubles that have messed me up"—even to the point of despair.

So even beyond the anguish that Jesus Christ, the Son of God, felt, the Bible is full of faithful people who go through hard times and strive with great darkness. We can take comfort in knowing that despondency does not signal the loss of our faith or our salvation. We might even say it is a normal part of working out our salvation.

What Makes Us Feel Forsaken?

When we feel forsaken, we tend to believe no one can understand what we're going through. While it's true our individual experiences are unique, it's also true that there are commonalities to the things that cause us to feel abandoned or desperate, and knowing this can help us hold on through the dark times.

Loneliness and Isolation

Isolation is that space we can all enter at times when we need the support of others but also feel agitated by their presence. In this place, our feelings can trump perspective, and negativity can run wild, producing critical thoughts that only serve to maintain and reinforce our distance from others. Consumed by our negative thoughts, we may come to believe that people just don't want to be around us, and we may also convince ourselves that isolating will somehow protect others from our miserable mood. But isolation only breeds depression, and depression, in turn, breeds more isolation. It becomes such a vicious cycle that, even if we are in a room full of people, we can still feel emotionally isolated and alone because ours is the only voice we hear.

Even when we are not isolating on purpose due to depression, despair, or simply a miserable mood, here in the US we tend to live very isolated lives. It is ironic that we are very much not alone in feeling alone. According to a new nationwide survey performed by global health service company Cigna, America is currently undergoing a "loneliness epidemic," with almost 50 percent of participants feeling lonely.[35] It is the paradox of our age that although we have more connections than ever before through digital media, we feel lonelier than at any point in human history.

This is concerning because *the first problem the Bible identified was not sin, it was being alone.* In Genesis chapter 1, God created everything. And at the end of all His work, He declared His creation to be "very good" (Gen. 1:31). Then, in chapter 2, God made man. And for the first time in all creation, God saw something that was not good. He said, "It is not good that the man should be alone" (Gen. 2:18). *And so, God made woman.* Yet, so often we think of everything as perfect up until the Fall of Adam and Eve in Genesis 3. But what God specified as "not good" had nothing to do with sin or with what Adam had done or not done. It was simply not good that Adam was alone. Like Adam, it is not good for us either, and when we are cut off from other people, we can feel cut off from and forsaken by God, too.

---

35 Susie Demarinis, "Loneliness at Epidemic Levels in America," *Explore* 16, no. 5 (September–October 2020): 278–279.

Unhealthy Comparisons

Trying to live up to the standards of this world often leaves us far from happy—and far from the intended path God has in mind for our lives. We look at other people's lives on social media and suddenly begin to feel disappointed in our own life. "Why doesn't my life look like this?" "Why am I not married to that kind of man?" "Why don't I have that many friends?" "Why aren't we going on that type of vacation?" "Why aren't we as happy as they look?" "Why don't my kids have that kind of success?" "Why, God, are You not helping me fulfill my dreams?" "Why do things never work out for me?"

When we compare ourselves to others, we are unaware of our blessings, which can make us feel forsaken by God as if He has not given us the blessings He has given to others. Comparisons can also leave us prioritizing things we were never meant to prioritize and changing our lives to resemble someone else's. Over time, we end up living a life that God never intended for us to live, a life where God might be looking at us and asking: "Who are you? What are you doing? I had plans for you. Why are you trying to be someone else? I don't recognize you as I have made you."

Saint Paul challenges our focus on comparisons with this question: "For am I now seeking the approval of man, or of God? Or am I trying to please man? If I were still trying to please man, I would not be a servant of Christ" (Gal. 1:10).

Faulty Thinking Habits

Our own thinking can also make us feel forsaken, especially when something upsets us, doesn't go our way, or doesn't have an easy solution. When these things happen, our thinking can fill our minds with our most familiar reactions, whether helpful or not. We might simmer unproductively about the awfulness of a certain situation or beat ourselves up with familiar critical narratives like "I don't have what it takes" or "This kind of thing always happens to me." It can also be common to generalize and predict more defeat: "This is just my life. I can't see it ever changing." In this space, we begin to lose our ability to hear God's voice because we can only hear our own faulty thinking.

One of Fr. Nicholas's professors in college used to say, "We are living magnets. Where our thoughts are is where we are heading." When we aren't intentional about confronting our own voice through life's storms, we often don't even realize the negativity that is leading us. As such, we can become fixated on and stuck in negative places that we aren't confronting enough to realign our thought life with God's wisdom. The field of psychology calls this *ruminating*: repetitively thinking or dwelling on negative and distressing thoughts and feelings. Ruminating animals chew and chew their food, then after swallowing, regurgitate their food, only to chew on that same food again and again to try to break it down. Interestingly, one of those animals is a sheep. Isn't it ironic that over five hundred times in the Bible, God actually refers to us as sheep. We act like sheep when we ruminate on our problems instead of working to break out of our faulty thinking patterns, calling upon God to help us, and listening to His voice.

Unexpected Challenges

Unexpected challenges in our lives can make our hearts grow weary, especially as we contend with plans that don't come to fruition despite our best intentions and our thoughtful diligence and perseverance. This happens when we have put something fully in God's hands and have prayed diligently about it, and for some reason it just doesn't seem to be working out. In these moments, we begin to feel like God has forsaken us—like He's just not listening, and we can find ourselves saying, "I've done everything right. I've put this fully in your hands. Why, God? Why is this not working out?" Sometimes we can become so self-important in our plan that our pride can fan the flame of our frustration, and we reject the opportunities God might be using to try to grow us.

Other times life seems to strike us with one problem after another, and we just don't feel we have the strength to meet the challenges. We feel so overwhelmed, we can't see where God is in it all. Here's the takeaway: It's okay to not be okay. Our difficulties are not our identity. They do not define us. With each difficulty we experience, our goal is to manage it in ways that do not separate us from God, but instead help us to grow in ways that leave more beauty in the world, keep our purpose intact, and preserve our souls.

What Can We Do When We Feel Despair?

While we can't always avoid feeling despair, we can certainly learn how to make it an unwelcome guest.

Draw Closer to God. The problem is that we have lost God at the center of our lives. —ST. PAISIOS OF MOUNT ATHOS[36]

Sometimes in all our pain and uncertainty, our hearts can feel so heavy that we don't even have the words to describe our experience. Yet we are called to bring everything to God in prayer, and this is still true when the weight of our heart immobilizes our best efforts to put words to feelings. In these moments, we desperately need God—which is why we have been given His Holy Spirit, who, as we have referenced before, "intercedes for us" and speaks for us, making clear our prayers even when they are unclear to us (Rom. 8:26). So even if we have no idea what to say, as we draw near to God's presence, the Holy Spirit helps us. When we draw near to Him, God promises us that He will be a "shield about [us]," "the lifter of [our] head," and will answer us "from His holy hill" (Ps. 3:3–4). So, no matter how low you feel, trust that God hears you, loves you, and will answer the worries of your heart—even if your emotions are trying to convince you otherwise. The first place we should turn in times of darkness is to the Source of all light and life.

---

36 St. Paisios, *With Pain and Love for Contemporary Man,* trans. Cornelia A. Tsakiridou and Maria Spanou, ed. Eleftheria Kaimakliotis (Thessaloniki, Greece: Monastery of St. John the Theologian, 2011), 167–168.

Jesus encouraged His followers to do this, even in their darkest hour when He would be taken from them. When He was about to be arrested and crucified, He could sense their distress, and so He said to them:

> Truly, truly, I say to you, you will weep and lament, but the world will rejoice. You will be sorrowful, but your sorrow will turn into joy. When a woman is giving birth, she has sorrow because her hour has come, but when she has delivered the baby, she no longer remembers the anguish, for joy that a human being has been born into the world. So also you have sorrow now, but I will see you again, and your hearts will rejoice, and no one will take your joy from you. (John 16:20–22)

Jesus' response to His followers' distress revealed to them that they would be transformed in an unprecedented way by what was distressing them. Although sorrow would fill their hearts, Jesus assured them of His never yielding presence, through His Holy Spirit, who would be their "Helper" and trusted guide and would never leave them:

> When the Spirit of truth comes, he will guide you into all the truth, for he will not speak on his own authority, but whatever he hears he will speak, and he will declare to you the things that are to come. He will glorify me, for he will take what is mine and declare it to you. (John 16:13–14)

Jesus left us the gift of His Holy Spirit so that we can know Him and draw closer to Him during times of distress, even though He would physically no longer be with us on this earth.

With the help of the Holy Spirit, we draw closer to God when we open our hearts to Him in every affliction, in every anxiety, and in every moment of distress and remember, as Paul assures us, that "the sufferings of this present time are not worth comparing with the glory that is to be revealed to us" (Rom. 8:18). And we must *choose every day*, even in the midst of our troubles, to draw closer to Him. We must choose to remember that He walks beside us and knows our deepest sufferings. We must choose to remember that His power remains in all things, along with His deep, penetrating love for us, which is ever-present through triumph and trial. We must choose to remember that, no matter how we have failed, our relationship with Him is not dependent on our works or our character but on His goodness and grace, because His love for us is not earned—it is freely given.

And lastly, we must remember that in darkness, when the twists and turns of life steal our joy, we need less of us and more of Him—especially when our circumstances and our own voice seem bigger than our God. Yet in our struggles, we often realize it's been a long time since we've truly talked to God, truly connected to His presence and tried to consciously remember His goodness, even though He's been waiting there all along to give us purpose and bring us life in darkness. Or perhaps we may know intellectually that God is present in all things, but we do not always connect more deeply to the experience of His presence. Ironically, our times of darkness, our hurt and brokenness, can actually help us become more sensitive to the experience of His presence, which can help us draw closer to Him.

How do we go about finding God in the midst of our dark times, though? We can open ourselves up to God and cry out for His comfort, saying, "Hear my prayer, O LORD; / let my cry come to you!" (Ps. 102:1), and then wait as the comfort of the Holy Spirit takes control, illuminates our path, and brings us back to a place of peace again. Also, don't be afraid to specifically ask for God's help, for He knows what we need before we even ask Him: "Before they call I will answer; / while they are yet speaking I will hear" (Is. 65:24). And Christ promises us that God will give us what we need, as He told His followers before His voluntary death: "Truly, truly, I say to you, whatever you ask of the Father in my name, he will give it to you. Until now you have asked nothing in my name. Ask, and you will receive, that your joy may be full" (John 16:23–24).

In your struggle, let your worry and despair serve as an invitation for God's presence to enter into your present awareness. Cry out to the one who promises, "Call upon me in the day of trouble; / I will deliver you, and you shall glorify me" (Ps. 50:15). As Fr. Nicholas likes to put it: "God can handle your mess. God can handle your complaining. He can even handle your lies and your mistakes. All you need to do is come and pour your heart out to God." We don't need to wait until we have it all together to reach out. Keeping it all inside and trying to manage it all on our own sets us up for failure—and that's how the devil can take advantage of us

CHAPTER 4: *My God, My God, Why Have You Forsaken Me?*

and get a foothold in our lives. But Jesus says, "Come to me, all who labor and are heavy laden, and I will give you rest. Take my yoke upon you, and learn from me, for I am gentle and lowly in heart, and you will find rest for your souls" (Matt. 11:28–29). So, when your spirit feels enveloped with a darkness you can't seem to shake, remember to pray Psalm 51:10: "Create in me a clean heart, O God, / and renew a right spirit within me." Set your eyes and your heart on the presence of the one true God who has promised to carry you through every hurt in this life. Know that He is already there with you, as the psalmist tells us:

> Where shall I go from your Spirit?
>   Or where shall I flee from your presence?
> If I ascend to heaven, you are there!
>   If I make my bed in [the depths] Sheol, you are
>   there!
> If I take the wings of the morning,
>   and dwell in the uttermost parts of the sea,
> even there your hand shall lead me,
>   and your right hand shall hold me.
> If I say, "Surely the darkness shall cover me,
>   and the light about me be night,"
> even the darkness is not dark to you;
>   the night is bright as the day,
>   for darkness is as light with you. (Ps. 139:7–12)

We can also draw near to God in the midst of our dark times by engaging in these helpful spiritual practices:

- **Read about Him every day in your study Bible.**
  It's hard to know how to respond in dark seasons
  if we aren't regularly filling ourselves with Scripture
  during less difficult seasons. We learn how to
  respond to times of despair in more life-giving ways
  when we have been chasing a more intimate relationship with God in more neutral seasons of life. Here
  are some examples for how you can begin your journey in the Word:

  — Begin with the Gospels, reading about the life
    of Christ (one-third of which are read during
    Holy Week). If you read three chapters a day,
    you can finish the Gospels in one month.

  — Read through the Book of Proverbs, a book of
    practical wisdom. If you read one chapter a day,
    you can finish it in one month.

  — Read through the Book of Isaiah, who is con-
    sidered one of the greatest of the Old Testament
    prophets and whom the New Testament quotes
    411 times. If you read two chapters a day, you
    will finish in a little over one month.

  — Read the Book of Psalms, which pretty much
    contains the entire spectrum of human emotion.
    If you read five chapters a day, you will be done
    in a month.

- **Reach out as often as possible in prayer.** Pray Psalm
  51. Pray the Jesus Prayer. Pray for people you come
  across. Pray for what you hear on the news. Pray
  for the driver in front of you. Pray for the person

standing next to you. Praying unceasingly means looking for every opportunity to connect to God in prayer.

- **Read other devotional books.** Try reading about the lives of the saints. There are many apps that give daily readings on the saints. Try out a new book each month on how to better live your faith. Give yourself five to ten minutes at the start or end of your day to read.

- **Know His promises and let them be written on your heart.** In order to reframe our struggles, we must remember that God promises to go before us and reminds us to trust in His goodness. To help you remember them in your heart, write as many of His promises down as you can think of and add to the list as you encounter new ones. Keep a log of your worries. Look back over them every now and again to write down how God delivered you in those worries. Read back through these during difficult times.

With these practices we are saying to God, "I am going to spend more time listening to You as You speak to me. I am going to spend more time in prayer, listening to You guide me, and more time reading the Bible and letting Your Word guide my life. I am going to spend more time in the house of the Lord."

When we draw near to God, He promises to draw near to us. So when we feel despair coming upon us, attempting to seize our soul, we don't have to fret because we can remember God's promise to us. We can also remember that while we can't always control the *arrival* of a difficult emotion, we can control *whether or not we welcome it into our hearts and fuel its story.* Saint Isaac the Syrian says that we need to remain watchful because:

> Not all the passions wage war by means of assault. For there are passions that only cause the soul affliction. Listlessness, despondency, and grief do not attack, whether by an assault proper, or through relaxation; rather they simply lay a weight upon the soul. The strength of our soul is proven, however, by victory over those passions which wage war by assault. A man must have a refined knowledge of all these, and recognize their symptoms, so that with every step he takes he may be conscious of the place he has reached, and in what terrain his soul has begun to walk.[37]

We can remember, too, that it is in these very moments of despair that God yearns for us to seek Him, to not try to manage everything all on our own. To find rest for our souls, we ask His Holy Spirit to renew our thoughts and cleanse us from everything that torments us. We were never meant to endure these dark and lonely places alone. We were intended to "pour out [our] heart before Him, for God is our refuge for us" (Ps. 62:8).

---

37 *The Ascetical Homilies of Saint Isaac the Syrian,* Homily 68 (Boston, MA: Holy Transfiguration Monastery, 2011), 332.

Regulate Our Thoughts and Feelings

The truth is, we can't always trust our thinking, and we especially can't trust it in dark times. Dark feelings give birth to dark thoughts, and dark thoughts give birth to dark feelings. So our thinking is dangerous when we feel forsaken because it can become a vicious cycle of negativity. Perhaps this is why the Bible includes so much guidance about being mindful of what we allow ourselves to think about. Paul counsels us to think about "whatever is true, whatever is honorable, whatever is just, whatever is pure, whatever is lovely, whatever is commendable, if there is any excellence, if there is anything worthy of praise, think about these things. What you have learned and received and heard and seen in me—practice these things, and the God of peace will be with you" (Phil. 4:8–9).

Fortunately, God gives us tremendous power to regulate our thoughts through life's ups and downs with the help of His Holy Spirit. But part of finding this regulation is knowing how to tune into it. How do we do that? We listen carefully to our inner stories, to how we think about things, and consider whether our thinking aligns with God's voice. God has given us the ability to *think about our thinking*, and we can use this gift to listen to how we explain things to ourselves. Because of this gift, we don't have to be paralyzed by our thoughts. Rather, we can challenge any thoughts that aren't rational, life-giving, or productive and choose not to act on them. Sometimes, our feelings take time to catch up with our choices and our more reasonable thoughts, but that's okay. We can still choose to make decisions based on our rational and life-giving thoughts, knowing that our goal is to step into problem-solving what we can change and learning how to adapt to what we can't. Either way, God has armed us with the power to not be held hostage by our thoughts.

If you are battling thoughts you can't seem to shake, take a moment to pause, tune in, and listen. What do you hear? What is occupying space in your mind? What are your thoughts telling you? How are you thinking about the things that worry or upset you? How are you explaining your hurt or disappointment? Now, make a choice to let the hope you have in Christ transcend your negative thinking. Make a choice to "not be conformed to this world, but transformed by the renewal of your mind, that by testing you may discern what is the will of God, what is good and acceptable and perfect" (Rom. 12:2).

As we saw at the beginning of this section, our thoughts and feelings are closely tied together, so it's important to also tune in to our emotions in order to detect our thinking. Often it is difficult for us to know what we are feeling, because while we feel some emotions strongly, others operate just beneath the surface of our awareness. Doctor Roxanne has found that she can ask someone who seems to be managing all the demands of life a simple question, "So, how are you doing?" and, all of a sudden, the tears begin to fall. People are always surprised when this happens because only seconds before they thought they felt "fine." In reality, they were not aware of feelings that were living just beneath the surface. Our emotions, whether we notice them or not, affect us in powerful ways. They can quickly shift the will of our spirit, especially when they lead us blindly. They affect the way we think, the decisions we make, and the spirit we operate out of. This is true for most of us. As we manage everything in our outer world, we don't necessarily notice our inner world, yet our inner world is affecting the outer nonetheless.

Even when we do notice what we are feeling, we often don't know how to respond productively to it. Most of us have learned to either ignore what we notice or to simmer unproductively in negative or irrational feelings. But it's important to learn to identify and name our feelings. MRI studies of the brain have shown that the simple act of labeling our emotions and putting words to our experience can help calm the brain region involved in emotional outbursts, which helps us regain control of ourselves. When we do this, we also see increased neural activity in brain regions more geared to reason, problem-solving, and logic.[38]

Labeling our emotions helps us regulate them so that we don't unconsciously fuel thoughts and narratives that make us feel worse. It can also help us learn something. Perhaps our emotions are pointing us toward something we need to address, to a problem that needs solving, or to an issue we need to air out. Other times, our feelings might not make any sense at all, and in that case, it's even more important that we notice them so we don't fuel anything negative or unhealthy.

---

38 Naomi I. Eisenberger et al., "Putting Feelings into Words," *Psychological Science* 18, no. 5 (May 2007): 421–8.

To figure out what you are feeling, try doing an emotional self-check. Take time throughout the day to ask yourself:

- How am I feeling?
- Is there anything heavy on my heart right now?
- Do I feel short tempered, agitated, or easily bothered lately? If so, why?
- Do I feel close or distant to the people I love? Why?
- Do I feel close to God or distant? Why? What am I telling myself about this situation?
- Am I scared or worried about anything?

Also, simply take a moment the next time you notice yourself feeling sad, upset, scared, disengaged, or otherwise not at peace. Sit back and just listen to your inner voice, and try applying James 3:17 to it: "But the wisdom from above is first pure, then peaceable, gentle, open to reason, full of mercy and good fruits, impartial and sincere." When you tune into your thoughts in the midst of strong feelings, is what you hear pure of heart? Encouraging? Does it solve problems or create them? Is it tainted with unrighteousness? Is it peaceable and gentle or harsh and divisive? Is it open to reason and logic? Is it leading you to good fruit or to be merciful? Is it helping you or making you feel even worse? Remember, the mind is the battlefield of the enemy.

In order to regulate our emotions, we need to go beyond just tuning into them and learn how to distinguish between our feelings themselves and the actual basis for those feelings—the narratives beneath them. When we find negative narratives, we need to reach for more life-giving thoughts to help reframe or adjust our emotional responses. Once we label our emotions, we turn away from anything that's not from God because we know that is of the enemy. "A stranger [we] will not follow, but [we] will flee from him, for [we] do not know the voice of strangers [the enemy]" (John 10:5). Even if we don't yet believe the positive thoughts or more plausible interpretations, we must keep trying to change the direction of our thoughts until we land on something that sounds more like God's voice.

Tuning in to, labeling, and understanding the narrative behind our emotions lays the foundation for discernment so that we don't just listen to any voice, but to the one true voice of the Person who loved us so much that He gave us life. As we do these things, we are striving to contain every emotion and thought inside a heart that knows Christ. We know that our thoughts and emotions can mislead us and turn our hearts away from Christ, as Proverbs says: "Whoever trusts in his own mind is a fool, / but he who walks in wisdom will be delivered" (Prov. 28:26). So we need to turn away from the voice of the enemy which divides, doubts, condemns, judges, discourages, confuses, frightens, torments, and overwhelms us. Instead, we listen for God's voice, which calms, comforts, convicts, encourages, enlightens, leads, reassures, and stills us. His is also the voice of peace, mercy, and love, and we know that "You keep him in perfect peace / whose mind is stayed on you, / because he trusts in you" (Is. 26:3).

To help us turn away from the voice of the enemy, we need to listen for anything that makes us lose our peace—things like faultfinding, emotional reasoning, resentments, self-disparagement, criticism, and doubt. Imagine that on your left is the voice of the enemy, which says, "You are alone in this," and on your right is the voice of Christ that is saying, "Let Me walk with you. Let Me give you hope. Draw near to Me, and I will draw near to you. I will fight for you. Call on Me, and I will answer. It is I who will give you rest. My love never leaves you. I will make all things work together for good." Know that whoever we listen to the most has power over our life, so we want to listen to thoughts that allow us to serve God. We can always identify a thought that is not from God if, when following it, it wouldn't allow us to serve Him in our actions. A thought is *not* from God if:

- It does not urge what the Spirit desires: forgiveness, grace, humility, peacefulness, goodness, gentleness, kindness, and self-control.
- It does not follow Christ's instructions to be merciful, pure of heart, and a peacemaker.
- It does not allow us to use our gifts for the good of others and the glory of God.
- It does not reflect God's voice.

We listen to and test our inner voice because spiritual warfare is very real, and the enemy sets us up to fail. The Book of James reminds us that sometimes our thoughts are really temptations trying to take root, and the devil uses such temptations to energize sin. This is why the Bible encourages us to "be attentive to my wisdom; / incline your ear to my understanding, / that you may keep discretion, / and your lips may guard knowledge" (Prov. 5:1–2). It is also why St. Paul tells us to "destroy arguments and every lofty opinion raised against the knowledge of God, and take every thought captive to obey Christ" (2 Cor. 10:5). To further help you regulate your emotions and protect yourself against temptation, consider listening for whether your thoughts are helping or hurting your situation from the perspective of your faith. Consider whether your thoughts create problems or solve them. Here we might ask ourselves:

- What is this thought urging me to do? Is that helpful? Where am I headed if I believe this thought?
- Could there be any other way to look at this situation?
- Are there any costs to thinking this way?
- Could there be a more productive way of interpreting this same situation that leaves me more at peace?
- Am I finding solutions or just indulging the urge to blame, accuse, or stew?
- Is this thought serving my goals?
- Does this sound like who God calls me to be?

Proverbs 2:10–12 says: "For wisdom will come into your heart, / and knowledge will be pleasant to your soul; / discretion will watch over you, / understanding will guard you." Our thinking should rescue us from sin, not lead us into it.

Reach Out to Someone

And though a man might prevail against one who is alone, two will withstand him—a threefold cord is not quickly broken. —ECCLESIASTES 4:12

Above all, when we feel despair we need God, but even God knows that we need other people; that's why He made Eve as a companion for Adam. The truth is, we all need someone in our life who understands us, who makes us feel like we are not alone and that we belong. We need this especially when we are struggling. When we are battling something within, we don't have to tell *everybody*, but we need to tell *somebody*.

Many of us, however, keep our struggles to ourselves instead of reaching out to others. Consider for a moment: What untold stories live within you? What realities do people not know about you when you smile and shake hands with them on a Sunday morning? What feelings are perhaps too tough to put into words? What truths about yourself feel too vulnerable to be exposed to the light? The truth is, most of us have secret stories that live beneath our smiles, stories we don't reveal to anyone because we fear judgment or because we think we need to be strong lest we cause others discomfort. But in reality, sharing our weaknesses will bind us together more powerfully than any show of strength. The enemy knows this and works to keep us isolated.

Moreover, many of us have never learned *how* to share our struggles with transparency, vulnerability, and authenticity—or have never cultivated a space for it. We see a lot of adults who have difficulty dealing with emotion due to having been raised in a household that did not allow for

open emotional expression, either because emotions esca-
lated too quickly or too often, or because emotions were
just never talked about in the open. As adults, these individuals often experience anxiety anytime they experience strong
emotions because they were never taught how to healthfully
express how and what they felt. That doesn't change the fact
that we still need to share our untold stories with others
because otherwise they can plague us, leaving us prone to
waves of sadness, worry, and negativity that can derail the
plans God has for us. Remember that emotions don't van-
ish because we banish them, and experiencing darkness in
isolation leaves us alone in our suffering without any other
voices, without perspective. In our untold stories, in every
burden, and in every experience, let us remember that God
is always with us, and He places people all along our path
to be expressions of His love for us. But it's up to us to
receive them—to open our heart to the experience of a good
listener, a comforting presence, or a warm hug. (For more
information about connecting with others and how to do it,
please see chapter 3.)

Remember Our Purpose

Let not your hearts be troubled. Believe in God; believe also in me. —JOHN 14:1

In seasons of darkness, depression, and despair, it's so easy to
feel we have nothing to live for. And when we feel forsaken,
it doesn't just make us tired and unmotivated, it can affect
our sense of purpose and meaning. You may know the story

of Victor Frankl—his story can help us think about how we need to hold on to our purpose, whether we are walking in times of darkness or light. Father Nicholas tells Frankl's story in this way:

> May 8, 1945, marked the end of one of the most horrific programs of violence ever implemented in human history. It was the end of the Holocaust, in which some 6.5 million people lost their lives. Men, women, and children were killed through starvation, scientific experimentation, and gas chambers.
>
> And then there were another 3.5 million people who survived the camps, and they were left with the horrors in their minds. In the weeks and years after the Holocaust, many of those who survived committed suicide—so many, that a famed psychologist named Victor Frankl set up a clinic in Austria to help Holocaust survivors. He studied them and he found in his research that pleasure is not the point of life; rather, people need *meaning and purpose* in their lives. The problem for many survivors was that life had lost its meaning for them. "People have enough to live by, but nothing to live for," he said. "They have the means, but no meaning."[39]

39 Viktor E. Frankl, *Man's Search for Meaning* (New York: Pocket Books, 1985), 165.

So when we feel despair, as if life has lost its meaning for us, rather than letting our feelings turn us inward, we must work to shift them into a larger context of hope that keeps our focus on our greater purpose in this life. Because it is our faith (not our feelings) that must ground our response to the existential questions that come from feeling forsaken, especially if we begin to question our life's meaning and purpose. God tells us that no matter how purposeless we feel, He has a plan for us. He created us with purpose, on purpose, for a purpose, and His plan is not contingent on our feelings or our circumstances. One of the greatest gifts God has given us is that we know what we live for: to be conformed to His image, becoming in thought, word, and deed what we already are in spirit. And as we allow our life experiences to grow us more and more into the image of Christ, we make manifest the words of St. Paul, to "put on the new self, which is being renewed in knowledge after the image of its creator" (Col. 3:10).

In everything we experience, good and bad, we must open ourselves up to experiencing it through a lens of this foundation. And though Jesus' life gives us many examples of how to grow into that image, He tells us His two most important commandments for our life: " 'You shall love the Lord your God with all your heart and with all your soul and with all your mind. This is the great and first commandment. And a second is like it: You shall love your neighbor as yourself. On these two commandments depend all the Law and the Prophets' " (Matt. 22:37–40). So although the Pharisees found 613 commandments in the Scriptures and debated about which one was the most important,[40] Jesus set forth for us the two most important things we can do to live out our faith. God has an overarching purpose for all of us: to conform us to the image of Christ, and that purpose remains, whether we are in darkness or in light.

We also remember our purpose when we focus not just on what is happening *to* us but on what God might be using it for *within* us. It is often in weakness where God's glory is made manifest, as 2 Corinthians 12:9 says: "My grace is sufficient for you, for my power is made perfect in weakness." Our trials lay the foundation for our ability to share Christ's love with others and bring us closer to our potential through Christ, to depend more fully on Him and to love others with more fullness. If you are facing a time of despair, let your hope in God ground you and carry you through it, for when we keep our eyes on the light, we have His promise that darkness will never overtake us. Additionally, we need to remember that we are not products of our circumstances; rather, as the Bible often reminds us, we are products of God's promises.

So, as you meet obstacles, try to let go of worry, hopelessness, and despair. Avoid the question of "Why me?" and instead say, "Okay, what now? What does God still yearn to do within me? What beauty can I bring to the world because of this pain?" Consider the questions about God's purpose

---

40 *The Orthodox Study Bible* (Nashville: Thomas Nelson, 2008), 1312.

for you. Trust in His goodness and remain open to the work of His hands.

Turn Our Despair into Something Beautiful

When life leaves us feeling forsaken and despairing, we can choose to be either a seed or a stone. If we are a seed, we let our circumstances grow us and create something beautiful. If we are a stone, we let our despair bury us beneath its weight. We can turn our despair into something beautiful by choosing to be a seed, allowing our struggles to produce something good, as the Apostle Peter says: "Let those who suffer according to God's will entrust their souls to a faithful Creator while doing good" (I Pet. 4:19). So, not only are we instructed to trust God in our despair but we are also instructed to use our struggles and afflictions to help others, like 2 Corinthians 1:3–7 tells us:

> Blessed be the God and Father of our Lord Jesus Christ, the Father of mercies and God of all comfort, who comforts us in all our affliction, so that we may be able to comfort those who are in any affliction, with the comfort with which we ourselves are comforted by God. For as we share abundantly in Christ's sufferings, so through Christ we share abundantly in comfort too. If we are afflicted, it is for your comfort and salvation; and if we are comforted, it is for your comfort, which you experience when you patiently endure the same sufferings that we suffer. Our hope

for you is unshaken, for we know that as you share in our sufferings, you will also share in our comfort.

If we stay connected to our faith, we can become better vessels of light through dark times. Look around. After enduring difficulty, we often see something beautiful emerge. For example, gratitude can be born when we experience being without. Authentic compassion is often born when we experience emotional pain, struggle, and hardship. In hardship, God preserves us, and the comfort and growth we receive is what helps us enter the afflictions of others with empathy. And if we look far enough into the stories that are truly beautiful in the eyes of the Spirit, we usually find seasons of difficulty along the way.

So, if you are struggling and feeling forsaken, try to find a way to let the experience yield something beautiful in this world. Perhaps your pain can birth a deeper dependence and reliance on Christ. Perhaps your pain can become a place where God's mercy finds you. Perhaps a painful past will become the reason you are now convicted about something that matters to you in the present. Perhaps experiencing a discouraging inner voice in the midst of your own struggle can become the reason you so intentionally lift up others today. The list can go on.

The point is, if we don't let our pain harden our hearts, it softens our hearts. We become more sensitive to experiencing God and to the experiences of others as we draw nearer to the potential God has designed in us to bring beauty into this world.

Embrace Our Strengths

Though God has an overarching purpose for all of us, He has also equipped each of us for a specific plan that He yearns to fulfill in our own individual lives. When we feel forsaken, we mustn't forget this but rather try to refocus our energies on using what we've been uniquely equipped for to better the world in some way. Living life in ways that help us express our unique spiritual gifts helps us transcend our earthly existence and reminds us of our spiritual existence. As we use our gifts, we become more aware of God's unique design for our lives and can spend more time being guided by that design. This helps to reveal His greater plans for our lives and can bring back meaning amidst any struggle.

But when we go through periods of despair, it can cloud our vision, making it easy for us to forget the gifts God designed us with. This leaves us questioning our value and feeling insecure in our abilities. Interestingly, using our gifts can help us combat despairing feelings because our psychological well-being increases when we contribute meaningfully to the world around us. Not surprisingly, research backs this. Studies have found that using our inherent gifts can help with emotional well-being, bolster happiness, and contribute to a life of growth and purpose.[41] So it makes sense that as

---

41 Carolina M. Azañedo et al., "Character Strengths Predict Subjective Well-Being, Psychological Well-Being, and Psychopathological Symptoms, Over and Above Functional Social Support," *Frontiers in Psychology* 12 (September 2021).

we ground ourselves in faith, we can begin doing what we were uniquely suited for and use it to serve one another. "As each has received a gift, use it to serve one another, as good stewards of God's varied grace" (I Pet. 4:10).

If you are struggling to remember your gifts, remember that self-disparagement is from the enemy. And if you have fallen into thinking about only what you lack, you may be falling into the trap of allowing the world to affect your identity, since the world often tells us to value things that are not the things of God.

When temptations like these go unmanaged, we end up yearning only to be rich in *this* world—being seen, valued, admired, and accepted by humankind at the cost of being rich in spirit and devoted to God's purpose in our lives. And because desires often give birth to sin, we must watch our desires so that we don't allow ourselves to be deceived (James 1:15–16). We cannot serve two masters. No, we must "choose this day whom you will serve" (Josh. 24:15). We do this by regularly managing the temptation to self-disparage about everything we lack and simultaneously remaining aware of what we have been wired to do in this life—the things that drive us and afford us a better spiritual, emotional, psychological, and intellectual life.

What if instead of trying to live up to someone else's highlight reel, we try to reset our focus on creating our own? Doing this would mean following God's design for our life, concentrating on our own purpose, capitalizing on our unique gifts and abilities, and celebrating the gifts we see in others—all for the purpose of God's glory. You see,

God has placed on all of our hearts certain desires and gifts. It may not always be clear to us what our gifts are, what our purpose in this life is, but we must take the long-range view and remember God's promise to bring His purpose into fruition in our lives, for He does have plans for us (Jer. 29:11). (If you struggle to know your strengths, try taking a strengths assessment at www.viacharacter.org.) He reminds us that we were fearfully and wonderfully made and that He "will fulfill His purpose for [us]" because He does not "forsake the work of His hands" (Ps. 138:8). "For it is God who works in you, both to will and to work for his good pleasure" (Phil. 2:13).

So even when we are depressed, we must remember to keep honoring God by never letting go of the gifts He has given us and to use them with humility and obedience. Remember, your gifts were never meant to be about you; they were meant to glorify God—so how we use our gifts is our gift back to Him. We shouldn't let our insecurity outweigh our responsibility.

To focus our energies more in this direction, we need to consider what we are feeding on. For instance, what's on your social media feed? What types of things do you watch and read? Are they mostly things that inspire you, reset your focus, or breed encouragement? Or are they mostly highlight reels of other people's lives that only remind you of what you are lacking?

We also need a mind that yearns to support the good things we see in others—the good God yearns to do within them—rather than seeing their good as something we need to compete with. After all, when God made man, He saw the need to give man a *helper*, not a *competitor*. As we look to live alongside one another, we aren't looking for who we can compete with; we are looking to support each other and to help others become the best version of themselves. So, we celebrate their wins, encourage their joy, and fan the flame of their gifts for the betterment of the world, so that it all brings God glory.

You see, our lives were never meant to be about us. We aren't here to prove our worth or seek our own glory. We are here to discover and water the seeds of goodness God has planted in us—and it's easier to celebrate our goodness and the good we see in others when we live as authentic beings, comfortable with our imperfections. We are all beautifully broken in some way, but God can and does use everything within us for good. Therefore, you can remove the stress you place on yourself to project the perfect image. Instead, work to accept your brokenness, and embrace and develop the strengths you do have. After all, we all possess different strengths and were meant to work together as one Body of Christ, as the Bible says: "For as in one body we have many members, and the members do not all have the same function, so we, though many, are one body in Christ, and individually members of one another. Having gifts that differ according to the grace given to us, let us use them" (Rom. 12:4–6). So if you have forgotten your purpose and meaning in the midst of your despair, try to remember how God has uniquely equipped you to share your strengths with the world. It can help to ask yourself the following questions:

- How can I focus more on serving God rather than competing with others?
- What has God uniquely equipped me with so that I can serve and love others?
- What has He placed on my heart?
- What used to drive me or fulfill me before I began to feel depressed and forsaken?
- What are my strengths? What am I good at?
- How do I relate to others in my own, unique way?
- What motivates me?
- When asked to serve in some way, what do I not usually say "no" to?
- What is one thing that people always compliment me for?
- What do I do seamlessly? What are my natural abilities and talents?

These are your gifts that become your responsibility to share for the betterment of others and the Church. In the Bible, when God gets the angriest, it is not with the unfaithful people but with faithful people who are not using their inherent gifts for His glory.

What Can We Do When Someone We Love Is Struggling?

You make known to me the path of life; / in your presence there is fullness of joy; / at your right hand are pleasures forevermore. —PSALM 16:11

We have looked at how to ward off despair when we feel it ourselves, but what about when someone we love is in the depths of despair? It's hard enough to handle darkness in ourselves; what are we supposed to do when it overtakes someone else? When joy leaves a person we love, it's important to recognize that our first response may not be compassion but discomfort, and that may make us want to withdraw from that person. It's hard to be around the suffering of others, and it's easy to back away and, forgetting our own struggles, permit ourselves to craft negative narratives about them.

If we understand and acknowledge this impulse, we can resist it. We know from our own experience that when someone is in a dark place, that is when they need love most. So, refuse to let those you love struggle alone in their negativity—love them through it. Draw near to suffering people. Approach them with loving concern and without judgment, and bring comfort and gentle encouragement. Offer a hug. Take a walk with them. Remind them of their value and that they are always loved. Appreciate the goodness and joy that remains in their lives—but don't require them to feel it in that moment.

In God's presence, there truly is fullness of joy, though someone who is struggling can't always feel it. So, with joy in your heart, be His presence for others. When we are God's arms of love in this world, we see that "a joyful heart is good medicine" (Prov. 17:22).

Here are a few more suggestions for how to love others when they're down:

- **Be merciful with them!** Pray that you will find mercy for them during their moments of inflexibility or strong emotion. Some good questions to ask yourself are, "Could this be their depression or despair talking?" "Are they having a hard time managing the pressures they face today?" "How can I help?" Remember, depression and anxiety can result in irritability, reactivity, and inflexibility just as much as in sadness.
- **Pray with them**, over them, and for them.
- **Encourage them to take small steps** rather than challenging them to break free from their despair all at once. Remember, it takes time to move through emotions.
- **Meet their struggle with your peace.** Getting upset with someone who is anxious or depressed *never* helps because intensity only breeds intensity. And telling someone they "shouldn't" feel the way they do or yelling at them to "get over it" or "move on" only creates more pressure and breeds confusion. When we meet others in their struggle with peace, we let go of trying to control the struggle or force them out of their experience by telling them what to do. This kind of calm is very grounding and can prompt reason to return organically as emotions begin to settle. So instead of taking on their emotionality, stay calm and let those struggling talk freely about what they are feeling to clarify their experience, and keep in mind that perspective often comes in time.

A Word on Joy

Happiness *happens*, but at times it can truly feel less natural to *choose* joy. Sometimes choosing joy takes more work than at other times. We encourage you today to work toward it by taking notice of your blessings, even in your angst. Hug those you love, acknowledge the growth that comes from disappointment, thank those who support you and have been part of your journey, give back to the world in small ways, appreciate the things around you, and never spend too long on any one thought that might keep you from the fulfillment you can find through gratitude.

When we pour joy into the world by noticing our blessings and letting goodness, mercy, and love lead our hearts, we neutralize any negativity that threatens to deplete us. It's been said that the heart is a very good fertilizer because anything we plant—whether love, hate, fear, hope, revenge, or jealousy—bears fruit. It is up to us to decide what to harvest. This goes for both ourselves and what we elicit from others.

To pour joy into the world, try praying sincerely and openly as you reflectively examine yourself in light of God's light. Consider His voice amidst your own. As we surrender our circumstances to God, He reminds us to turn our lives over to Him, to let go of oppressive and legalistic approaches to our burdens that put too much pressure on ourselves. God invites us to find rest in Him (Matt. 11:28–30). Why must we remember this? Because life isn't perfect. It isn't a fairytale or a storybook. And it doesn't always have easy answers.

Living a life of joy means letting the Spirit lead in everything we do. Remember that our joy doesn't come from *something*, it comes from *Someone*—our Savior. Whether in depression, strife, or offense; in challenging situations or moments we sail through with ease; in fighting for peace or resting in it, joy is constantly taking notice of our blessings and remembering we are never alone. So, choose joy today, and watch the transformation that takes place both within you and within every heart you affect.

For Discussion: The Three Rs—
Rest, Reflect, and Respond

1. What situation has brought up the feeling of being forsaken?

2. What do you find yourself saying or thinking about God during these times?

3. What issues do you struggle with that might be feeding your feelings? (For example: isolation, unhealthy comparisons, faulty thinking.)

4. Label the feelings you're facing right now: anger, hurt, sadness, worry, despair (E.g., "I'm angry.")

5. What's the story attached to the feeling? What are you telling yourself about your circumstance, about why you feel what you feel? How are you explaining your hurt or disappointment? (E.g., "Things never work out for me.")

6. Why is it so upsetting? (E.g., "Because I'm tired of being the underdog.")

7. Why is it important to fight that feeling? (E.g., "Because God has plans for my life, and this feeling can derail His plans for me if I keep engaging it.")

8. Why is it important to accept the situation you're dealing with? (E.g., "Because fighting it unproductively doesn't allow me to move on from it and have hope and trust in what God could be using it for.")

9. Is there anything you can do differently in light of this struggle?

10. What's the next best thing you can do right now? (E.g., "To try to hear God's voice in this.")

11. What steps could you take to help you draw closer to God and hear His voice? What book of the Bible could you delve into?

12. What is one thing you can remember that God promises you in times of despair?

13. How has God resolved your dark feelings in past situations? Name one example of how God has kept His promises in your own life.

14. When you tune into your thoughts during times of despair, what voice do you hear? Do you hear things the Spirit desires within you (forgiveness, hope, grace, mercy, humility, peacefulness, or goodness)? Do you hear things the enemy encourages (faultfinding, unproductive guilt, resentment, self-disparagement, hopelessness, condemnation, criticism, or doubt)?

15. What could God be using this situation for within you?

16. How could you use what you are experiencing for something beautiful in this world?

17. What is your greatest temptation during times of despair?

Prayer: Lord of the Powers

In the name of the Father, Son, and Holy Spirit.

O heavenly Father, some of Your greatest miracles take place in darkness. It was in the darkness of a cave that You sent Your Son to be born. It was in darkness that You hung on the Cross just before Your Resurrection. It was in the darkness of the Tomb that You destroyed the power of Hades. You, O Lord, reveal to us that darkness can never overtake the light and that no matter what the enemy tries to use against us, it is not more powerful than You. I call upon you, O Lord, because at times I experience the darkness of despair, and dark clouds sometimes cover every area of my life. Help me to remember that absolutely nothing can separate me from Your light. Remind me of the words of the hymnographer who prayed, "Lord of the Powers, be with us [pause and take a breath], for other helper have we not, in tribulations but you [pause and take a breath]. Lord of the Powers, have mercy on us." In the holy and sacred name of the Father, Son, and Holy Spirit I pray, Amen.

CHAPTER 5

I Thirst

*Jesus, knowing that all was now finished, said (to fulfill
the Scripture), "I thirst."* —JOHN 19:28

WHEN SOMEONE ASKS the common question, "How are you?" most of us reply with the default response, "Great, how are you?" Of course, our default reply doesn't reflect what is truly going on inside of us. If someone asked it differently—"How are you doing . . . really?"—and we wanted to give an honest answer, it might be more accurate to say "tired," "overwhelmed," "drained," or "scattered." This is how many of us feel as we try to manage our day-to-day responsibilities and expectations.

In light of this, one of the most misunderstood aspects of our walk of faith is the importance of tending to ourselves. It's easy to fall into the trap of thinking that self-care is selfish and that if we want to fulfill God's purpose for our lives, it's better to deprive ourselves—especially if it means serving others. For this reason, the fifth statement on the Cross is powerful and revealing. Christ, the King of Glory who breathed the stars into their courses, who knows the exact number of hairs on our head, who designed every animal and organism, and whose love for us is never tired, shares with us two powerful words that reveal His vulnerability: "I thirst." Jesus, as fully God and fully human, was willing to acknowledge and express a need of His earthly nature. His words remind us to be open to our own needs, willing to both acknowledge and express them as we tend to the gardens of our own humanity.

You see, we are the instruments by which God transforms this world. The questions we must ask ourselves, then, are, "What is the cost of *not* tending to ourselves? How well can we fulfill God's calling in our lives if we don't care for the very body the soul depends on?"

Self-Care Is Not Self-Indulgence

*So teach us to number our days, / that we may get
a heart of wisdom.* —PSALM 90:12

Self-care is not about indulging ourselves; it's about making the choice to build a lifestyle that better supports our ability to live more in the image of Christ. We can't ignore the fact that our soul is housed within our body, and although the Holy Spirit is always at work within us, our bodies—and the decisions we freely make with them—affect the work the Spirit yearns to do within us. So, when we put ourselves back on our own radar by committing to life-giving sources of renewal and by respecting our own capacity (the amount we can handle while still remaining emotionally, spiritually, and psychologically healthy), we create a better foundation for the Holy Spirit to thrive in our lives and thus to manifest the fruit of the Spirit.

Self-care then is about caring for our body and soul to help our life to flourish in God's promised abundance. As Jesus said, "I came that they may have life and have it abundantly" (John 10:10). We aren't gratifying the flesh, since that leads only to destruction. Self-care isn't about giving in to our vices, and it's not about any other kind of indulgence like selfish ambition, lack of discipline, sexual immorality, idolatry, dissension, drunkenness, or impurity. In our self-care, we "crucify the flesh" (Gal. 5:24) to gain a body belonging to Christ that functions to support the work of the Holy Spirit within us, ultimately to bring to fruition the things pleasing to the Spirit.

If self-care is working as it should, we should begin to see more of the Holy Spirit present in our lives and directing our lives. So ultimately, self-care is about seeing more of God and less of us. For example, we might find that we are more patient and loving in our relationships. We might find that we are led more by peace and gentleness in moments of conflict. We might find ourselves more open to connection with others, rather than aggravated by their presence. We might begin feeling more intrinsic joy—joy that isn't based on external things. We might find ourselves purer of heart, more open to forgiveness, our thinking laced with more goodness. Or perhaps we might find ourselves exercising more self-control around temptations we usually struggle with.

Self-Care Means Slowing Down and Making Space

Life in the world today is stressful and hectic. Many of us live in noisy environments and have more demands than we have the capacity to manage. And as we try to manage it all anyway, we don't realize just how much our souls are affected by going too long without renewal. We forget that our soul depends on the body in which it is housed and that the aim of the Christian life is for Christ to shine through us. So instead of losing ourselves in the busyness of our lives, we must take time to study ourselves in relation to how well we see Christ within us. To do this, we first need to slow down and make the space and find the quiet for contemplation. And second, we need to remove the obstacles our body often presents to living more closely in Christ's image: we need to get out of our own way so that we can see God in us.

When demands press on us and our internal reserves run low, it's hard to hit the pause button. But that's what we need most to enter the kind of quiet contemplation our souls require for realignment so that more of God's righteousness can direct our steps. Without this, we will find ourselves behaving in ways that don't reflect Christ. For example, even something as simple as being in a hurry can make us less likely to stop to help someone in need. Being exhausted can leave us more prone to agitation, impatience, or irritability. Chronically working can make us so restless that we can't relax even when the work stops. Overextending ourselves in general can make it hard to connect in positive ways to people we love. We might even find ourselves pushing away the very people we love and need most, which only worsens the depletion. Without sufficient renewal to counter the effects of stress, we are left relying on willpower alone to live as children of the light.

Think about the qualities expressed by the Holy Spirit. They motivate us to be liberal in our giving and tend to prompt practical expressions of love, goodwill, and graciousness. The Spirit leads us in ways opposite of selfishness, pride, and a me-first attitude. These qualities are only born in our behavior, through an intimate relationship with Christ and with a body, free of carnal desire, that doesn't inhibit the fruit of that relationship.

When our spirit is thriving, we express our generosity organically through kindness, allowing others to go before us, doing what is best for all and not just what is best for us, having the willingness to carry each other's burdens, to compliment others freely, and to use our inherent gifts in ways that make the world a better place. This type of generosity that is born in a spirit that is thriving liberates us to lead others to a light they may have never known or may have simply forgotten.

But unchecked stress from pushing ourselves to operate at the edge of our capacity for far too long can lead to burnout and chronic exhaustion. And when we are burned out, we don't open our eyes and hearts to the people who stand right before us, whose wounds need our compassion. When we are burned out, we don't give unconditionally because we don't have anything left to give.

Self-Care Helps Us Resist Taking on the Values of the World

Self-care is soul-care not only because the body houses the soul but because if we don't take care of ourselves, then we will slowly, unconsciously take on the values of the world. The values most of us contend with epitomize the greater struggle we are seeing in our world today. We unconsciously subject ourselves to living beyond our natural capacity, and we aren't drawing healthy lines that allow us to effectively manage our own needs. We're not deciding what really matters or setting boundaries around what doesn't. Most of us wear busyness as a badge of honor, let chronic hurry drive our day, and chase the "more is better" mentality that leaves us unsatisfied. These are the default settings of our culture. The world is constantly trying to define us with temptations of every kind: to live for the now, to place our reputation over our character, to overvalue our image, to seek academic/career success for our own glory, to desire wealth, to seek status, and, yes, to be liked and accepted. But as Christians, we know we shouldn't be deceived by the things of this world and that it is often our own desires that ultimately give birth to sin (James 1:15–16).

Yet we also know that we cannot "serve two masters" (Matt. 6:24). So, if we want to live out our purpose, we must examine what we do and why we do it. We must think about what motivates us and run it all back through a lens of what is actually pleasing to God. Saint John of Kronstadt wrote,

> How will it be with us in the future life, when everything that has gratified us in this world: riches, honours, food and drink, dress, beautifully furnished dwellings, and all attractive objects—how will it be, I say, when all these things leave us—when they will all seem to us a dream, and when works of faith and virtue, of abstinence, purity, meekness, humility, mercy, patience, obedience, and others will be required of us?[42]

Think about your own life, and consider what the world has encouraged you to make a god out of. How have you let the world define the things you prioritize? What are you protecting or overvaluing? How does it derail your life in Christ? Let today be a moment of redirection for you to "choose this day whom you will serve" (Josh. 24:15).

Here are some values we unconsciously take on, that we should guard against:

Feeling Pressed for Time

We are living in an age where we never have enough time and everything feels rushed. We have become impatient. We can't seem to get what we want or where we need to be quickly enough. The world has incentivized us to get *through* our day

---

42 Sergiev, *My Life in Christ*, 243.

at the expense of being present, caring, and compassionate *within* our day.

Being Driven by the Numbers

We are also living in a time when *consumption is valued over compassion*. A physician friend once shared with Dr. Roxanne, "Unfortunately, we don't get paid to pace ourselves—we get paid to see more patients." Sadly, this is true for far too many of us. We can be so consumed with making a living that we are not making a life. Whether it's the things we want to buy, the bills we have to pay, or wanting to increase our investments, we can become so focused on the numbers that we lose sight of our own capacity.

Overvaluing Things That Don't Matter

Modern life is becoming less and less personal, less and less meaningful, and less and less focused on what really matters. We let all sorts of forces claim importance in our lives rather than God. We can unconsciously find ourselves overvaluing what's unimportant (errands, responsibilities, and to-do lists) and undervaluing what truly matters (connection, meaning, and purpose). Spiritually, we stop making time for God and might feel disconnected from our faith. Life can start to lack meaning. Professionally, we may find ourselves getting things on our to-do list done rather than investing in what we are doing, because we have nothing left to give toward what used to bring us meaning. Relationally, we might find ourselves tuning out or not being present with loved ones, or withdrawing from others out of sheer exhaustion because we have less to give to our relationships. We become less generous. We may not desire to spend more than a few minutes a day engaging with quality relationships or having conversations. Or we may find ourselves agitated, short-tempered, or reactive.

Doing More than We Can Reasonably Handle

Studies show we have less than thirty minutes each day to manage our own needs, but we are called to care for others for more than ten hours.[43] This creates a supply-and-demand imbalance because we can't effectively care for others if we don't have enough time to care for ourselves. The enemy loves this because *if he can't make us sin, he'll make us busy* so that we stop prioritizing our soul, we stop connecting to people around us in positive ways, and we stop prioritizing our physical and mental health.

How to Recognize What Kind of Self-Care We Need

In our day-to-day busyness, it can be hard to recognize that we need to take some time for ourselves—or to know just what, exactly, we need. Often, we think what we need is to

---

43 Habib Yaribeygi et al., "The Impact of Stress on Body Function: A Review," *Experimental and Clinical Sciences Journal* 16 (July 21, 2017): 1057–1072.

check off all the items on our to-do list, but in reality, our to-do lists are never ending. There will be more to do tomorrow and the day after. We will never feel completely rested if we place our peace in our to-do list.

What works better is to know ourselves well enough to see what needs replenishing and to heed the warning signs of exhaustion *before* it derails us. To do this, start by just reflecting on what makes you feel truly rested and replenished. Then, plan ahead to make time for those things, scheduling them just like you would any other appointment.

Next, keep an eye out for stress signals: irritability, despair, lack of desire, and struggling to give and receive love as usual. These are all signs that our soul is depleted, because unhealthy emotions thrive more in bodies that are not well cared for. We might also dread our responsibilities or feel overwhelmed by our usual to-do lists. Conversely, we might feel complete apathy.

Emotionally, we might find ourselves tuning out or not being present with loved ones—maybe even withdrawing out of sheer exhaustion because we have less to give to our relationships. We might even find ourselves paralyzed by incessant worry or more critical than usual toward ourselves and others, battling silent narratives that trigger misplaced anger and magnified aggravations. And because we tend to have lower levels of empathy when we're stressed, we may have less grace and be less patient, which leaves us shorter tempered and reactive to all the little things.

Physically, we might feel restless and have trouble relaxing even when we have time to. We may find ourselves sacrificing everything that usually keeps us healthy and whole, like adequate sleep, rest, quiet, physical activity, and wholesome nutrition. We may have stopped going to the doctor for routine visits or nagging symptoms because we just don't have the time. We might even confuse physical symptoms—like headaches, physical exhaustion, or trouble sleeping—with age or typical fatigue, when these are really just signs our body uses to get our attention.

In more extreme cases, we may find life starting to lack meaning, or we may become stuck in a vicious cycle of avoidance, not wanting to contend with daily responsibilities. Or we may find ourselves drawn toward destructive habits that we just can't seem to shake. When this happens, we don't need blame, self-condemnation, or judgment; that only adds to the stress. We only need to do the next right thing by choosing to invite rest, reflection, and restoration. When we listen, we are better able to respect our body enough to draw back and do what we need to do in order to keep our soul nourished.

Spiritually, another stress signal is feeling distant from God and not being able to hear His voice. Perhaps this is why Jesus so often went away by Himself to pray—to get away from the noise and better hear God's voice. In the Gospel of Mark, Jesus calls His disciples to get away from the crowds: "'Come away by yourselves to a desolate place and rest a while'" (Mark 6:31). Just like the disciples, we too do not always see the need for rest. Sometimes we are so busy overextending ourselves that we don't see the collateral damage it has in our own lives. But when we rest, we are better able to seek God's will because we can better hear His voice. It is this process of finding rest and reenergizing ourselves that keeps us serving Him in whatever capacity we have been called to serve.

In order to find this time for rest, we must set boundaries to keep the busyness at bay. If you have trouble setting healthy boundaries, remind yourself that to keep going, to keep moving toward God's purpose for your life, to love others well, and to better put on the image of Christ, we must take time to listen to our bodies. Setting boundaries is not selfish; it is the self-care we need to nourish the efforts of our soul in trying to better live in Christ's image.

What Self-Care Is and What It's Not

Christians are so often told to be self*less* that a concept like self-care can feel very self*ish*. As we've been trying to explain, however, self-care keeps our body at its best so we can be a conduit for the Holy Spirit. Our culture has learned to prey upon self-care, however, and has attempted to redefine self-care as something hollow and unhealthy. We might hear that self-care means rewarding ourselves with food, pampering ourselves (via massages, facials, gifts, etc.), or engaging in destructive habits (like drinking, vaping, overuse of social media/gaming, drugs, or any other form of escape) in order to escape our stress. But true self-care is not about escaping stress; it's about acknowledging it and addressing it in healthy ways. Not only can many of these false promises of relief harm us physically by placing added stress on our body, they can also harm our spirit because they don't allow us to confront our stress in ways that truly heal.

So, as opposed to what our culture might tell us is self-care, true self-care nourishes our body, mind, and spirit in substantial ways, which may look like doing things such as:

- making yourself a healthy lunch
- replacing your running shoes
- going to bed early
- making and keeping doctors' appointments you have been putting off
- spending more time in nature
- scheduling a weekly lunch with a good friend who nourishes your soul and replenishes your spirit
- solving problems rather than just naming them or letting them simmer
- protecting time for your faith through attending church, reading your Bible, and/or engaging in regular prayer

Think about it. When we exercise daily and take the time to prepare wholesome, nutritious meals, we fuel the body and facilitate the type of restful sleep we need to handle life's changing demands with a spirit of goodness. A healthy awareness of our emotions prompts the understanding we need to lead our feelings, rather than allowing our feelings to unconsciously lead us. Maintaining supportive networks of people can help break cycles of despair we could otherwise enter. Protecting practices that nourish our soul and deepen our faith helps us relate our faith to our everyday circumstances in meaningful ways that sanctify us. You see, we can't rely on life slowing down or going well as conditions we must have in order to live our faith. Rather, it's up to us to build our lives around the life-giving habits we need, in order for our flesh to not hold our spirits hostage.

So in this way, true self-care is about supporting our ability to live the life Christ intended for us to live. It is about setting ourselves up to draw near to others and remain someone others can draw near to.

Good self-care also means having self-compassion. For instance, in tough times, instead of judging ourselves we could acknowledge what we feel and make space for it in a compassionate way. When we have self-compassion, rather than engaging an unkind, harsh, or judgmental voice, we can talk to ourselves in life-giving ways that encourage, comfort, calm, and keep us pushing forward toward our goals even if we feel nervous, defeated, or afraid. You see, our participation is required in order to experience the comfort of God's presence. Self-compassion helps us find the wisdom, peace, strength, and courage we need to walk through difficulties, because it replaces our voice with God's voice. And instead of adding more feelings to the situation we already face, we gain clarity. So in stress, allow mercy and compassion to live in your heart, and let it build the foundation of your thoughts so that what flows out is from the Holy Spirit and brings healing rather than more hurting.

Whatever self-care methods we use, we should use all of them with the right goal in mind: to care for our life in ways that allow our soul to flourish. Remember, unhealthy emotions thrive in unhealthy bodies. All our best intentions and willpower won't help us follow God's will for our lives if we haven't taken good care of ourselves. Because when we can't calm a storm in our life, self-care helps us calm ourselves within that storm.

Dimensions of Self-Care

True self-care involves putting ourselves back on our own radar—our whole selves. It's remaining mindful of what we truly need in order to thrive, rather than trying to will ourselves into a life of faith. And self-care is not as simple as eating healthily and taking warm baths. We are complex beings, and self-care has as many dimensions as we do.

Physical

A medical student recently told us he wasn't allowed to have water all day in preparation for not having time to drink during twelve-hour shifts as a physician. So in our culture, healthcare professionals are being taught not to take care of their own health! We live in strange times if we believe this is normal or acceptable. We certainly wouldn't want to have a malnourished, sleep-deprived doctor who isn't thinking clearly caring for our health in our most vulnerable time, so why should that be any different for being a parent, a spouse, a friend, or a servant of God? We have to take care of our physical needs if we ever expect to be able to effectively care for others.

Remember, the primary purpose of the human body is to provide a healthy residence for the Holy Spirit to reside within us. So in caring for our bodies, we are literally caring for the Holy Spirit. So it's important to respect our limitations and to honor what we can reasonably take on, because we weren't meant for the kind of sustained stress that epitomizes our world today. In fact, it's literally killing us by causing the release of damaging stress hormones like cortisol. Prolonged exposure to high levels of cortisol is associated with higher blood pressure, lowered immunity, inflammatory responses in the body, decreased bone density, blood sugar imbalances, impaired cognitive performance, and suppressed thyroid function.[44] In fact, even our blood-brain barrier, which plays a critical role in controlling the influx of blood-borne pathogens into our central nervous systems, can begin to allow foreign toxic bodies to enter the brain during times of heightened stress.[45] With all of this going on in our body, we feel less able to unwind and slow down—even when we can—which makes us feel anxious and overwhelmed even by the simplest of tasks.

Our bodies need us to slow down so that we can seek balance with regular self-care habits. Through this balance, we

---

44 Yaribeygi, et al.
45 Menizibeya O. Welcome and Nikos E. Mastorakis, "Stress-Induced Blood Brain Barrier Disruption: Molecular Mechanisms and Signaling Pathways," *Pharmacological Research* (July 2020): 157.

provide a better foundation for our bodies to have the capacity to serve God's will for our lives. We need walks. We need activity. We need to go outside. We need to look up and be transformed by the majesty of nature that surrounds us. Taking care of our bodies physically could also mean making things like adequate sleep and exercise prescriptive rather than convenient. It could mean resting when our body demands it, or taking an extra-long shower when our body aches. It also means going to the doctor as we should, respecting our body's warning signs when we've done too much, and taking the time to prepare wholesome, nutritious meals that fuel the body.

Keep in mind that physical self-care should be implemented both *reactively* (in response to emotional exhaustion or the need for rest) and *proactively* (as a consistent prescribed practice we follow daily, regardless of our mood or circumstance).

One final consideration: St. Paul instructs us not to be an unnecessary burden on others. If we are physically unwell because of our own poor choices, we are in effect relying on others to pick up the slack by caring for our unmanaged emotions and difficult demeanors or to take on more of the housework. While we are not responsible for everything that happens to our body, we should take responsibility where we can.

Emotional

Keep your heart with all vigilance, / for from it flow the springs of life. —PROVERBS 4:23

While emotions can prompt goodness, love, mercy, and compassion, they can also prompt unhealthy reactions that leave us so entrenched in self-preservation that we forget about relationship preservation, not only with others but with God. And although we tend to think about feelings as being buried deep down inside us, in reality, much emotion lives just below the surface. That's why when we are overwhelmed or stressed, it can be seen on our face or witnessed in our nonverbal reactions. Our negative emotions can make us feel out of sorts and cause us to react in ways that negatively impact our walk of faith.

And while it's easy to act in accordance with our faith when all is well, when we don't take adequate care of our emotional lives, our unstable, negative emotions can crowd out virtues—like patience, goodwill, grace, and mercy—despite our best intentions. At those times, rather than feeling the kind of remorse that prompts us to turn back to faith, we can find ourselves rationalizing our behavior, reasoning that it was okay and perhaps even warranted because of "what we were dealing with" at the time. Yet, this kind of reasoning leaves us connecting more with the one who hurt us than the One who promises to fight for us and heal us.

And because we know that two wrongs do not make a right, we have to learn how to regulate our own emotions. God never said, "If others falter, it's okay for you to lose your way and react in sin." No, we are called, as the prophet Jeremiah puts it, to "test and examine our ways, and return to the LORD!" (Lam. 3:40). But without tending to our emotions, we are less able to realign ourselves with the Holy

Spirit and more vulnerable to aligning with the behavior of others who have fallen into temptation.

Without emotional self-care, we can have a hard time remembering that our souls are worth more than the offense, more valuable than our fleeting anger. Our emotions can make us forget who we are and who we are called to be. Emotional self-care helps us remain grounded so we can better separate from the angst in someone else and maintain calm even when others are not. This helps us do more of what works to help tough situations, rather than escalating them by our own unhealthy reactions.

Social

This type of self-care is about connecting to people in positive ways that renew our spirits. That involves not only prioritizing our own need for connection as human beings but also being mindful of the influence we have on others, because what we bring to relationships relies heavily on the peace we are able to receive from those connections. Ultimately, we derive benefit from relationships when we are someone who can draw near to others and someone who others want to draw near to.

And while we've already discussed (in chapter 3) how much loneliness can affect our souls and our well-being, it's also important to look at our relationships from the standpoint of how much stress can affect our ability to connect. In stressful times, many of us feel we just have too much to do and are too tired to devote energy to quality time with others. Even trying to keep up with the daily demands that life brings can create exhaustion and general moodiness. This makes it easy for disconnection to set in. Once we feel disconnected, it becomes easy to forget what's good about our relationships, and we may tend to simmer in minor aggravations. Because of this, we start to forget the last time we laughed together or shared fond feelings for one another. But because the world is never going to slow down to create a better foundation for us to prioritize our relationships, self-care when it comes to relationships is all about taking the time to do exactly that: to seek quality time, to share the funny moments we had in our week, or the compliment we were given by a friend, or the worries we have hidden down deep. It also means prioritizing an emotional climate that others feel safe to enter, by being mindful of the climate we allow our own stress to create.

In times of stress, we often require more love and support, not less. But when we are depleted, our connections with others suffer because we just can't seem to dial down our own intensity well enough to connect in positive ways. This may cause people to hesitate to connect with us, since most people have an intuitive sense of when someone feels unsafe to approach. Perhaps this is precisely why St. Paul notes this duality when on the one hand he encourages us to carry each other's burdens, but just a few verses later he says, "for each will have to bear his own load" (Gal. 6:2, 5). Both are true. Both are necessary. And keep in mind that someone who doesn't manage their stress is indirectly asking people around them to do it for them. There is a fine line between being responsible *to* each other and becoming responsible *for* each other. We aren't managing our own load when we are short fused, hurtful in our reactions, irritable and snapping at all the little things, avoiding those we love, or forcing others to walk on eggshells. The truth is, connection always goes better when we dial down our own intensity, because we become approachable. And no matter how much we will ourselves to connect for self-care, if we aren't safe to connect with, people will keep their distance at a time when we need them most.

Intellectual

Intellectual self-care involves focusing on what brings meaning to our lives, but our default setting is to pursue most things according to whether they are useful or pleasurable. Because both of these motivations are very self-oriented, it's quite easy for boredom to ensue again, once the pleasure of something or its usefulness wears off. This happens because we no longer see the value in it. But a meaningful life cultivates something much more lasting within us because it acquaints us with our deeper interests and convictions, which keep us engaged with life through growing, learning, and understanding the things God has uniquely equipped us for.

In fact, a meaningful life requires that we feed the desire within us for things that move us deep within our soul, things that inspire us, that expose us to good, that bring significance, that help us follow Christ, and that motivate us to want to be our best selves. These things do not wear off, because meaning and goodness leave lasting impressions on our hearts. When we pursue things that are meaningful to us and to God, we change our hearts in lasting ways, reinforcing our values and igniting our strengths, while deepening our connection to the world. In this way, we get to discover our own unique strengths and how God meant us to use them in the world.

So we should make time to pursue lives filled with active virtue, living in ways that touch our hearts and energize our spirits. That might mean taking up a new cause related to justice, empathy, or compassion. It could also mean using our gifts to pursue interests God has placed on our hearts or tapping into our generosity where we feel moved to do good in this world.

Professional

> Whatever you do, work heartily, as for the Lord and not for men, knowing that from the Lord you will receive the inheritance as your reward. You are serving the Lord Christ. —COLOSSIANS 3:23–24

Being mindful of self-care as it relates to our professional lives is about living with one mind by bringing our faith and our calling into our secular lives. This not only leaves us feeling more fulfilled but also more at peace because different values aren't competing to define who we are. Sometimes we can compartmentalize our faith, but that leaves us with just a Sunday morning experience, and we never make our faith a lifestyle that grounds us. In doing so, we grow more distant from God's design for our lives and can feel less settled, even taking on the world's values.

So, caring for ourselves professionally is about making sure that our actions and our unseen motives remain accountable to our soul. This minimizes stress because we are letting God be Lord over all of our lives, not just moments of our lives. This is how we catch ourselves from falling into unhealthy values that exist in the world, which can begin reaping a harvest that God never intended for our lives—whether that be focusing on the bottom line, our earnings, our status, or just on getting our work done at the expense of doing it with loving care.

When we live undivided, we honor what is most important to God because we live with integrity and feel fulfilled by making a difference in this world, rather than just making a living in this world. Jesus reminds us of this when He chastises the religious leaders of His time for their lack of genuineness and holiness, saying, "Woe to you, scribes and Pharisees, hypocrites! For you clean the outside of the cup and the plate, but inside they are full of greed and self-indulgence. You blind Pharisee! First clean the inside of the cup and the plate, that the outside also may be clean" (Matt. 23:25–26). You see, the Pharisees were missing the mark. They were more concerned with how they appeared than with what was guiding them. They were "ungodly, coldhearted and vainglorious," and "Jesus charges them with inverting God's values and with being mean-spirited, greedy, ambitious, absorbed in externals, hypocritical, and blindly self-righteous."[46]

---

46 *The Orthodox Study Bible* (Nashville: Thomas Nelson, 2008), 62.

Think of your own workplace. Do you have to contend with any of these values in your work life? When we remain mindful in our professional lives, we are better prepared to stay true to ourselves and not be molded by the values of this world, which can dilute the values of our faith. In our professional lives (as well as in the rest of our lives), we need to pay attention to our heart, which guides our inner life, our attitudes, and our unseen motives. We need to strive to be pure in heart because when we are pure of heart, our outward actions and our unseen motives come into alignment. When we fall out of alignment, we often don't sleep well, we experience stress and worry, we might feel guilt, and we can even have a hard time praying.

Self-care in our professional lives is also about setting boundaries that help us remain our best selves. That means trying to strike a balance between what we expend and what we put back in. This doesn't necessarily involve removing our stress, but rather, being discerning with how much we do and why we are doing it, and learning to seek comparable amounts of renewal. As Christians, even though we may tell ourselves that we're doing good work or that we're being sacrificial, we can end up running on the same hamster wheel as everyone else. We can overdo it, even when it comes to doing good. Instead, any virtuous behavior is usually best expressed as the mean between two vices. For example, being overly kind can lead to passivity in the name of conflict avoidance, which could leave us unwilling to speak up for what's right, to say no, or to set a boundary even when its necessary to do so. Virtues exist best when we are doing just enough to help us better put on the character of Christ, but not so much that we lose our light. In other words, too much of a good thing can often inhibit our purpose and create collateral damage. It can make us lose sight of the very life-giving habits we need to keep us renewed enough to continue moving toward our purpose.

At times, we get caught up in saying "yes" far too much. When we become that busy, we can no longer hear His voice guiding our lives, and we end up taking on a lot of unnecessary things that use up all of our energy needed for things He is calling us to actually do. First Kings 19:12 says that God speaks in a whisper. So, if we aren't exiting the noise long enough to hear the things God is whispering on our hearts in conversation with others, in our prayers, or in our reading of Scripture, then we miss all the ways He might be trying to lead our lives. We envision His whisper to be a soft, gentle tug on our heart, a quiet impression, a gut feeling, or a thought that keeps returning.

Spiritual

The other day I (Roxanne) was driving my son to school and feeling pretty sorry for myself. It had been a long week of everyone fighting off a terrible cold, and today, it was my turn. My throat was sore, and I had a throbbing headache. I felt frustrated and put upon. "How will I get everything done?" I thought. "I just don't have time to get sick." Then my son said, "Mom, look at that rainbow." Directly ahead of us was the most vibrant rainbow streaking across the sky in a solid vertical line, like nothing I'd ever seen. It made me smile, cross myself, and utter, "God loves us, doesn't He?"

In a moment where I had lost perspective, I was reminded of God's unyielding presence—but only because something got my attention. Caring for ourselves spiritually is about finding the time and space to be still and tune in to God's presence so we don't get caught up in our own problems. As we make time for stillness, we are better able to contemplate and reflect on our life in relation to our faith. Spiritual self-care opens us up to renewal when we have allowed mental clutter to separate us from God's presence.

Examples of spiritual self-care might include beginning a daily habit of prayer and Bible reading, seeking stillness and solitude on walks, or taking mini-breaks throughout the day to tune into a Christian podcast, Christian music, or a daily reading in accordance with our liturgical calendar. If you don't know where to start with prayer, try reading a pre-scribed prayer or using the Lord's Prayer to guide you.

How to Practice Self-Care

We've seen that proper self-care is a Christian virtue that keeps the body well so the Spirit can do its work, and we've given several quick examples of forms of self-care across multiple dimensions of the self. But now let's look more closely at how to practice those different dimensions of self-care.

As you read this section, we encourage you to think about your own life. Let it prompt an awareness about the things you've been prioritizing, both consciously and unconsciously. And keep in mind, change starts with digging deep within ourselves, taking an active look at our lives, and acknowledging what we're up against. We need to be honest about the type and amount of stress we have in our lives, how we typically respond to it, what we tend to prioritize, and the real reasons we don't take better care of ourselves. In this process, we may also need to acknowledge our own inherent dispositions that might leave us more prone to stress, or the things we may have come into adulthood with that make self-care harder. All these things can affect our efforts at trying to take care of ourselves, so it's not just about willpower.

For example, let's say you want to become more present in your important relationships. But you were also brought up to place a strong value on getting things done, even when it came at the expense of meaningful connection. Perhaps you feel a strong sense of time urgency around things that need to get done, and you can't relax in everyday life until they are done. As a result, you tend to prioritize your workload or to-do list over being present with the people in your life, and you may even feel easily irritated by their interruptions. Trying to be more present in this situation would require more than just good intention, because the behavior is deeply rooted in values that may or may not be conscious. Choosing to be present, then, would have to be a conscious choice to leave undone what isn't done, in lieu of the choice to place a new value on the people standing right before you. It might also need to involve a bit more planning to create protected pockets of time for both getting things done and spending time in meaningful connection, so that neither value competes for your time.

Or, let's say you want to take better care of yourself by not overcommitting to things. But you were also brought up in a home that didn't give you much space to make choices for yourself, like how you spend your time, when you do things, and how you choose to do them. Perhaps you often had to accommodate someone else's wishes whose needs seemed bigger or more important than your own, and their negative reactions to your having an opinion made you anxious and uncomfortable. As a result, you may have learned it was just easier to accommodate whatever need was outside of you. And now you may have a hard time knowing how not to overcommit, because you never learned to attend to what you needed or how you felt. As a result, you may not even be used to hearing your own body's stress signals.

And yet, what if we find, after digging deeply, that our struggle to be present isn't related to a value of getting things done but is about a general feeling of irritability or agitation that feels ever present. Or perhaps our overcommitment is about avoidance or not being happy in other parts of our life. So it's not that we are overvaluing tasks; rather, we are avoiding ourselves. Ultimately, if we are trying to take better care of ourselves, we need to be curious about the underlying values, struggles, or beliefs that might be serving as our primary opposition before we can adequately address making changes that last.

So before delving into the next section on ways to practice self-care, take a moment to pause and reflect on what might be the root of your own struggle with self-care. What comes to mind? Also, try to reflect on why changing it matters to your life—namely, your spiritual life.

In this section, we will list a lot of ways to practice self-care. You don't need to do all of them, but perhaps one or two will resonate with you. Give yourself room to experiment and find the best practices for your life and soul. And remember that fundamentally, self-care begins with boundaries. It's about striking a balance between what we expend and what we put back in. True self-care doesn't necessarily involve removing our stress but, rather, learning to find comparable amounts of renewal.

Physical Self-Care

Physical self-care begins with self-awareness. The body alerts us when we are stressed, so we must listen to it and heed the warning signs. Then we need to slow down and replenish.

Signals

Stress signals are different for everyone, so we each should know our own. They may include:

- Agitation, irritability, or general moodiness (Remember, unhealthy emotions tend to thrive more in bodies that are not well cared for.)

- Inability to fall or stay asleep, or wanting to sleep too much
- Disconnection, apathy, lack of motivation or zest for life
- Feeling a lack of purpose or that life is no longer meaningful
- Dreading or avoiding responsibilities
- Difficulty making decisions, or overthinking everything
- Tuning out; inability to stay present
- Becoming hypercritical of yourself or others
- Recurrent headaches
- Fatigue and exhaustion despite sufficient rest
- Muscle tension, especially in specific places such as the upper shoulders, jaw, back
- Decreased levels of empathy
- Withdrawal from friends and family
- Feeling overwhelmed
- Nervous habits (nail biting, overeating)
- Restlessness; being unable to wind down, relax, or fall asleep at night

TACTICS

There are countless ways to practice physical self-care (without lapsing into escapism or indulgence). While many are easy and free, all involve prioritizing yourself and taking time out of your day, week, or month.

- **Check in with your body.** Mindfulness exercises teach people to recognize what they are feeling in their bodies in real time so that they can release it. To check in with your body, sit back in your chair, take a breath, and notice what's tense. Neurologically, tuning into our body and its sensations pulls us out of verbal activity, which is a driver of rumination and worry, so even this step can help release stress. It also helps you identify whether you need to take a moment for yourself. Check in again later to see if the tension feels any different.

- **Seek your sabbath daily.** Find time during your day to quiet the noise around you and re-center yourself. It can be as little as five or ten minutes—whatever works for you.

- **Take a mini-break.** Stop what you are doing, sit back in your chair, relax your shoulders, and breathe slowly for five to ten minutes.

- **Wait in silence.** If you have to wait somewhere, actually wait. Don't fill the time by grabbing your phone. Choose instead to just be still. Perhaps say the Jesus Prayer.

- **Take a walk.** We recommend walking early in the morning or after the sun has gone down. These are times when your mind is freer to wander, to wonder, to connect to God, and to make new insights.

- **Sit outside in nature.** Don't underestimate the power of fresh air and natural beauty.

- **Take a long shower.**

- **Use your commute.** I know for me (Roxanne) personally, I find stillness on my commute to and from work. It's often quiet, and I can hear my thoughts, regain perspective, process how I feel about things, and connect back to God in prayer. Music often begins this process for me; I have a favorite Christian artist I listen to every morning whose words turn down the volume in the world and help me refocus, drawing my soul into Christ.

- **Take "reset breaths."** When we are stressed, we stop breathing naturally because we enter a fight-or-flight state. Deep breathing activates the vagus nerve and counters this. Regular breathing also reduces blood pressure, promotes relaxation, and helps us generally de-stress. To stimulate the vagus nerve, use the "reset breath": take a deep breath in for three seconds, hold for a moment, then exhale for four seconds. Long exhalations naturally slow the heart rate, so the exhale is more important than the inhale in taking a reset breath. As few as one to two breaths can make a difference, then return to normal breathing.

- **Reconnect with former pleasures.** Who were you before your career? How did you enjoy spending time then? How did you replenish? Was it bike rides, lunch dates with a friend, philosophical discussions, going to bookstores, getting involved in volunteer work? When was the last time you did any of those things? Try participating in hobbies you once enjoyed. If it helps, create a schedule for yourself that feels life-giving.

- **Exercise.** This should be an absolute must because it is so good for our body. Try to get thirty to forty minutes of exercise, four to six times per week. Start anywhere, even with just a walk outside.
- **Eat nutritious foods.** Eat more whole foods that are less processed, focusing on a return to food as it was intended for us. Begin a renewed commitment to approach food as fuel for the body through balance, mindful eating, and goodness.

If you don't know what helps or what recharges you when you need refueling, try responding to these prompts:

- I feel best when . . .
- I am happiest when . . .
- I feel rested when . . .
- The last best day was when I . . .
- My day goes best when I start it by . . .
- What time of day is best for me to seek refueling?
- What time of day do I need it most?

Emotional Self-Care

Emotional self-care is about learning to interact with our emotions in life-giving ways.

Emotional self-care prioritizes thinking and acting in ways that protect our soul so that we do not become our emotions, but rather, can distance ourselves enough to inter- act with our feelings with level-headedness, intention, and spiritual discernment. To do this, we can't feel too much or too little. We don't want to become so numb to our feelings that we miss important moments where God calls us to stand for something. But we also don't want to be so over-taken by emotion that we can't respond in ways that heal. Emotional self-care involves monitoring our feelings and keeping an encouraging, helpful, and life-giving inner voice, toward ourselves and others. Simply said, when we remain aware of emotions, we are better equipped to lead what we do in relation to them so that they don't blindly lead us.

We often don't recognize how much our emotions are affecting us, because whatever we are focused on seems so important that we feel justified in the experience of it, at the expense of our willingness to evaluate it. But those negative emotions typically signal that we need to attend to our emotional life. Just like our bodies, our emotions give us information about how we're really doing. Emotional self-care is about tuning in to our emotions and letting wisdom lead us in processing them.

SIGNALS
- Feeling irritable or impatient all the time
- Feeling critical of ourselves and others
- Snapping at people with little or no provocation
- Crying for no apparent reason
- Avoiding activities you usually enjoy
- Blaming others
- Apathy
- Intense worry that won't remit

- Feeling despair or hopelessness
- Feeling confused and being unable to articulate what's wrong
- Feeling overwhelmed
- Friends, family, and/or peers ask if you're okay

TACTICS

Have you ever taken the time to tune in to how you are feeling? Consider taking a little emotional self-assessment:

- Do you find yourself stressed a lot? If so, what is it usually about?
- Does your stress bleed into your home life? If so, how?
- Do you struggle with worry? Can you unpack what's really going on?
- Do you often feel like you need a break? Do you take one?

During your day, you can proactively ask yourself:

- How am I feeling?
- Is there anything heavy on my heart?
- Do I feel short-tempered/agitated or easily bothered lately? If so, what might be causing that?
- Do I feel close or distant to the people I love? If I feel distant, why might that be?
- Do I feel distant from God?
- Am I worried about anything?

If you are already aware that you are feeling upset, irritated, disengaged, or otherwise not at peace in your heart,
sit back and listen to your inner voice. What do you hear?
Is it encouraging? Is it pure, peaceable, gentle, open to reason, merciful, leading you to good fruit? Then let it lead you.
Is it only making your situation worse? Then identify the
false beliefs you're holding and replace them with true beliefs
about the grace and love of God. It may help you to reflect
on I John 2:

> Do not love the world or the things in the world.
> If anyone loves the world, the love of the Father is
> not in him. For all that is in the world—the desires
> of the flesh and the desires of the eyes and pride in
> possessions—is not from the Father but is from the
> world. And the world is passing away along with its
> desires, but whoever does the will of God abides for-
> ever. (15–17)

Also, for every problem that stresses you out, try identifying
any worldly love that may be competing with God. Then think
of something God loves and look upon it with love yourself.

Try these useful practices:

- **Journal when you feel anger or irritation.** We can
write our inner world to life, in a way that allows us
to confront it enough to work through it. The act of
putting words on our experience can calm the part of
our brain that keeps us reacting to it, and involve the

part of our brain that helps us start responding to it. We can't hide from lingering feelings; they have a way of catching up to us and impacting our decisions, our connections, and our presence.

- **Take time to process hurt or anger before reacting to it with someone.** Ideally, we never want to express feelings while we feel them. We are better able to talk about feelings when we separate a bit from them first. The goal is for our mind to separate from strong feelings long enough to pray and regain perspective, reason, compassion, ownership, and humility before trying to share. Be sure to wait for dark and bitter thoughts to soften, and become led by goodness, before sharing.

Here are some ideas for letting the mind separate:

— Go for a walk
— Pray, pray, and pray again; ask God to give you the words to communicate with love, grace, and unity
— Breathe deeply to settle your emotions and your heart rate
— Get your mind on something else
— Go for a ride
— Do some work
— Organize something
— Go to the gym
— Sleep on it

— Read something that resets your inner voice (the Bible) or that distracts (an interesting article)

— Examine your inner voice when you make mistakes. Be sure it's helpful, merciful and re-centering. Keep in mind: if you wouldn't say it to someone you love, you shouldn't say it to yourself.

- **Start a daily habit of gratitude.** This can be as simple as writing down three things you are grateful for each morning and why you are grateful for them.

Social Self-Care

We know that God made us for relationship, but for relationships to help with self-care, our connections need to focus on replenishing our spirit. That means reaching out to people who are committed to our well-being, emotionally and spiritually, and who bring out our inherent good by their inherent good. It may be their contagious joy, their comforting presence, or their desire to help with anything large or small. When we tap into each other's spiritual gifts in ways that honor God, we experience self-care through the power of relationship.

We can start by trying to prioritize our important relationships and scheduling quality time so that we can be fully present at some point with someone who is important to us. Whether it be initiating a walk together, meeting up for a cup of coffee, having a conversation by phone, or taking on a household project together, as long as we give it our full attention, it has the power to feel like loving care for our soul.

We must be careful to not allow our stress to be so uncontained that we negatively affect the people who are trying to love us. What does that mean? It means remembering that our stress can't be permission to let go of kindness, courtesy, gentleness, or basic manners. It also means our stress can't create eggshells for everyone to walk on. Rather, if we want connection to feel possible, and like something that renews our soul, we must do our best to show an easy manner, despite our stress. So, even amidst everyday irritations, if we meet those hassles with acceptance rather than with short tempers and aggravation, people are much more likely to stick around and help us realign our spirit—whether it's being stuck in traffic, forgetting something at home, having to wait longer than we expected for something, or having made a mistake. If we take ownership of attempting to create a more peaceful environment for others to love us, even amidst our stress, we participate in relationship self-care. Not only does this free up our own resources for promoting positive connection, it also opens up others to remain connected to us. Remember, much of the time, others move away from us not because they don't *want* to love us but because they don't know *how* to love us in the middle of our stress.

One red flag to pay attention to, that can inhibit relationship self-care, is blaming others for why we feel less than our best. In stress, it can be easy to reach for the most superficial reason when it comes to defining why we are upset. We can suddenly shift our focus to what someone else needs to be doing differently, in order for us to be less stressed. And if we get consumed by the fog of chasing other people's improvements, we miss the boat on managing the true root of our stress and being able to enjoy the people whom God has placed on our path to love us. This only adds to our stress because we begin chasing outcomes that others are not necessarily seeking for themselves, and maybe aren't even aware of. And blaming others only exacerbates our stress because it leaves our minds spinning in frustration, despair, and disappointment, when what we really need is loving connection. For relationship self-care to work, we must let our connection to God be the foundation of our connection to others.

So try connecting to God instead and study where to start yourself. Ask in prayer, "How do I want to feel in this relationship?" "What needs to change for me, so that I can feel that way?" "What could I begin doing to improve the good they do bring?" "What could I stop or start doing in this relationship that might help me enjoy their good?" Consider all the small ways you could better begin navigating your situation with more peace, wisdom, and well-being. Approaching our relationships in this way lets us love others more unconditionally, judge a little less, find a little more of their good, and leave more positivity not only within our own souls but in the souls of everyone around us. The longer we remain in a state of trying to change someone else, the worse we feel, and the more we delay the care that relationships can bring to our soul. So, seek the good in others, change what you can within yourself to enjoy your relationships more, and lean into God to intervene where you cannot. "These things I have spoken to you, that my joy may be in you, and that your joy may be full" (John 15:11).

SIGNALS

- Consistently prioritizing work over relationships
- Saying "I'm too busy to connect" without committing to another time when you could
- Ignoring opportunities to connect—giving one-word answers, not truly being present when someone does initiate connection
- Actively isolating or avoiding connection
- Being too focused on everything that's wrong with others when it comes to opportunities to connect
- Blaming people for your stress
- Choosing the wrong people to connect with, who don't bring out your inherent good

TACTICS

To get out of your isolation, try these tactics:

- Make room in your calendar. What you make time for shows what you value. If you're a busy person, then you'll need to schedule in your social time. For the people most important to you, we recommend:
  — Something small *daily* (15–30 minutes)
  — Something bigger *weekly* (around 2 hours)

- — Something big *once a month* (a full evening or a whole day)
- Connect with life-giving people. Find people who radiate goodness and inspire you to be better in some way.
- Make a practice of sharing with others and asking them to share things like:
  - — A funny moment from the week
  - — A compliment you recently received
  - — Something that's been worrying you lately
- Try being fully present with someone for at least some time each day. You can do this in a conversation, cook together, or play a game. Practice good listening skills and work at being completely present:
  - — Put away phones or computers
  - — Put aside other tasks and responsibilities
  - — Mirror the other's emotions
  - — Show interest in what they share
  - — Ask questions that deepen the conversation
  - — Encourage the other to say more
  - — Pay enough attention that you remember what they said they liked, what they are looking forward to, etc. Remember the next time their birthday comes around, or follow up on a life event they told you about.

Intellectual Self-Care

Intellectual self-care is not simply about using our brain; it is about finding meaning. So, we want to encounter things that activate not only our mind but also our heart and bring everything into alignment with our spirit and our calling. Intellectual self-care is about making the time to pursue opportunities that help us actively live out the virtues.

SIGNALS

- Feeling that your life or daily activities have become meaningless
- Sensing a lack of purpose or that you're simply going through the motions
- Being restless and bored during meetings or social gatherings
- Experiencing boredom because you're not feeding your mind enough

TACTICS

Intellectual self-care means doing things that cultivate the spiritual strengths and the inner goodness God designed us with. When we do this, we embrace our true beauty, because when goodness, convictions, and strengths guide our heart, our soul moves toward things that inspire growth and bring meaning to our lives. Try giving yourself permission to follow your curiosities and to engage positive interests and convictions.

- **Take up a new cause.** Invest in something you have always felt strongly about or moved by.
- **Read that book you have been wanting to read** because it touches on something that matters to you.

- **Take a class.** Find a topic that stretches you where you want to grow.
- **Visit an art museum** to prompt wonder, thought, and deeper connections.
- **Pursue active involvement in the things God has placed on your heart.**
- **Practice journaling.** Putting your thoughts on paper can help you clarify ideas that have only been notions in your head up to now. If you find yourself wrestling with negative beliefs or criticisms, try to "destroy arguments and every lofty opinion raised against the knowledge of God, and take every thought captive to obey Christ" (2 Cor. 10:5).

Professional Self-Care

We typically associate stress at work with burnout, but ideally, we can notice professional stressors long before we reach the burnout stage.

SIGNALS

You may need to practice professional self-care if you find yourself:

- Working many late nights, which keeps you away from your family or friends
- Talking about how busy you are, and being proud of it
- Often feeling bored or irritable at work
- Having a hard time getting out of bed on workdays

- Realizing you're saying "yes" all the time despite not having time for everything

In short, we need professional self-care when we feel we have nothing left to give to things that really matter. We lose sight of our goal of being a positive force in people's lives and over-value the mere act of getting things done rather than investing in what we are doing and the people we are with.

TACTICS

- **Stay connected to your purpose.** Know your "Why" and keep it front and center when confronted with difficult professional decisions. If a choice doesn't align with your Why, have the courage to say no or to let it go.
- **Establish clear boundaries for yourself around work.** What is work time, and what is family time? Protect family time as if it's a precious resource (because it is!).
- **Learn to say "no."** If something will interfere with that precious time, it needs to go so that we don't unravel due to stress and overcommitment, leaving little capacity for what truly matters.
- **Take some time to reflect on your God-given gifts.** What are you good at? What makes you feel alive? What do people say about you? Take a personality or strengths test if you need to. That can help you identify what you are called to.
- **Consider moving on to a different job or rethinking your current one.** In some cases, professional self-care

CHAPTER 5: *I Thirst*

means leaving your current position. Sometimes it means changing industries. Other times it means committing to your current role with a renewed sense of personal mission. Saint Paul left behind a role among the powerful Pharisees to become an itinerant missionary. He said, "But I do not account my life of any value nor as precious to myself, if only I may finish my course and the ministry that I received from the Lord Jesus, to testify to the gospel of the grace of God" (Acts 20:24).

Spiritual Self-Care

Do not be conformed to this world, but be transformed by the renewal of your mind, that by testing you may discern what is the will of God, what is good and acceptable and perfect. —ROMANS 12:2

It's amazing how easy it is to walk through life without realizing our blessings; we experience many good things without truly reflecting on them. When our prayers get answered, when a loved one we were worried about comes through a difficult battle, when a relationship is healed, when God gently nudges us in the right direction, or when we find ourselves in a moment of peace amidst a hectic day, it's all too easy to be relieved but not reflective. We forget to thank the One who made that experience possible.

SIGNALS

You may need some spiritual self-care if you find yourself:

- Unable to remember the last time you prayed
- Unable to remember the last time you opened your Bible
- Feeling distant from God or as if God has gone silent
- Never experiencing silence in your day or week
- Looking upon other people critically instead of with love

TACTICS

Since the early days of the Faith, we have been told to seek God in *silence*. In a world premised on barraging us with noise, silence is countercultural in addition to being life-giving. Saint John Climacus says that

> deliberate silence is the mother of prayer, a recall from captivity, preservation of fire, a supervisor of thoughts, a watch against enemies, a prison of mourning, a friend of tears, effective remembrance of death, a depicter of punishment, a meddler with judgment, an aid to anguish, an enemy of freedom of speech, a companion of quiet, an opponent of desire to teach, increase of knowledge, a creator of contemplation, unseen progress, secret ascent.[47]

It is in silence that our inner person is illuminated, exposing our will. It is also in silence that our spirit is rejuvenated in the presence of the Holy Spirit.

So choose not to be held hostage by this world.

---

47 *The Ladder of Divine Ascent* (New York: Paulist Press, 1982), 157.

- **Take a break from the noise.** Let the tasks wait, and set aside a portion of your day to simply be still. Breathe deeply, relax your body, and open up your mind in prayer. Part of finding our peace in this world is realizing that God has equipped us with everything we need to connect to His voice.

- **Make prayer a part of your daily routine.** Try praying for everyone you come across. Pray for people in news stories. Pray for the person in front of you in line at the store. Pray for other drivers on the road. Pray for your children's future relationships. Pray for the thoughts that fill people's minds. Pray for the words you need before a conversation. Pray for the sick, the suffering, and specific afflictions you hear about. Pray for your relationships. Pray for God's will in your life and to hear His whispers. The list is never ending.

- **Pray the Jesus Prayer: "Lord Jesus Christ, Son of God, have mercy upon me."** It's one of the simplest prayers you can pray. It's easy to remember and is almost universally applicable; the prayer for mercy is a prayer for God to manifest Himself in your life, which we always need. Saint Gregory of Sinai (who gave us this prayer) and his disciples would use it to usher them into stillness. They would inhale while praying, "Lord Jesus Christ, Son of God," and exhale while praying, "have mercy upon me." This can help you slow down and focus your mind on God.

- **Prioritize reading that edifies you.** There are many schedules and apps to help you with daily reading. You can read according to our liturgical calendar, or you can read the lives of the saints. You can even listen to a Bible-in-a-year app on your commute. The amount you read is not as important as reading well and reading something that feeds your spirit.

- **Develop a gratitude practice.** Feeling grateful has many benefits for your heart and soul, and it's not always something that you just feel spontaneously. You can learn gratitude. Begin by taking a moment to notice the good things around you, the small things that make your day a little lighter, a little brighter. Thank God for those things. Notice the small gestures people make. Don't just say "Thank you" reflexively; note the action and thank the person sincerely.

- **Think twice before complaining.** Move on quickly from thoughts that could lead to crankiness or discontent. Hug those you love and tell them what you appreciate about them. Gratitude is not about pretending everything is fine or that bad things aren't happening. It's about recognizing God's presence and blessing even in the hard times. James says, "Count it all joy, my brothers, when you meet trials of various kinds" (1:2) because God's goodness and grace are ever present. God promises us that He is always with us, working things out for good. So, we can choose to take notice today of what could change tomorrow; we can take notice not only of the multitude of blessings that God has given us but of the people and things He has surrounded us with.

Conclusion

Our bodies are temples of the Holy Spirit, so we cannot say often enough that self-care is not selfishly gratifying the flesh. It is a holy act of maintaining God's temple so He can use us in the world.

Of course, not every temple is identical, and that's okay. God does not require us to be in perfect physical and mental health in order to do good work through us. We are not saying that we need to be capable of playing a body double in a superhero movie in order to be godly on this score. But no matter our physical and mental limitations, we can all find ways to take care of ourselves and be the best we can be.

And take heart! Self-care is not a burden, it's not just something else you need to accomplish during your day. It's the gift of rest and recovery. Remember that when Christ says, "I thirst," He gives us all permission to get our needs met.

FOR DISCUSSION: THE THREE Rs— REST, REFLECT, AND RESPOND

1. If you had to rate your stress on a scale of 1–10, where would you fall?

2. What stresses you out the most?

3. How much time do you devote to your own needs each day?

4. What do you spend most of your time thinking about in your day?

5. What worries you the most when that part of your life is not going well?

6. What are you most motivated to protect time for each day?

7. What are two things you prioritize each and every day? Are they important?

8. How are you most likely to spend your day if no one makes demands on it?

9. What do others see you as caring about?

10. What reasons do you name for not taking better care of yourself?

11. Is there really nothing different you could be doing?

12. What is a fruit your spirit yearns for, but your unmanaged stress keeps blocking?

PRAYER

O Lord Our God, as we journey through this book, we can't help but praise You for sharing each of Your statements from the Cross with us, Your beloved children. On one of the darkest days in history, You once again revealed Your love for us, because You knew that these statements would help us through the dark seasons of our own lives.

You knew that Your words would give comfort in our crisis. You knew that it would be easy to simply neglect ourselves, or worse yet, indulge in unhealthy reactions to the stressful experiences that leave our mind, body, and soul deprived of its true needs. You, indeed, have "searched me and known me! / You know when I sit down and when I rise up; / you discern my thoughts from afar. / You search out my path and my lying down / and are acquainted with all my ways. / Even before a word is on my tongue, / behold, O LORD, you know it altogether" (Ps. 139:1–4).

You also know how difficult it often is to put into practice the words of the many who say amidst our stress, "Take care of yourself." For this reason, You give us permission through Your sacred words of "I thirst," to seek the care we need. In our weakness and during our most vulnerable times, grant us opportunities to draw near to people who can care for us. Also, strengthen us to be people whom others can, in turn, draw near to, so that all of us can experience Your love and care when we need it most. Help us to tend to our physical bodies, our emotions, and our spirits in ways that give life meaning and give You glory. Through the prayers of our Holy Fathers, O Lord Jesus Christ our God, have mercy on us. Amen.

CHAPTER 6

It Is Finished

It is finished. —JOHN 19:30

WE COME NOW to one of Jesus' most resonant and powerful statements from the Cross: "It is finished." Jesus says this almost as if to Himself, or maybe in direct dialogue with the Father—but we feel the impact of those words across millennia. Jesus speaks with a finality and certainty that assures us of His authority, but what did He mean by this statement? In this moment, Jesus our Savior declares that the divine plan of salvation has been fulfilled. He has completed what He was sent here to do—conquering sin, the demons, and death by His own death. These words commemorate His voluntary death, which would free all humanity from the hands of death and reconcile humankind with God.

Interestingly, "It is finished" translates the Greek τετέλεσται (*tetelestai*), from τελέω (*teleo*), which is a verb in the perfect tense and passive voice. It's a reasonably literal translation, except Greek understands the perfect tense in a different way than English. In English, the perfect tense indicates an action has been completed and is in the past: "He has graduated," "She has won." The event referred to is no longer in progress. In Greek, the perfect tense is a little more nuanced. It refers to an action that took place in the past but that has an impact we still feel in the present. It speaks of an action that both has taken place and, in a sense, is still taking place. To say "She has won," for instance, would mean both that she won something and that her victory is part of her current status.

Where are we going with this? Well, when Christ declares, "It is finished," He is saying that all the Old Testament prophecies about the Messiah coming to liberate His people have been fulfilled and also that the present is now impacted by this completion. Perhaps a more accurate translation would be, "It has, is, and will always be complete." It is accomplished for all time. Everything He was sent to do, He has done. He has conquered death by His own death, and His victory rescues us from us.

With this announcement that He has completed His earthly mission and has become victorious over darkness, Jesus declares Himself King over our lives. From now on, all who put their faith in Him will share in His promises.

The King Claims His Kingdom

Though the world recently witnessed the coronation of a new king of England, interestingly, he was crowned king *after* he had already assumed his new role. He was *already* the monarch; he just hadn't been formally crowned in the eyes of the public. In much the same way, when Christ says, "It is finished," though He is already our King, His words formally mark an event in time, which we will only fully understand upon His Resurrection.

In one moment, Christ overthrows the ruler of death and reveals Himself as the King of life who destroyed death and liberates His people. On Holy Saturday in the Orthodox Church—that is, on the day we remember the disciples' grief and fear at the death of their Lord, the day *before* Jesus descended into death and rose from the dead, and before this rising was revealed to the disciples and changed everything—we read one of the most iconic sermons in Christianity, which encapsulates this idea perfectly: St. John Chrysostom's Easter message. There he says:

> Let no one fear death, for the Savior's death has set us free. He that was taken by death has annihilated it! He descended into hades and took hades captive! He embittered it when it tasted his flesh! And anticipating this Isaiah exclaimed, "Hades was embittered when it encountered thee in the lower regions." It was embittered, for it was abolished! It was embittered, for it was mocked! It was embittered, for it was purged! It was embittered, for it was despoiled! It was embittered, for it was bound in chains! It took a body and, face to face, met God! It took earth and encountered heaven! It took what it saw but crumbled before

what it had not seen! "O death, where is thy sting? O hades, where is thy victory? Christ is risen, and you are *overthrown!*" (emphasis added)[48]

So, what the world meant for the ultimate evil, Jesus used for the ultimate victory. His death made it possible for us to live an eternal life with Him in His heavenly Kingdom. And although Jesus' coronation wasn't a beautiful ceremony but a public execution, our Faith is full of attestations of Jesus as King. For example, in Orthodox worship, the Prayer of St. Ephraim calls out to Jesus, "Yes, Lord and King, grant me to see my own faults and not to judge my brother." We say during Holy Week services, "for you are the King of peace." In the Matins service, the reading of the Psalms begins with, "Come, let us worship and bow down to our King and God," and the introductions to the liturgies of St. John Chrysostom and St. Basil the Great begin with, "Blessed is the Kingdom." Even the penitent thief on the Cross recognizes the kingship of Christ when he pleads with Him, "Remember me when You come into Your Kingdom" (Luke 23:42). But perhaps the most powerful example comes when Jesus says, "Repent, for the kingdom of God is at hand" (Matt. 4:17). Without drawing the attention of the authorities at that early stage, Jesus hints at who the real King of heaven and earth is. But what does it mean that the Kingdom of God is at hand?

---

48   Johanna Manley, ed., *The Bible and the Holy Fathers for Orthodox: Daily Scripture Readings and Commentary for Orthodox Christians* (Crestwood, NY: Monastery Books, 1990), 11.

Well, humans are worshipping creatures; every day when we get up in the morning, we bow down to something, and that something is either God or not-God. God has given us free will to choose what we bow down to. But to live in the freedom that God has granted to us, we must voluntarily submit our lives to Him, declaring Him King over all of our lives, not just some of our lives. When we do this, we do our part in the plan for salvation. And while our faith reminds us to keep ourselves God-centered rather than self-centered, we are living in a world that is filled with distractions, many of which want to play the role of God in our lives. We call these the *weapons of mass distraction*, and they confuse our concept of what's important. Through these distractions, the world tries to define us, drive us, and consume us with temptations of every kind: to live only for the now, to place acceptance over character, to overvalue our image, to seek success for our own glory, to acquire wealth, and to seek status. As Christians, we must remember that it is often our own desires that give birth to sin in the first place (James 1:15–16).

So ask yourself, what are you bowing down to today? Christ tells us that we cannot "serve two masters" (Matt. 6:24). Trying to maintain an attachment to both earthly and spiritual things eventually creates conflict, because both demand our full allegiance. One will eventually have control over the other. And when earthly things become the throne of our happiness, we do not leave a place for God, as St. Nektarios says:

How mistaken are those people who seek happiness outside of themselves, in foreign lands and journeys,

in riches and glory, in great possessions and pleasures, in diversions and vain things, which have a
bitter end! [It is] the same thing to construct the
tower of happiness outside of ourselves as it is to
build a house in a place that is consistently shaken
by earthquakes. Happiness is found within ourselves,
and blessed is the man who has understood this.
Happiness is a pure heart, for such a heart becomes
the throne of God.[49]

So, if we want to live an "it is fulfilled" lifestyle, we must
think about what motivates us and run it all back through
a lens of what would actually be pleasing to God, our King
and our Savior.

Because although Christ has conquered death and made
it possible for us to live in His Kingdom, if we have not formally crowned Christ King over our own lives, we will never
experience the peace He yearns to give us. Putting God on
the throne of our lives means that we are willing to repent,
change direction, and put the real King back on the throne
when anything other than God seems to have a hold over us.
Imagine God saying, "You have someone or something sitting in the place where only I belong."

---

49 "St. Nektarios: How mistaken are those people who seek happiness," *Orthodox Church Quotes* (blog), accessed September 22,
2023, https://orthodoxchurchquotes.wordpress.com/2013/07
/12/st-nektarios-how-mistken-are-those-people-who-seek
-happiness/.

How do we crown Christ King and live an "it is finished" lifestyle? Let's look at four important things we can do.

Crown Him by Being Still

Life is full. Good, but full. Days are long, but time feels fleeting. And like so many others who try to derive meaning from their role in life, we [Fr. Nicholas and Dr. Roxanne] feel we have been blessed to lead lives that offer fulfilling work and opportunities to learn and grow at every turn through the wisdom we encounter in others who are sprinkled all throughout our midst. Because no matter our occupation in this life, God has a way of speaking to us through those we meet. One such nugget of wisdom Dr. Roxanne will never forget was once offered by a woman who turned to her and said, "How do you keep up with all you are doing?" And before she could even respond, the woman said something so beautiful. She said, "If I could give you any one gift, I would give you the gift of time." And at that moment, Dr. Roxanne's thoughts came to a complete stop as she rested in the comforting thought of this beautiful offering.

Her insightful gift couldn't have felt more fitting to Dr. Roxanne; it was as if she could see something her heart needed but couldn't articulate. Yes, the gift of time. It's an incredible gift that we all wish we had more of. Every day seems to go by so fast, and there is never enough time to get everything done or to place the type of value on things we wish we could. Seasons of life come and go, changing so fast that we often look back and don't know where the time has gone. And the woman was right—time is one of the most powerful resources God gives us. It is so powerful because we get to choose what to do with it—but when it is gone, it's gone and doesn't return. One moment we are here; the next, we are a memory. And while we know this, we don't always live like we know this. Most of us move at a pace of life that doesn't allow stillness. We run from one thing to another, reacting to the demands of life rather than proactively seeking time with the giver of life.

We once heard a story at a seminar we attended about a monk, which illustrates this well. One day a monk took dirt and added it to a glass of water and began to stir it. The dirt spiraled up until the water was cloudy. He then put the glass on a shelf and after five minutes, asked his visitors to look at the glass. They noted that the dirt that was previously swirling had begun to settle, and after about ten minutes, the dirt had totally settled, and the water was clear. In the same way, the monk said, our busyness can make it feel like we're swirling around in dirty water. Finding stillness allows the dirt to settle and our minds to clear.

If the dust were to settle in your own life, what might need to fall to the bottom of your glass? What seems to regularly intrude upon your stillness? If you are having trouble seeing it, the story of Mary and Martha may help you reset your priorities. One day, Christ is visiting His dear friends Mary, Martha, and Lazarus. At this gathering, Martha works diligently in the kitchen, preparing a meal for Christ and the guests. At the same time, her sister, Mary, is sitting right next to Christ listening to His words. Eventually, Martha has had enough and interrupts the conversation to complain that her sister isn't helping. In an extraordinary moment, Christ looks into her eyes and says, "Martha, Martha, you are anxious and troubled about many things, but one thing is necessary. Mary has chosen the good portion, which will not be taken away from her" (Luke 10:41–42).

Sometimes we feel like Martha, as if everything we're doing is important, but could Christ be seeing those things we deem important as interruptions to what truly matters? God says only one thing is needed: "Just come and sit right next to me." So in a world that is constantly vying for our time, it is paramount that we are intentional about dedicating time for God. Seeking stillness is one way we crown God as King of our lives, because as we quiet the world, we better hear His voice, His guidance, and His leadership so that we can obey His reign over our lives. Saint John Climacus talks about this when he speaks of the value of stillness, stating, "The friend of silence draws near to God, and by secretly conversing with Him, is enlightened by God."[50] So how we spend our time is of great importance because it can literally affect the direction our lives will take.

Each year, we try to take some kind of family vacation with the hope that it will recharge us so that we can come back with renewed energy and the capacity to continue in some way with the work we believe is God's will for our lives. This year, our only prayer for our annual vacation was that it would bring this sense of renewal. And somehow,

---

50 *The Ladder of Divine Ascent*, 77.

despite every unexpected tribulation on vacation (and there were many), as we returned home, we felt a sense of peace we couldn't describe. It was as if everything had slowed to a different pace than we had felt before. What happened? We found stillness. And it was in that stillness that God's voice became clear. Suddenly, things that once felt overwhelming became manageable. New perspectives were revealed, and we felt drawn in new directions and toward renewed priorities.

We see Jesus modeling this stillness in His own life when, after He was baptized, He went into the desert. Interestingly, it is there that He was tempted by the devil. The Greek word that we translate as "desert" is *eremos*, which can mean a deserted place, a solitary place, or a quiet place. Sometimes it's translated as "wilderness." The desert here isn't typified by its harshness but by being apart from human activity. And Jesus shows us that we can find our strength in stillness and in quiet places, as drawing near to God through forty days of prayer and fasting gave Him the power to defeat the devil. For most of us, the cares of this world keep us from this kind of closeness with God, and it is challenging to find our own quiet place to pray. Where is your *eremos*, your quiet place that you can retreat to and be apart from human activity? If you don't have a place like this right now, consider where you might find or create one.

The quieter we become, the louder God becomes; the stiller we become, the more we hear God's voice resonate within our soul. You see, stillness cultivates our ability to hear the gentle whisper of God and to experience the calm, reassuring sense of His presence. This is why the Bible says

to "pray without ceasing" (I Thess. 5:17). One of the patris-
tic fathers, St. Gregory Nazianzus, puts it in starker terms:
"Remember God more often than you breathe."[51] So all
throughout our day, we should be in conversation with the
King, acknowledging His love and grace, and protecting time
for stillness so that we may listen to His guidance and Spirit.

We can find stillness at any time of the day by praying.
Saint John Climacus states that "deliberate silence is the
mother of prayer, a recall from captivity, preservation of fire,
a supervisor of thoughts, a watch against enemies."[52] We
can reach out in prayer in simple conversation with God. Or
we can always say the Jesus Prayer, one of the most ancient
and recited prayers in Christianity, which is prayed purpose-
fully to create stillness through the inhaling and exhaling
of breath. As we pray and breathe, we find our minds and
spirits slowing down as we free ourselves from competing
thoughts. In early Christianity, this practice was known as
hesychasm, from the Greek word *hesychia*, meaning "stillness":
a purposeful effort to descend with the mind into the heart
through bodily stillness and watchful, concentrated prayer.

Another way to find stillness is to be active in the House
of God. Taking the time to participate in the worship service stills us because it brings everything that occupies us
and attempts to reign over us to a sudden stop. Our attention becomes freed up to refocus on prayer within a greater

---

51 Kallistos Ware, *The Inner Kingdom: Volume 1 of the Collected Works*
(Crestwood, NY: St. Vladimir's Seminary Press, 2000), 67.
52 *The Ladder of Divine Ascent*, 76.

community of believers. Liturgy is also our weekly opportunity to pause in reverence to remember Christ's sacrifice for us on the Cross. We can't forget that Christ established the Church to help us walk more fully toward our salvation, and it is not just a place we go to learn about God but a place where we find the stillness of His presence as we experience and participate more fully in the life of Christ, since it is in the Church that He is pleased to dwell most fully among us upon the earth in this age. Saint Cyprian of Carthage once said, "No one can have God for His father, who has not the Church for His mother."[53]

Scripture says, "Draw near to God, and He will draw near to you" (James 4:8). In stillness, in church, in prayer, and in reading the Scriptures, we come close to God so He can come close to us. If you haven't done so already today, take a few moments to practice stillness. Go ahead and stop everything you are doing or were about to do and refocus your attention on simply connecting to God. Set a timer for three to five minutes.

Crown Him by Protecting Our Mind and Body

In addition to taking the time to draw closer to God, we have to make sure we are crowning Christ King by filtering what we allow to come into our mind and body. Christ shares in the

---

53 Geoffrey Wainwright and Karen B. Westerfield Tucker, *The Oxford History of Christian Worship* (Oxford, UK: Oxford University Press, 2006), 43.

Sermon on the Mount, "The eye is the lamp of the body. So, if your eye is healthy, your whole body will be full of light, but if your eye is bad, your whole body will be full of darkness. If then the light in you is darkness, how great is the darkness?" (Matt. 6:22–23). So the lens we look through affects us greatly. Our minds affect us greatly, as the *Orthodox Study Bible* puts it: "As the eye is the lamp of the body, so the mind is the spiritual eye of the soul: it illuminates the whole inner man and governs the will. Keeping our spiritual eyes good, that is, wholesome and pure, is fundamental to a Christian life."[54] But our world constantly barrages us with images that feed the flesh. Whether it's television, streaming videos, video games, social media, or the internet, an ocean of temptations is waiting to compromise our values and contaminate our soul. This is why St. John Climacus tells us, "The guarding of the thoughts is one thing, and the custody of the mind is another. As far as the East is from the West, so much higher is the latter than the former, even if it is more laborious."[55] So ultimately, we must protect ourselves from being occupied by anything other than the Holy Spirit. The cost of not doing so is allowing the enemy into our sphere of influence, from the thoughts we fuel to the images we allow ourselves to interact with to the things we allow ourselves to idolize, and the rationalizing we do through all of it. If we're not careful, we can give glory, honor, and worship to all the wrong things that derail our life in Christ.

---

54 *The Orthodox Study Bible* (Nashville: Thomas Nelson, 2008), 1327.
55 *The Ladder of Divine Ascent,* 140.

And we all have work to do when it comes to avoiding interaction with things that feed negative impulses within us, whether envy, pride, self-sufficiency, idolatry, vanity, greed, selfishness, hostile anger, or any other facet of the flesh that can destroy us. We have to stay alert to our inner captors so that we don't give free reign to just any value, as the values we come up against in the world can and will contaminate our soul.

And although Christ has given us everything we need to live honorable lives, because of our free will, we must actively decide how we will live, what we will allow ourselves to focus on, to interact with, to think about, to see, and to hear— which all ultimately either help us or hinder us in living out the life God has in store for us.

If we want to live an "it is finished" lifestyle, we have to be willing to die to ourselves so that Christ can live within us. We have to remember who and what we are living for. We also have to acknowledge that we have been bought at a price, that our freedom isn't free. Christ died in order to free us from death and grant us the possibility of eternal life. But when we don't allow our bodies and minds to be temples for His glory, we are not dying to ourselves in order to live for Him; we are choosing to be vessels for the world's values and agenda. Saint Paul says, "I have been crucified with Christ" (meaning our sinful passions and desires). "It is no longer I who live" (under the dominion of sinful passions and desires), "but Christ who lives in me. The life I now live in the flesh I live by faith in the Son of God" (Gal. 2:20).

For some of us, instead of living an "it is finished" life, we forget what Christ has accomplished for us, and we fall into being "all in" on this earth. But earth is not our homeland; heaven is. And if we give ourselves over to things of this earth, we are forgetting the gift that has been made possible for us. Saint John Climacus said, "He who has died to all things remembers death, but whoever is still tied to the world does not cease plotting against himself."[56] We don't live once. We live twice, and the world that we will go to after this life doesn't end. Christ wants us to experience that life; He wants us to have a throne in the Kingdom of heaven. And because so much of what we choose to do in this world is not always a conscious decision, but rather something we allow ourselves to fall into without true discernment, we must make sure that in all the things we subject our minds and bodies to, we are seeking to glorify Him. In this way, we crown Him King over all our life on this earth.

If you are struggling to crown God in an issue you face, remember that temptations and unhealthy habits have a knack for sticking around unless we confront them head on. So don't fall for the temptation of avoidance: we can't win battles we aren't fighting. If you feel like you keep falling prey to the same struggles, try these tools the next time it happens:

- **Track it, learn about it, get curious about it.** When did it start? Why did it start? What keeps you going back?

---

56 *The Ladder of Divine Ascent,* 59.

- **Pay attention to what triggers it and keeps it around.** Why does this have power over you? Why do you allow this to be on the throne where only God should remain? Are there certain times when you seem to be more likely to engage in the behavior? Why do you feed this struggle and place it on the throne only God should be on?

- **Retrain yourself to pause and notice what's going on when it surfaces,** and take inventory of what you might really need instead. What else is usually going on for you at the time you turn to it?

- **Notice it, but don't engage it!** Engage God instead. Ask God to help you choose with intention a more life-giving action rather than continuing to engage your default setting.

- **Forgive yourself, and don't get caught up in unproductive guilt.** Remember God promises us a way out (Matt. 11:28–30). He forgives us and "[blots] out our transgressions" (Is. 44:22–23).

Here are a few additional tips to help you monitor what goes into your mind and body:

- **Don't battle alone.** "Without counsel plans fail, / but with many advisers they succeed" (Prov. 15:22). Seek a spiritual father and prayer from friends. Choose life-giving friends.

- **Flee.** "So flee youthful passions and pursue righteousness [a right relationship with God], faith, love, and

6 HOURS, 7 LESSONS

peace, along with those who call on the Lord from a pure heart" (2 Tim. 2:22). "Put to death therefore what is earthly in you: sexual immorality, impurity, passion, evil desire, and covetousness, which is idolatry" (Col. 3:5).

- **Remember to watch your eyes.** The Psalmist said, "I will not set before my eyes / anything that is worthless" (Ps. 101:3).

- **Remember you can overcome anything; God provides the way out.** "No temptation has overtaken you that is not common to man. God is faithful, and he will not let you be tempted beyond your ability, but with the temptation he will also provide the way of escape, that you may be able to endure it" (1 Cor. 10:13).

- **Depend on God's strength daily to revamp your choices.** Pray both proactively and reactively in the moment you struggle.

- **Never forget 1 Corinthians 6:19.** Our bodies are a temple of the Holy Spirit. The temple was important because it was the symbolic dwelling place of God. It was where God and humanity met. Through Christ we are now called to be the temple, the dwelling place of God.

Crown Him by Being Pure of Heart

Because life can suddenly shift us into dark spaces, we may not always be able to stop certain thoughts from entering our mind, but we can choose the thoughts we fuel. And God tells us that He knows our heart. He knows our words before they are even on our tongues, and He is familiar with all our ways. He knows where we are most likely to stumble and falter and where the enemy attempts to get a foothold in our lives. All we need to do to access His presence is to turn to Him, because He reigns through it all. And we must do so before our unhealthy thoughts implant in our hearts and threaten to turn our lives away from Him. You see, God's power to direct our lives is affected by our freewill decisions—by the things we allow to simmer in our hearts and what we allow to overtake us.

And it's easy to live one way on the outside but be guided by inner thoughts and feelings that contradict that impression on the inside. Because the heart is the deep-seated center of our soul, it directs and is responsible for everything we do. The heart guides our inner thought life, our passions, our attitudes, and our unseen motives. When we are pure of heart, our outward actions and our unseen motives are *both* accountable to wisdom. When we are pure of heart, we catch bad seeds before they are sown in our lives so that we may actively and willfully prevent their growth within us. Remaining pure of heart is a process of listening and constantly resetting our thoughts to what the Spirit desires. In this way, we gain the opportunity to decide what will realign us with the image of God, because His aim is not to reform us from the outside in but to change us from the inside out.

Our character is not defined by our actions but by our heart. And who we are deep within our soul matters more to God than what we show to others, for "man looks on the outward appearance, but the LORD looks on the heart" (I Sam. 16:7). So, "Keep your heart with all vigilance, / for from it flow the springs of life" (Prov. 4:23). So the next time the enemy tries to attack your life, see it as nothing more than a temptation threatening to take root and change your heart. Whether it's an important relationship that suddenly angers you, or one of your children is pushing back in ways that leave you less than compassionate, choose not to give the enemy power by watering those seeds. Let God reign by remaining pure of heart. Do not let anger blindly lead you into sin; choose instead to pray for the one who upset you. Crown Him by not allowing the stress to divide your spirit but to open your spirit. Turn to God and ask Him to lead the way, to purify your heart, and to help you handle the situation according to His goodness and wisdom.

Crown Him by the Way We Live Our Lives

There is perhaps no better way to impact people's lives than by living in the King's light ourselves—as Christ says, "All people will know that you are my disciples, if you have love for one another" (John 13:35). Metropolitan Anthony Bloom expresses a similar sentiment when he says, "We should try to live in such a way that, if the Gospels were lost, they could be rewritten by looking at us."[57] And we also have

---

57 His Eminence Archbishop Elpidophoros, "Homily for the Eighth Sunday of Matthew," *Orthodox Observer News*, August 2, 2020,

CHAPTER 6: It Is Finished

the old adage, "Actions speak louder than words." In each case, the emphasis is not on what we say (or don't say) but on what we do.

Christ challenges us to let our light shine throughout the world, as He says, "Let your light shine before others, so that they may see your good works and give glory to your Father who is in heaven" (Matt. 5:16). Yet many people feel their relationship with God is a private matter. Of course, there is a privacy to it that comes from intimacy, but we mustn't forget that if the disciples and the saints of Christianity had kept their faith to themselves and stayed in Jerusalem and in the Mediterranean, we would not have Christianity anywhere. They shared their faith through their words, and more importantly, through their actions. In the same way, Christ calls us to be His ambassadors, His witnesses, inviting people to a life with the King of Glory. People will never talk about Christ the King with you if they don't see Christ the King in you.

One way we crown God in our daily lives is by remaining conscious of what we are motivated by. Are we trying to please God or other people? Choosing to please God before people helps us chase righteousness over social acceptance. Look at what happened to Pontius Pilate: he knew Jesus was innocent, and on two occasions he tried to get out of allowing Jesus to be crucified. But in the end, he was too weak to act as his conscience led. For the sake of his own reputation and position, he caved in to the demands of the crowd and turned Jesus over to be crucified (John 18).

---

https://www.goarch.org/-/homily-eighth-sunday-matthew-2020.

Ultimately, when we crown Him by the way we live our lives, the focus becomes less about ourselves and more about Jesus. And yes, we have all probably been driven to become greater in some way: more important, more honored, more prestigious, better than others. But we must know that focusing on ourselves sways our daily ambitions, changes what we see as important, and affects how we live our life. We have to decide whose glory we are seeking: is it about us or about Jesus? To do this, ask yourself, "Who do I want people to see when they see me?" One of the most beautiful examples of this is when John the Baptist was tempted by others to glorify himself instead of Jesus. His followers were getting competitive and envious of Jesus' success, and they came out and said to Him, "He's now competing with us. Everyone's going to Him instead of us" (John 3:22–36). John responded, "He must increase, but I must decrease" (John 3:30).

To live in the light of Christ also might mean sacrificing your immediate desires. To see this in action, here's a story Fr. Nicholas shares from his youth that many of us can relate to:

> In high school, I wasn't a very popular kid, but I wanted to be. I wanted to hang out with all those good-looking and athletic kids, partying late into the night on weekends. At the same time, I was also growing in my faith. I began to read the Bible and pray and learn more about my faith. I felt like I was on fire for God. Then one day, one of the most

popular boys at school invited me to a huge party at his house that weekend. All the cool kids would be there; there would be loud music, girls, and probably illicit substances, too. I was torn. On the one hand, I had wanted to go to one of these parties for a long time. On the other hand, I knew that what was going to happen at that party would not glorify Christ. Well, my impulses won out.

On that night, as I opened the front door to leave the house, my father came up to me and said, "Nick, where are you going?"

I knew my father wouldn't approve of this party, so I told him I was going over to a friend's house to study.

My father looked into my eyes and said, "Nick, when you walk out that door, you don't walk out as simply Nicholas. You walk out as my son, as a member of the Louh family. Don't bring any shame to our name." That final statement stopped me in my tracks. I decided not to attend the party, knowing that had I done so, I would have brought shame to the family name.

Like Fr. Nicholas learned in this story, we need to realize that every day when we go out into the world, we are representing our Lord and Savior, the King of our lives. We have opportunities to bring glory or shame to His holy name.

As representatives of Christ's family, our conduct provides an example for others. Saint Paul writes in the Book of I Timothy, "Let no one despise you for your youth, but set the believers an example in speech, in conduct, in love, in faith, in purity" (4:12). So whomever you meet, wherever you go, allow Christ to create in you a new identity as one who lives in the light of Christ. Then when people see you, they will see not only someone who has crowned Christ King—they will see the King of Glory in you.

Crown Him by Shining Brightly

On Holy Saturday in the Orthodox Church, at around midnight the lights go out and the priest emerges from the altar holding a large, lit candle and proclaims to the congregation, "Come receive the light, the never waning light, for Christ is Risen from the Dead." He approaches the faithful, all of whom hold candles, and lights one. This person then lights their neighbor's candle, and so on, and before long, the church, once in darkness, is now filled with the light that originated from the light of the Resurrection. And even when someone comes inside the church for a worship service on a typical Sunday, the custom is to take a candle and light it from a previously lit candle—which represents the light of Christ—and place it in the sandbox while saying a prayer.

This is a beautiful representation of how, in the darkness of the world, the light of Christ comes and is shared from one person to another. As we share the light, we are also reigniting our own light as we recommit to living our whole life for Christ and sharing His light with others, making manifest His words: "I am the light of the world; he who follows me will not walk in darkness but will have the light of life" (John 8:12).

To live an "it is finished" lifestyle, we must resolve to take the light of the Resurrected Christ into a dark world—to light one another's candles, because for many people, life can be a battlefield. Perhaps you, too, are feeling overwhelmed, exhausted, worried, and defeated. In such times, we need people in our corner who speak life into us, who remind us that we "can do all things through him who strengthens [us]" (Phil. 4:13), who remind us that God will be with us "always, to the end of the age" (Matt. 28:20), and who can remind us that we worship the King of Glory who holds us all in the palm of His hand (Is. 49:16). When we have people in our corner who can share with us a word of encouragement and inspiration, it brings us comfort, peace, and strength. In the same way, God calls us, too, to be in someone's corner, shining brightly in the lives of people who are going through the battle of life.

Maybe you're not in a dark place right now, but chances are, someone you know is. We don't have to look far for pain, and when we truly strive to live with Christ on the throne of our lives, we look to use what we've been given to do good when we can. Choosing how to share Christ's light sometimes feels overwhelming, but remember, oftentimes, the little things are the very things that hold significance to God.

If you don't know where to start, think about one thing that people always compliment you for. Think about what you do effortlessly. Those are the spiritual gifts you are supposed to unwrap in the world. You see, God places spiritual gifts in our hands to share with the world around us, but so often, we keep our gifts to ourselves because we are so busy prioritizing everything else. But remember that the greatest sermon preached is not what people hear on a Sunday, it is what people experience through us on a Monday. So go out today and look around. Be willing to see the needs of those God places on your path. Be willing to let those needs interrupt your day or your plans. And choose every day to live in such a way that when people see you, they see the light of the world, Jesus Christ.

The Three Nots

Unfortunately, it's easy in our culture to empathize from a distance. We feel bad for others' suffering, but we avoid taking direct action. Then we rationalize our behavior, usually in one of three ways that we call the Three Nots.

1. **Not on my schedule.** We convince ourselves we are too busy to help, so hurry becomes the enemy of help. We once heard someone make an acronym of the word *busy*: Bound Under Satan's Yoke. The enemy wants us to be so busy in our life that we don't have time to make a difference in someone's else's life.

2. **Not my purpose.** We tell ourselves that helping isn't part of our five-year plan. We're all out there trying to achieve the "American Dream," which has some fine qualities, but it doesn't leave a lot of space for

other people's needs. As a result, we have replaced compassion with consumption, service with status, and helping with hoarding.

3. **Not my problem.** We live in a major military town, and the soldiers have a mantra: "Leave no man behind." In ancient Greece, Spartans were given a helmet, a sword, and a shield. It was okay for them to lose the helmet and sword in battle but not to lose their shield, because the shield was supposed to protect the brother soldier to their left when they stood in formation. Compare that to our culture's attitude of every man and woman for themselves. In the battlefield of modern life, we don't say, "No man left behind"; we say, "Not my problem." Christ says, "Love your neighbor," but we shrug and say, "Yeah, but who's my neighbor, really?"

You can see how the "nots" interfere with living our created purpose of a resurrected, "it is finished" life. Again, we are called to let Christ reign over all our life, not just when it is convenient.

How to Share the King's Light

Here are some practical ways to crown our King by shining brightly.

SEE WHO PEOPLE ARE

We live in a polarized world where we are constantly encouraged to judge others based on their values, lifestyle, political affiliation, marital status, wealth, poverty, etc. We often see sides, not souls. But we don't know what people's stories are, and we shouldn't presume to decide who should and who should not receive God's grace. We are not called to judge; we are called to love. All we need to know is that each person is beloved of God since, as St. John Chrysostom says, "If you cannot find Christ in the beggar at the Church door, you will not find Him in the chalice." Christ modeled this in His life. He would frequently interact with lepers, bleeding women, prostitutes, tax collectors, and so on, despite religious laws that considered them unclean or social norms that considered them enemies. He chose uneducated, lower-class fishermen who were considered dirty, and He used them to transform the world. He shared the hope of the Kingdom with the Samaritan woman at the well, not letting her past, her religion, or her ethnicity be a barrier. Christ didn't have favorites, and neither should we. We are called to see people the way God sees them. In the writings of the first-century Greek philosopher Aristides, we see the early Christians excelled at this. "These Christians . . . love one another," he writes:

> They never fail to help widows; they save orphans from those who would hurt them. If a man has something, he gives freely to the man who has nothing. If they see a stranger, Christians take him home and are happy, as though he were a real brother. They don't consider themselves brothers in the usual sense, but brothers instead through the Spirit of God. And if

they hear that one of them is in jail, or persecuted for professing the name of their redeemer, they all give him what he needs. If it is possible, they bail him out. If one of them is poor and there isn't enough food to go around, they fast several days to give him the food he needs. This is really a new kind of person. There is something divine in them.[58]

So, look around you. The person who needs your light may be the widow or the recent divorcée. It could be the cashier at the local supermarket or a child who sits by himself at school. We should have the attitude that what is important to Christ the King should be important to us. We don't need to be judges but rather witnesses of the King's light.

LEARN WHAT PEOPLE NEED

We once heard a speaker exploring the questions that Christ posed as compared to the answers He gave. He had discovered that in the Gospels, Christ asks over 330 questions but only answers three that are posed to Him. Christ wanted to get to know people's stories: how they got to where they were and what they were going through. Yet how often do we assume we know what others need rather than following Christ's model by asking?

During Fr. Nicholas's dissertation research on pastoral counseling in urban ministry, he spoke with people living

---

58 Bruce Milne, *Dynamic Diversity: Bridging Class, Age, Race and Gender in the Church* (Downers Grove, IL: InterVarsity Press, 2007), 51.

on the streets in Boston. On one occasion, he met a young woman who was living in a refrigerator box with her child. He shares:

> I gently told her that I wanted to help her, then I asked her how she ended up there. She told me she grew up in a middle-class neighborhood and did well in school, but then she began hanging around the wrong people. Someone drugged her drink at a party and raped her, and she got pregnant. Her family didn't want her to have the child, but she refused to get rid of it or give it up, and through a series of unfortunate circumstances, she landed on the streets.

This experience taught Fr. Nicholas not to jump to conclusions about people. Whatever he may have assumed about that young woman's story, it wasn't close to the reality. It taught him that when we talk to people, we hear their stories and their struggles and can understand what they really need from us.

The comedian Robin Williams, who sadly took his own life, said, "Everyone you meet is fighting a battle you know nothing about. Be kind. Always."[59] We can be like Christ by doing a lot less talking and a lot more listening. Ask gentle, open-ended questions that communicate it is safe to open up to you. At an appropriate time or moment, say, "How are

---

59 Adrian Webster, *Tiny Noticeable Things: The Secret Weapon to Making a Difference in Business* (Chichester, UK: Wiley, 2021), 69.

you doing, *really*?" or "Tell me your story." Don't force them to share more than they are comfortable. You might simply ask, "What is a practical way that I can help you today?" Then take a moment to simply pray for them. We like to say that your location is your vocation—in other words, divine interruptions can happen anywhere, at any time. We need only be willing to stop.

REMEMBER WHY

In the Passion narrative, we hear and experience the love God has for us. We hear how Christ endured the physical and emotional pains of betrayal, deception, scourging, spitting, and whipping. We hear that after His entire body was mangled and destroyed, He was forced to carry the Cross nearly the length of eight football fields on an uneven road, eventually to be hung on that same Cross. And yet, in all of that, He never wavered in His love for us. Saint Paul encapsulates this steady love when he writes, "God shows his love for us in that while we were still sinners, Christ died for us" (Rom. 5:8).

And on the other side of His death is His Resurrection. In the Orthodox Church, at the Agape service on Easter Sunday morning, we chant, "The gates of death opened to You for fear, and the doorkeepers of Hades quaked when they saw You. For You crushed the gates of bronze and You shattered the bars of iron, and You brought us out of darkness and the shadow of death, and You broke our chains to pieces." In fact, Christ's life, death, and Resurrection were His rescue mission for us to experience His love through the Church and sacraments and, ultimately, to be welcomed into heaven. Christ's dream is that we would extend His witness to all people. His desire is that we would feel welling up within us a desire to extend His love and mercy toward others. He saved our life so that we can help Him save other people's lives. We can shine His light by remembering our why—the life and work of Christ—and knowing that we are in this work on earth together.

In 2011, we toured Redwood National Park outside of San Francisco. These famous redwood trees are some of the largest trees in the world, and they are magnificent. But did you know that, though these trees can reach heights of over 300 feet and can live for over two thousand years, their root systems are only about six to twelve feet deep? It doesn't seem like enough support. However, instead of growing deeper, the roots of these trees grow horizontally, intermingling with the root systems of other redwood trees. In fact, the root systems within the forest are all intertwined. For this reason, when a storm or an earthquake hits that region, very rarely do the trees fall. They rely on one another for support.

When Christ died on the Cross, He called us His sons and daughters. He tells us that we are all interlinked, that we are connected to one another as one body. If we are truly the King's children, and if the King has truly finished a work in such a way that it resonates into the present, then we need to live our lives in such a way that we rise and fall with each other.

The darkness of this world can be overwhelming and daunting. If we are not careful, we can slip into helplessness and hopelessness, opting to do nothing rather than risk burning out with yet one more thing on our to-do list. But let us remind you that the darkness of the world is no match for the light of Christ. Living out our purpose feeds us when all the wrong distractions deplete us. Saint John the Theologian writes, "In Him was life, and the life was the light of men. The light shines in the darkness, and the darkness has not overcome it" (John 1:4–5). When Christ utters those words, "It is finished," He is declaring that the darkness of the world, what was thought to have destroyed and killed Him, is simply the tool that He used to resurrect and give life to the world.

Let us place the crowns of our life upon the true King of our life. Let us bow down and worship Him by growing closer to Him in our walk of faith while finding stillness; bow down and worship Him by bringing Him into every situation, by watching what we take in and living our lives intentionally; and bow down and be His shining lights who go out and help change the world.

For Discussion: The Three Rs—
Rest, Reflect, and Respond

1. What are you bowing down to today that is of this world and tries to demand your full allegiance? What sits on the throne where only God should be?

2. How are you doing with seeking stillness in your life?

3. What might need to settle to the bottom of your priority list in order for you to have more time for stillness?

4. Where might you go to find stillness? What time of day are you most likely to stick to a routine of stillness?

5. Where, when, and with whom are you most likely to be tempted to see and hear things that barrage your flesh with images and ideas that contaminate your soul? What freewill choices put you in the face of temptation?

6. What could you do differently to limit your exposure to these things?

7. What did you learn when you tracked it, learned about it, and got curious about it? What priorities does this behavior protect in your life? Are those

values important to God? How does it hurt your ability to live for Him? To serve Him? To prioritize what matters?

8. Where might you struggle most with being pure of heart? How could you change your narrative in that situation?

9. Where are you tempted to seek your own glory? How might you point the focus back to God in those moments?

10. What do you think others see when they see you? When are you most likely to emanate the light of Christ? Where might you struggle more to do so? What is one area of your life where you could be a light for others?

11. Which of the "three nots" do you struggle with the most, when it comes to helping those in need?

PRAYER

Lord, today I am crowning You by giving You **my mind.** Let my mind not think on things that are negative, that are unholy and unrighteous. When a thought comes over me that doesn't honor Your Spirit within me, let me catch it and not fuel it. Rather, fill me with "whatever is honorable, whatever is just, whatever is pure, whatever is lovely, whatever is commendable" (Phil. 4:8).

I am crowning You by giving You **my ears.** Allow me to be sensitive to Your whisper. Help me to remember that the quieter I become, the better I can hear You. Direct me away from listening to things that can corrupt my soul.

I am crowning You by giving You **my mouth.** Let me not speak negative things about anyone, but let me use my words to be a blessing to others.

I am crowning You by giving You **my eyes.** Let me not look lustfully at anything that corrupts my soul.

Allow me to have eyes that look straight forward, not to the left or to the right. Allow me to have eyes that are fixed on You.

I am crowning You by giving You **my hands**. Let my hands be used to do good deeds in this world and to bring help, relief, love, and comfort to those who need You most.

I am crowning You by giving You **my feet.** Let my feet be guided by You. Direct my path, lead me to the places I need to be and away from the places I shouldn't be. Let my every step be subject to You.

Lord, let Your values pave the way for my life. Let Your ways direct my ways—my motivations, my choices, my ambitions, and my cares. Let me know Your thoughts in every circumstance. Keep me grounded in what I am chasing and why, so that my identity doesn't change based on who and what I am around. Let me be guided by what is pleasing to You, so that I may be a light in this world. And let my life be made in Your image so that people who know me, but don't know You, will want to know You because they see You in me. In the name of the Father, Son, and Holy Spirit. Amen.

CHAPTER 7

Into Your Hands

Then Jesus, calling out with a loud voice, said, "Father, into your hands I commit my spirit!" And having said this he breathed his last. —LUKE 23:46

HOUSTON, WE HAVE a problem." These words echoed throughout America on April 13, 1970, as astronaut Jim Lovell reported that the Apollo 13 spacecraft had experienced a cascade of problems that happened as if in an instant. At one moment, things were going well, and a few moments later, a disaster threatened to leave the astronauts stranded in space. It took a lot of ingenuity, bravery, and faith in their equipment and one another to get back. Few of us will ever take as large a risk as flying into space, but all of us are susceptible to those moments when we suddenly realize we may not make it out. Life is precious, and it can also be capricious. None of us is guaranteed tomorrow, but oftentimes it takes a dramatic event to shock us into awareness of the fact.

On July 21, 2003, we experienced a shocking event of our own. Two days after our wedding, we set out on a once-in-a-lifetime trip to Italy. We were so excited, so happy—we were newlyweds! We had been flying for seven hours across the Atlantic and had a couple hours to go. Up to that point, it had been a very smooth, comfortable flight. But in an instant, we went from staring into each other's eyes to being afraid for our lives. The plane hit incredible turbulence and fell for what seemed like forever. Our stomachs were in our throats, and we gripped our seats and each other. Passengers were screaming in fear, babies were crying, compartments overhead were opening, and the plane was violently shaking. The lights on the plane were flashing on and off. It was like something out of a movie right before a plane crashes, and it felt like an eternity of instability, fear, and anxiety. We were more afraid than we'd ever been in our lives; we truly thought we weren't going to make it. Then, just as quickly as it had started, the turbulence ended. The flight smoothed out, and we soon arrived safely in the middle of what was deemed one of Italy's worst hailstorms. And life over the last twenty years has been no different. While we have experienced blessings too great to imagine that could have only been divinely orchestrated and planned, we have also endured suffering that felt too hard to hold at times and loss that has changed our lives in indescribable ways.

Nowadays, we are most likely to say, "Houston, we have a problem" in jest—a kind of dark humor that hides the discomfort of the actual event. But at some point in our life, most of us will experience a situation that rattles us, that shakes our faith and that creates a turbulence within that makes us keenly aware of how tenuous "normal life" can be. We wonder during those times how and whether we will get through it. But it is precisely these situations that remind us of the importance of Christ's seventh recorded statement that He makes on the Cross.

As He is about to take His last breath, Jesus gathers up the last of his strength and cries, "Father, into your hands I commit my spirit." While we do not know the exact order of all these statements, it is interesting that the Scriptures record this particular statement as the last one. Not only does it mark a dramatic conclusion to His Crucifixion, it also points us back to Scripture, which Jesus always does with conscious intent. In this case, He is referring to Psalm 31, which reads, "You take me out of the net they have hidden for me, / for you are my refuge. / Into your hand I commit my spirit; / you have redeemed me, O LORD, faithful God" (Ps. 31:4–5). Here, the psalmist reminds us that God is our refuge, and Christ, when He chooses this statement, tells us to put our whole life in the hands of an all-knowing, good, and life-giving God. So, if Christ's sixth recorded statement was all about triumph, then His final recorded statement is all about trust.

Why was it so important to end with this prayer? Why was it important for Christ to share this statement at this moment? Because life can take us from seasons of abundance in one moment, where we think "Glory to God, thank you Lord, I can see Your hand in everything"—to seasons of agony in the very next moment, where we cry out, "Lord, have mercy upon us, watch over us in our anguish."

God hears our agonies, our worries, our gratitude, and our cries for mercy. And He answers our prayers in so many ways. When something isn't right, He closes doors and alerts us to what we need to see. When it's not the right time for something, He slows us down and prepares us through patience. And when it is the right time, we see the wonders of His works, outcomes that only could have happened by His hands. It is important to remember that God never leaves us. His answers are compassionate, merciful, and benevolent. We feel His presence in our life, both in seasons of abundance and seasons of turbulence, when we stay close to Him. As James 4:8 says, "Draw near to God, and He will draw near to you." So "let us then with confidence draw near to the throne of grace, that we may receive mercy and find grace to help in time of need" (Heb. 4:16).

Battles and Blessings

We don't have to look far to find sadness in the world. As we write this very chapter our hearts are heavy. A young boy has just lost his life on a bike ride, and a man in the prime of his life has died within a month of a cancer diagnosis. A young woman found out her back pain is stage four cancer. A young girl has tragically died in a car accident. And a woman is trying to cope with having lost two members of her family from unrelated causes in the very same week. Pain is everywhere. But Scripture tells us to regard suffering as a normal part of this life (1 Pet. 4:12). Whether it's disease, natural disaster, unjust persecution, broken relationships, or tragic loss, dark seasons happen with disturbing regularity. And we are not immune just because we are faithful. Even St. Paul experienced tremendous suffering—through his great labors as a servant of Christ, through multiple imprisonments, and through countless beatings that often brought him near to death. He describes this in detail in 2 Corinthians 11:23–28:

> Five times I received at the hands of the Jews the forty lashes less one. Three times I was beaten with rods. Once I was stoned. Three times I was shipwrecked; a night and a day I was adrift at sea; on frequent journeys, in danger from rivers, danger from robbers, danger from my own people, danger from Gentiles, danger in the city, danger in the wilderness, danger at sea, danger from false brothers; in toil and hardship, through many a sleepless night, in hunger and thirst, often without food, in cold and exposure. And, apart from other things, there is the daily pressure on me of my anxiety for all the churches.

Yet we know that it was God who gave him the strength to get through it and provided a means of escape (2 Cor. 11:33).

So although we need to think of the Christian life in terms of battles as well as blessings, this isn't always easy. And when battles come our way, no matter how much we look for control, reassurance, and paths around them, we can still contend with things we don't understand in our own lives and in the lives of those around us. But what we do know is that it is in these dark seasons when we often learn to stop trying to manage everything on our own, and we truly begin to entrust our souls to God, depending more fully on Him.

Scripture tells us, in response to our battles, to trust God and remain committed to doing good (I Pet. 4:19). In chapter 4, Peter urges Christians to be fiercely committed to fulfilling God's purpose for their lives. He encourages us to endure our battles with a "spirit of death and resurrection" because "every trouble of life can be entered into as a baptismal experience, an ongoing acceptance of death in this life in order to grow in the qualities of the life to come."[60] In our own life, we can look back and see just how much our battles have transformed us, brought us deeper into a more profound understanding of our Faith, and prompted blessings in the lives of others. Through our own trials, we are better able to feel compassion for others in their dark seasons. And it's true that through trials, more beauty, love, and authentic compassion enter the world. Those who proclaim that "the light shines in the darkness" (John I:5) must be acquainted with darkness.

But sometimes our response to it all isn't like Peter or Paul. In the midst of our battles, our reactions sometimes create additional battles. Even though God surrounds us with His unyielding love and finds ways to remind us of His presence, our emotions can quickly shift our spirits into doubt, turbulence, willfulness, anger, and anxiety. As these feelings intensify, they can drown out the gentle guidance of God's whisper and the comfort of His presence, making it hard to remember all the ways He has responded to our worries and prayers in the past. That is why in all the battles we

---

60 *The Orthodox Study Bible* (Nashville: Thomas Nelson, 2008), 549.

encounter in this life, Jesus reminds us that as we surrender, He fights for us. We were never meant to battle alone.

He didn't, and we shouldn't.

Reactions That Mask Our Resistance to Surrender

More often than not, when things aren't going the way we hoped they would, we can find ourselves fighting our realities in unproductive ways rather than surrendering them to God. Our resistance often only makes our situation harder. Look out for these common forms of resistance.

We Get Stuck in Judgment

In tough situations, we can get stuck in bitterness and judgment about who and what is to blame for our circumstances, rather than dealing with the situation itself. It's getting stuck on what "should" have been that can leave us despairing and unable to move forward in ways that might help. But it's the "I refuse to accept what is happening" response that leaves us suffering, because our judgment only creates additional emotions that make our situation worse. Now, not only do we have our initial feelings about what's going on, but we have secondary emotions that distract us from coping with the real issue. Ultimately, this blocks the wisdom and discernment we need to move through it.

If we want to live out our faith during stressful times, we must try reaching deep within ourselves to unpack our struggle rather than getting stuck in the rabbit hole of judgment.

In this moment, we stop looking for who to blame. We start doing the more vulnerable work of acknowledging the truth of our struggles as well as the reality that some things in life just don't have easy answers, and that is why we were meant to trust in God and remember we are not alone.

We Get Stuck Asking "Why?"

When battles won't relent, our pain, worry, and upset sometimes morph into anger with God, and we blame Him for what is happening and get stuck asking that pesky three-letter question, "Why?" "Why is this happening? Why has God allowed this? Why has He not relieved my worry, my sorrow, my situation in general? Why is He punishing me?" And then we begin to wonder, "God, where are You in all of this?" And most of the time, on this side of heaven, we won't get the answer. Because although God can see everything from beginning to end, we weren't necessarily meant to. So, we get stuck questioning the things we don't understand and don't have good answers for.

We see that even the prophet Jeremiah struggled with this. He had a very difficult calling from God to preach to a rebellious people and urge them to turn back to God and repent of their ways. Jeremiah's prophecies prompted plots against him. He suffered and was ridiculed and mocked by people, and he became increasingly more discouraged that his efforts didn't seem to be making a difference to the people he was preaching to. He became discouraged even to the point of doubting God's promises (Jer. 15:18). We later even hear him ask, "Why did I come out from the womb / to see toil and sorrow, / and spend my days in shame?" (20:18). And even though God responded multiple times to Jeremiah's pleas, protecting him, revealing plots against him, giving him the words when he feared he wouldn't have them, and saving him on multiple occasions, Jeremiah couldn't see the bigger plan. He couldn't see that people would be talking about his life three thousand years later, and that his life would give hope to the hopeless. Like us, he struggled with not knowing the greater plan for his life and whether there would be purpose in his pain.

And all throughout Scripture, when Jesus responds to suffering—in addition to healing the sick, raising people from the dead, consoling the afflicted, comforting the broken-hearted, and liberating those oppressed by the devil—He also points us back to heaven and to the multitude of blessings that await us in the Kingdom (John 14:1).

We Get Stuck in Fear

When we are stuck in fear, we know it because we get knots in our stomach, racing thoughts keep us up at night, we get short of breath, and we struggle to focus on anything else. But what is fear, really? Fear is just an anxious feeling caused by our anticipation of a threat (either real or imagined). Once something makes us afraid, we can make the situation worse in our minds by dwelling on worst-case scenarios. Then we either try to exert some level of control or influence over the outcome or end up paralyzed by the anxiety of what appears to have no solution. We end up heading down a dark and lonely path that consumes our energy, clouds our judgment, and narrows our focus to what we are afraid of instead of who holds us in our fear.

And although fear is a normal response, and one of humanity's oldest emotions, we must remember that fear is a product of trying to trust our own resources. But having faith amidst our fear reminds us that we don't have to. And if you are struggling with fear that feels immobilizing, remember you are not alone. We see evidence of fear in the life of the Apostle Peter when he lashed out at the guard in the Garden of Gethsemane (fight), when he denied Christ three times despite all his earlier promises and vows (flight), and when Christ invited him to walk across the water (freeze). We also see fear in the disciples when Jesus was arrested. Though they had seen Him perform so many miracles, when it came down to it, even with their faith in Him, they still panicked and abandoned Him in His time of need. And in Moses, who, even with the power of God on his side (Ex. 4), was afraid to confront Pharoah. But in all these circumstances, God steps in and works on behalf of those in fear (Ex. 4:12; Matt. 14:32; John 20:19–23).

We Get Stuck Trying to Manage Everything on Our Own

This is one of the greatest struggles most of us face—the struggle between trusting in God and trusting in ourselves: we struggle to fight and surrender at the same time. Instead, we tend to remain on either side of the dichotomy, depending on what's happening. We trust in God when we feel His blessings, but we try to control and manage everything ourselves when battles strike. Yet it is in our battles that our life meets our faith, and we must learn to transcend this duality.

We see this dichotomy exemplified in the Bible between the Garden of Eden and the Garden of Gethsemane. In the Garden of Eden, Adam and Eve were with God. They had all the benefits of His love, guidance, and protection. However, when the serpent entered the picture and deceived them in a battle they didn't realize they were entering, they began to question God's intentions and engaged a desire to control their own lives and act apart from Him. We all know how that ended. It was in this garden that unhealthy fear, shame, and embarrassment entered the world. In fact, Adam and Eve wound up hiding from God, their Source and Creator (Gen. 3:10).

The opposite happened in the Garden of Gethsemane. Here Christ, dealing with the greatest struggle in the history of humankind, revealed His humanity by asking God to take this cup from Him. He shared His anguish at His impending death. But unlike Adam and Eve in the Garden of Eden, Christ chose the will of the Father and said, "Nevertheless, not my will, but yours, be done" (Luke 22:42).

When we face battles in this life, we are pulled between these two gardens: insisting on our own will or surrendering to God's. Whichever garden we spend the most time tilling will dictate our level of peace amidst struggle. We must strive to live in such a way that allows God to work in our lives, accepting that both our effort and our full dependence on Him in every situation can and should exist simultaneously.

It is only in this way that we find peace, transformation, and rest for our souls. This synergy between our work and His work is what gives rest for our souls as God begins to work out everything we cannot. It is He who produces the result of our efforts as He works within us.

God's Reaction to Our Battles

Of the thirty-seven miracles Christ performs that are recorded in the four Gospels, most of them are directed at bringing someone to faith in Him. And one common reaction Jesus has is to comment directly about the faith of the person He heals, emphasizing the importance of putting their trust in Him. In one such instance, Jesus had the disciples take Him across the sea after a day of preaching. A windstorm kicked up, and water started to fill the boat. The disciples were afraid, but Jesus was asleep. They woke Him up saying, " 'Save us, Lord; we are perishing.' And He said to them, 'Why are you afraid, O you of little faith?' Then He rose and rebuked the winds and the sea, and there was a great calm" (Matt. 8:23–27).

We hear of another time when the disciples were caught in a boat while the sea was experiencing wind and waves. In this instance, Jesus was not in the boat, but they saw Him walking toward them on the water and they were terrified:

> But immediately Jesus spoke to them, saying, "Take heart; it is I. Do not be afraid." And Peter answered him, "Lord, if it is you, command me to come to

you on the water." He said, "Come." So Peter got out of the boat and walked on the water and came to Jesus. But when he saw the wind, he was afraid, and beginning to sink he cried out, "Lord, save me." Jesus immediately reached out his hand and took hold of him, saying to him. "O you of little faith, why did you doubt?" And when they got into the boat, the wind ceased. (Matt. 14:27–32)

In other words, in both scenarios, before Jesus addressed the issue, He spoke to their faith.

So, here we can see that even Peter, who had just witnessed Christ walking on water, still became afraid as soon as he focused on the storm instead of focusing on Christ. And we too can feel like the disciples and wonder, "Are we going to be okay? Does God care that we are in this storm? Is He going to help us? Why is He not taking care of this?" Perhaps Jesus would say to all of us, "O you of little faith." But just like it was with the disciples, it is through encountering these storms that we will come to know more of His power, and our faith will be strengthened.

Entrusting Our Lives to Christ During Our Battles

Be strong and courageous. Do not be frightened, and do not be dismayed, for the LORD your God is with you wherever you go. —JOSHUA 1:9

So how do we commit our lives to Christ and remain trusting when we are going through the battles of this life? How do we remain grounded when we feel the earth beneath us shaking? The Book of Hebrews says that hope is "a sure and steadfast anchor of the soul" (6:19)—or we could say, Christ [our hope] is the anchor of the soul. Let us follow Christ's example.

Pray Without Ceasing

Rejoice always, pray without ceasing, give thanks in all circumstances; for this is the will of God in Christ Jesus for you. —1 THESSALONIANS 5:16–18

We can't expect never to feel distressed, but we can invite God into that space with us. We've all heard the expression "pray without ceasing," but what does that even mean, practically speaking? It means that handing our circumstances (and our whole lives) over to God is easier when we have remained close to Him and left the door of our hearts open to Him in every circumstance, every day. It means we invite God into our stream of consciousness regularly, just as we would our dearest friend. It means we open up both in our best moments and in our worst, in our silent pleas and deepest longings, in the midst of our tears and in every celebration. It means prayer fills our natural pauses throughout the day and that when we experience any hard feelings, we're prompted to ask for His mercy to wash over whatever we feel up against.

When we pray about our anxieties and our difficult feelings, we often remember all the times God has worked in our lives before, which prompts us to praise God and helps us feel connected to Him. Feeling His presence leads us to seek His voice more—in daily Scripture, Christian music, or devotionals—which helps us maintain the comfort of

His presence. Staying close to God in our struggles is the only protection we have during times when we experience circumstances we wish weren't happening, as it reminds us we aren't alone.

If you are feeling anxious about something today, turn your attention to God and ask Him to wrap you in the comfort of His presence. Remember, seasons change, but God's everlasting presence and love for us never does. When we feel distanced from Him, it's not because He moved but because we did. God surrounds us, knows everything about us, and is always in control. So when we pray, it isn't to remind God of our existence, it is to remind us of His.

To pray without ceasing, start from wherever you are in your prayer life and take one step further. If you are only praying in the morning and at night, try praying throughout the day. If you are only praying once a week in church, try praying in difficult moments throughout your week. If you already pray daily, try praying more often during your day: on your commute, while you exercise, at red lights, in grocery lines, or during any pause in your day. If you only pray for your own situation, try praying for those you come into contact with, both those you know and those you don't. And whenever you pray, do so with the fullness of your presence. Don't let your prayers be empty. Repetitive words that don't connect to their meaning become nothing more than rote performance. So when you pray, connect. Be emotionally present. Let your words have meaning.

We must never forget that prayer has power. In the words of St. John Chrysostom,

The potency of prayer hath subdued the strength of fire; it hath bridled the rage of lions, hushed anarchy to rest, extinguished wars, appeased the elements, expelled demons, burst the chains of death, expanded the gates of heaven, assuaged diseases, repelled frauds, rescued cities from destruction, stayed the sun in its course, and arrested the progress of the thunderbolt.[61]

Remember God Can Be Trusted

I am the vine; you are the branches. Whoever abides in me and I in him, he it is that bears much fruit, for apart from me you can do nothing. —JOHN 15:5

When we face battles, it's natural to want to change things we wish weren't happening or to feel blindsided by terror or overwhelmed with sadness about calamities we experience in this life. But we must remember that God is with us and is always in control. And that means we can surrender the things in this life that we don't understand and that don't go our way: our worries and burdens, the things that keep us up at night, and even our hopes and dreams that seem distant and out of reach.

Sometimes God answers our prayers in ways that heal, and sometimes He answers them in ways that feel difficult. But it also means that we don't have to carry our burdens alone,

---

61 Hugh Stuart Boyd, trans., *Select Passages of the Writings of St. Chrysostom, St. Gregory Nazianzen, and St. Basil* (London: Longman & Company, 1810), 30.

and we don't have to force anything to happen according to our own agendas. And it means that we can rest in knowing that God hears us, "that if we ask anything according to his will he hears us. And if we know that he hears us in whatever we ask, we know that we have the requests that we have asked of him" (I John 5:14–15). It also means remembering that when we do not receive what we ask for, God answers prayers based on an eternal perspective, not an earthly one. Sometimes with His answer He yearns to grow us or mature us in our faith, to increase our dependence on Him, to strengthen us where we are weak, or to remind us that it is to Him we give all the glory for what is to come.

As we grow in trust, we allow our realities to call us into a deeper relationship with God, which draws us closer to Him than we were before as our dependence and trust in Him grows. You see, God tells us that apart from Him we can do nothing, but it's often not until we can no longer influence a situation that we actually realize this fact. The synergy between our active submission and His compassionate will is what gives our souls rest as God works out what we cannot. It is He who produces the result of our efforts as He works within us.

Saint Paul writes to the Corinthians about his own struggles with things not going to plan:

> For we do not want you to be unaware, brothers, of the affliction we experienced in Asia. For we were so utterly burdened beyond our strength that we despaired of life itself. Indeed, we felt that we had

received the sentence of death. But that was to make us rely not on ourselves but on God who raises the dead. He delivered us from such a deadly peril, and he will deliver us. On him we have set our hope that he will deliver us again. You also must help us by prayer, so that many will give thanks on our behalf for the blessing granted us through the prayers of many. (2 Cor. 1:8–11)

Here, Paul insists that just because something bad is happening to him doesn't mean that God is not working. God was working in him so that he would learn not to rely solely on himself and would remember how God delivered him before and will do it again. He was saying, in effect: He has. He will.

Pause for a moment. What are you worried about in this moment? What have you not asked God to help you with and are trying to control and manage all by yourself? Decide today to release control over things you cannot control. Remember God knows your needs and hears your pleas. Trust that your prayers matter, because the Bible says, "When the righteous cry for help, the LORD hears / and delivers them out of all their troubles" (Ps. 34:17) and "Before they call, I will answer; / while they are yet speaking I will hear" (Is. 65:24). Know that no matter what you battle, God promises to ultimately use it for good, according to His will. So if you are worrying about something right now, look up and say, "Lord, You take over," and watch as He does.

Stop Fighting Your Reality

> *I believe in the sun even when it is not shining. I believe in love even when I cannot feel it. I believe in God even when He is silent.* — WRITTEN ON A CELLAR WALL DURING THE HOLOCAUST[62]

The Bible tries to prepare us for pain. In fact, God made it a point to tell us not only about His victory over the world but that we should be prepared for the tribulation we will face (John 16:33). And we read how the apostles suffered for their faith and in most cases died violent deaths, yet most of us chafe at having to face hardship ourselves. Because unfortunately, we can pray, and that person doesn't always get better. The things we plan in our lives don't always end up the way we want them to. Life doesn't always go in the direction we hoped it would. At times, what happens to us can absolutely feel unfair. It's human to feel sad or angry about suffering or to wish it weren't happening at all. Where we go wrong is in getting stuck there, placing a period where a comma should go. We get stuck dwelling on what we wish weren't true, which doesn't help us cope with it in ways that heal.

So what are we to do when we pray and yet still face disappointment and defeat? When our dreams are met with closed doors? How are we to contend with this seemingly difficult realization when God's will does not align with our own? What do we do when we can't make sense of why?

---

62 Maggy Whitehouse, *Total Kabbalah: Bring Balance and Happiness into Your Life* (San Francisco: Chronicle Books, 2008), 155.

Truthfully, these are some of the most difficult moments in life because we don't always know why God is allowing something to occur or how He will use it. Because we can't see our lives from beginning to end. We can't see how all the dominos are going to fall. And sometimes if we're honest, it's hard to remain in trust when life hurts or disappoints us. Many realities we have to contend with on this earth can be incredibly difficult for our bodies to hold.

But our worries can send us into a place of anger and anxious over-control when we refuse to accept our circumstances as they are. We stay fretting about how to bend life according to our will, rather than trying to submit to what we can't change, to the will that is already at hand. The anxious distress can cloud our judgment and make us lose sight of the sovereign nature of God's unyielding presence in our lives. And because our worries can often flow faster than our awareness of them, we sometimes forget to meet our anxieties with the presence of faith. For this reason, we must be aware of the kind of relationship we have with the situations we face.

Acceptance means finding a better relationship with "what is" rather than getting stuck on "what ought to be." This doesn't mean we like it or that we resign ourselves to injustice or defeat. It doesn't even mean that we shouldn't try to affect change *where we can*. It just means that we stop suffering about things we cannot change so that we can act meaningfully in ways that help us adapt to what it means for right now. It just means that we can acknowledge what's before us enough to engage our faith and continue to live into our next chapter, knowing there is still a plan for our lives, rather than suffering in relation to our resistance of it. You see, when we take the pain of an experience and add judgment, angst, and resistance, the result is suffering, not healing.

Think about it on a small scale, like getting stuck in traffic that isn't moving. We get frustrated and wish we weren't stuck. We can start obsessing over our choices: "If only I had exited. Why didn't I leave earlier? I can't believe I chose to go this way. If only I hadn't stopped to get gas." Thinking things like this doesn't change the traffic, but it definitely changes us as we become increasingly more aggravated by a situation that we can do nothing about. It makes us, in a sense, suffer through it instead of recognizing that traffic is a part of this life—something frustrating that we are asked to contend with that challenges our spirit.

Now consider something much worse: the pain of being in an abusive relationship. We can almost enter despair, thinking, "If only I had married someone else. I should have seen the signs. I'm stuck, and it's my own fault I'm in this." This kind of judgment and blame causes us to resist seeing our reality for what it is and prevents us from considering necessary steps to help us break free of an unchanging situation that's actually changing us.

When we fight against reality, we know it because we make judgmental statements about ourselves and our situation. We might think, "Things like this always happen to me," "Why can things never go my way?" or "It's never easy for me." "It's my own fault I'm in this mess." These thoughts all serve to distract us with unhealthy emotion, rather than helping us effectively deal with our reality through acceptance, problem-solving, and unbiased reasoning.

Acceptance is not pretending we are okay or trying to feel good about something that isn't good; it's just deciding to see it and act with intention rather than following the dead end of judgment. It frees up brain space and energy for us to make a positive impact where we can. And accepting our present circumstances helps us objectively look at our problems so we can approach them with wisdom. It's what frees us up to begin considering the solutions God places on our hearts or where He yearns for us to let go and rely on Him to fight our battles. You see, no amount of resistance has ever changed circumstances that were out of our hands. But again, the resistance can, however, change us.

Fighting our reality can surface in a lot of different ways that breed chronic negative emotion. Watch out for it in the form of words like "should," "wish," "must," or "can't." Even "why me" can be a trap, as we'll read about later. Watch out for the type of resistance that shows up in the form of attempting to blame or control someone else's behavior as a reason we can't change ourselves. Or extreme interpretations that leave us throwing up our hands in "complete" despair, refusing to do "anything" effective because "nothing" will help. Lastly, it can show up in the form of conditional "only-if" statements where we tell ourselves we can "only" be okay, "if" a certain thing happens. These are all ways we resist accepting the reality that is before us, and they stop us from engaging with our situations in ways that heal.

Accepting a difficult reality requires remembering that God is aware of our circumstances. He fights for us and holds us in His loving arms through every uncomfortable emotion. We are often reminded of His presence only when we stop judging our circumstance and truly look to Him to support us in it. We start to feel Him close to our fragile heart, our mind begins to clear, and we can see things we couldn't previously see. Acceptance of our reality is made easier when we embrace the idea that God is with us always, unconditionally, wholeheartedly, and continually, even when we can't see Him or feel Him. Learning to trust that happens often by experience.

Release Control

> Unless the Lord builds the house, those who build it labor in vain. Unless the Lord watches over the city, the watchman stays awake in vain. It is in vain that you rise up early and go late to rest, eating the bread of anxious toil; for he gives to his beloved sleep. —PSALM 127:1–2

People like to say that God never gives us more than we can handle, but if that were true, then we would never need God, right? We would just depend on ourselves because our own resources would be enough. Life throws a lot at us—often too much to bear on our own, by our own strength, ability, and perspective. Most of the time we encounter situations in which we need God more than ever. And when we try to live life controlling everything ourselves, trusting solely in our own ways, we often find ourselves struggling to succeed or facing the same trials again and again as we learn how to depend more fully on God.

And if we can keep God near in prayer, remember that He can be trusted, and accept reality as it is, then we can more easily release our need to be in control of every aspect of our lives, truly learning how to lay our worries at Christ's feet. In fact, God yearns for us to do so—we are to "cast all [our] anxieties on him because he cares for [us]" (1 Pet. 5:7) and accept God's gentle invitation to let him lighten our burden and relieve our worries by handing over everything that weighs us down (Matt. 11:28). Because with Him, we often learn that nothing is impossible (Luke 1:37).

But releasing control is easier said than done. In fact, it can be one of the hardest things to do—especially if you are someone who struggles with the need to be in control. We certainly struggle with this, ourselves! In fact, the idea of completely releasing something goes against our core, not because we lack faith but because our personalities make it more challenging. We can both be proactive, ambitious, conscientious, and very goal driven. It's easy for us to believe it's all about the choices *we* make and that *we* have to make everything happen.

What we have come to realize in trying circumstances is that God never expects us to sit back, give up, and do nothing. But He also never equipped us to be a one-man show, to navigate our troubles in self-dependent ways. He wanted us to be God-dependent. After all, God often uses our trials to remind us of His goodness, to reveal His glory, and to change us in ways we can't change ourselves. In our own lives, we have witnessed how little we can do without God, and the moment we choose to release control is often the moment we find rest in His presence and can watch as He works things out in ways we never could have imagined. And He often does so in much better ways than we ever could have done on our own. Looking back at our own lives, we can certainly see God's hand in everything we've had to walk through. The reminders are constant.

But to release the burden of control, we must work with the part of us that seeks control and believes that we hold all the power and responsibility for determining our destinies. How do we do that? We look up and remember to let go when we wrestle with things that feel impossible to manage. We remember what we cannot do, while remembering that God fights for us (Ex. 14:14), knows us intimately (Ps. 139:1–24, Heb. 4:12–13), and has power over our lives (Ps. 147:4–5; Jer. 32:17; I Cor. 2:5; Eph. 1:19). To release control is to honor the relationship we have with God, in every circumstance knowing He can and does use even the worst that comes against us in this life, for good (Rom. 8:28). The best example we have of this is the Cross. God took the great evil of the Crucifixion of our Lord, which was rooted in envy, power, and greed, and used it to bring salvation to the entire human race. To release control, we must meditate upon all of this, realizing in the midst of turmoil that we are held in the hands of an all-knowing and merciful God who acts with goodness to help us find rest as we abide in the fruit of His promises.

What does He promise?

- That when we are weak, He strengthens us (Is. 41:10)

- That as we sleep, He remains awake (Ps. 121:3)
- That He will be with us wherever we go (Josh. 1:9)
- That He will give us rest (Matt. 11:28)
- That as we submit to Him, He fights for us (Ps. 50:15; 1 Pet. 5:6–10)
- That He is faithful and will provide the way out (1 Cor. 10:13)
- That He will not fail or forsake us (Deut. 31:8)
- That for those who love Him, all things work together for good (Rom. 8:28)
- That He is always watching, listening, and knocking at the door of our hearts, just waiting for us to let Him in, so that He can direct our lives (Rev. 3:20)

God promises to work in our life to strengthen us and bring healing, perspective, and peace about the many tough moments we all experience in this life. But our peace in any circumstance can't begin until we turn back to God with all our heart and trust in Him to navigate our situation. When we rest in this relationship in the midst of our struggles, we feel God's presence and experience a deeper relationship with Him as we watch how He works things out. This is where trust is experienced and faith is developed.

God is our healer, and in all things, as we let go, we experience His promises. As 1 Peter 5:6–7 tells us, "Therefore humble yourselves under the mighty hand of God, that He may exalt you in due time, casting all your care upon Him, for He cares for you." Keep in mind, this cycle of letting go and finding rest is a circular one. When we release control, we find rest in God, and as we rest in our relationship with God, we feel more of His presence, which calls us further into faith and trust, reminding us to release control.

Keep the Right Perspective

The way we see our situations can make it easier or harder for us to surrender them to God. If we aren't careful, our difficulties can start to change us and make us lose perspective. When our soul is affected, we find ourselves angry and distant from God, forgetting all the ways He has worked in our life before. We may find ourselves praying less or not at all. When our heart is affected, we know it because our motivations shift. We may find ourselves feeling less pure of heart, and less led from a place of goodness, love, peace, and righteousness. When our mind is affected, we know it because our thoughts become more self-defeating, quarrelsome, bitter, lacking in mercy, or tainted with negativity or hopelessness. Perhaps this is why we hear in the Book of Isaiah that "You keep him in perfect peace / whose mind is stayed on you, / because he trusts in you" (Is. 26:3).

Keeping the right perspective greatly affects the peace with which we move through challenges and can affect the plans God has for our lives. This is why we are reminded to cling to our faith in all the ways we react to our most upsetting moments, which Paul says makes us "a vessel for honorable use, set apart as holy, useful to the master of the house, ready for every good work" (2 Tim. 2:21).

What ideas keep our perspectives grounded as we try to surrender our difficulties to Him?

GOD IS FAITHFUL

There's an aha moment I [Dr. Roxanne] experience every so often, when I suddenly realize God's presence in a storm. It's as if when the dust settles, I can suddenly see things clearly, and everything has come together exactly as it should— maybe not in all the ways I asked, but usually in ways I never could have planned. In all my worries, I can suddenly see God's goodness and faithfulness. Sometimes it's shortly after I've fallen to my knees in prayer; other times it's years later when I finally make the connection and can see His answer to my prayers, many of which I made long ago.

Think about your own life. Revisit the things that once worried you, and reflect on how they have worked out. This often reveals God's faithfulness. Sometimes God answers prayers with a simple "Yes." Other times He says "No." But He may also say, "Yes, but here's how," or, "Yes, but here's a better way." Sometimes, He says, "No, wait. This is not the time." He's always at work, even if we don't always see it through our pain. We may not see it until we are on the other side and our minds finally find rest. After all, a mind at rest is most capable of making connections.

Jot down your prayers from time to time. Go back and read through them, studying how God has worked to bring healing, reassurance, new perspectives, and peace. God always finds ways to remind us of His goodness, even in the greatest of storms. Whether the things we were worrying about resolved, or our perspective toward them changed, or we grew in ways we never expected, in hindsight we can always see how His light was present. So remembering that God is faithful is a perspective that helps us surrender.

GOD HAS EQUIPPED YOU

When we find some external circumstance upsetting, our stress can set into motion the narrative that something "must change" before we can be okay. But if we always seek our peace from the outside in, we remain in a constant state of stress, waiting on something to change for us to be okay. This leaves us feeling helpless and out of control, as if tossed by the waves of a storm. But Jesus didn't say "Don't worry" because there was nothing to worry about; He said "Don't worry" in spite of all the things there are to worry about.

We forget that God has equipped us to manage difficulty but not necessarily to think about having to do so. We often get the most stressed when we anticipate difficulty or envision worst-case scenarios. God has given us His Holy Spirit to help us manage anything we must confront, and He has equipped our minds with tremendous power to alter how we think about our circumstances when we are forced to confront them. Could it be that He knew we would stumble here instead of letting Him be our anchor?

If you are battling feelings you can't seem to shake, take a moment to pause, tune in, and listen. What do you hear? Are your thoughts helping you transcend your circumstance? Or are you envisioning worst-case scenarios? Don't forget the power of the Holy Spirit will be with you in anything you face. In the meantime, let your thoughts be led by God's voice.

GOD KNOWS AND LOVES YOU DEEPLY

The Bible says, "God shows his love for us in that while we were still sinners, Christ died for us" (Rom. 5:8). God didn't just say "I love you" on a postcard, but He demonstrated it. He came Himself, and He took on human form and was willing to experience pain and suffering and eventual crucifixion in order to grant us the ability to live with Him for eternity. He was willing to die in order for us to live.

Saint Paul reminds us that in effect, He was adopting us as sons and daughters. In all we endure in this life, the God we serve is close to us, close to the brokenhearted and familiar with suffering. In fact, it was because of our brokenness as a people that God sent His only begotten Son into this world to be our Savior and our Redeemer. He did this so that no matter what we face, no matter what we battle, no matter what we struggle with, He would meet us in the midst of all of it and walk with us by way of His Holy Spirit. And if you think God doesn't know your struggle, read Psalm 139, which begins, "O LORD, you have searched me and known me! / You know when I sit down and when I rise up; / you discern my thoughts from afar" (1–2). This psalm reminds us that God knows us deeply, our innermost thoughts and worries. He even knows our words before they are on our tongue. We read that we cannot flee from His presence not only because of His power but because of His great love for us.

So in our tougher moments, in order to remain undivided we must remember that we serve a God who is always on our side, stands at the door to our hearts, fights for us, walks with us, and yearns to lead us and give us eternal life. His only ask is that we turn back to Him in the midst of our turmoil and let Him lead the way, placing in His hands everything we are trying to unsuccessfully manage on our own. Today, let the peace of remembering whose you are help you feel His peace, despite circumstance, for as Scripture says, "Blessed are the people to whom such blessings fall! / Blessed are the people whose God is the Lord!" (Ps. 144:15), and "The Lord is near to all who call on him, / to all who call on him in truth" (Ps. 145:18). However bad things feel, no one can take God's love away from you.

God Always Wins

As we saw in the previous chapter, Christ has established His kingship over all creation and even over death. He has won, and His victory is still unfolding. Indeed, the Bible says:

> If God is for us, who can be against us? He who did not spare his own Son but gave him up for us all, how will he not also with him graciously give us all things? . . . Who shall separate us from the love of Christ? Shall tribulation, or distress, or persecution, or famine, or nakedness, or danger, or sword? . . . No, in all these things we are more than conquerors through him who loved us. (Rom. 8:31–32, 35–37)

God always wins. He has the last word. And we share in this victory when we choose to trust Him in our own battles so that we too will be victorious. Think about the story of Joseph in Genesis. He was sold into slavery and probably believed his life was over. But God lifted him up, and through a series of events, he became governor of Egypt. Seventeen years later there was a famine, and the very brothers who sold him into slavery were now coming to him, begging for food.

Look at the story of Peter in Matthew 26 and 28. Even after He denied Christ and was devastated by that choice, just a few days later Jesus invited him to a meal and said to him, "Peter, even though you denied Me, what I want you to do is feed my sheep." And look at Jesus, Himself. He was crucified and even cried out that God had abandoned Him. But on the third day He rose, and God's purpose prevailed.

DEATH IS NOT THE END

We know that because of the Resurrection, death is not the end. We know that there is life after death. It says in the Book of Hebrews, "Since therefore the children share in flesh and blood, he himself likewise partook of the same things, that through death he might destroy the one who has the power of death, that is, the devil, and deliver all those who through fear of death were subject to lifelong slavery" (Heb. 2:14–15). In other words, death is not the worst thing that can happen to us. We don't need to despair that our suffering might end us—because it is not really the end.

Also, we can remember that the present troubles we're going through right now won't last forever. But they are producing in us an eternal glory that is going to last forever (2 Cor. 4:14, 16–17). The worst thing life can do to us—kill us—only sends us into the arms of the Father who loves us without condition and beyond human understanding. So, as we struggle through our difficult moments, if we can't change our circumstances, we may need to confront and change our perspectives—to remember our faith—as we walk through them.

Wait and Hope

We want answers and solutions *now*, but the Bible counsels us to lean into God and to trust in Him fully as our refuge and our hope (Ps. 18:2). A refuge is a place of retreat to wait out trouble, and hope is always future-oriented. The peace we have is not in being free from trouble but in knowing our troubles will not last, are not greater than God, and will be made right in the end.

Beyond bringing us peace, in the waiting it helps to remember that God often uses our difficulties "so that [His works] might be displayed in [us]" (John 9:3). The Bible also tells us that "[His] power is made perfect in weakness" (2 Cor. 12:9), meaning we must expect to feel weak and be brought low sometimes if we are to experience God's power. It's easier to wait when we remember that God is working for our good and demonstrates His power best through us, when we are struggling, even if we can't see how it's all going to come together in the end.

It's also easier to wait when we remember that we are not products of our circumstances but of God's promises: "For I know the plans I have for you, declares the Lord, plans for welfare and not for evil, to give you a future and a hope" (Jer. 29:11).

So if you are feeling defeated or facing setback after setback, remember that God does not let go of us until He's accomplished His work in us. Remain steadfast in prayer, trust in His goodness, and never let go of the hope of His promises.

Remember That God Can Use Our Suffering for Good!

While God does not cause suffering, He knows it is inevitable. Life comes with so many ups and downs on the way to realizing our hopes and dreams, and the universality of human struggle is ever before us. Yet, because we know that God never leaves us, we must be open to how God will use it, rather than allowing our feelings to overtake our trust in God. You see, trusting God in defeat is never easy, but we also know that the development of good things within us rarely comes without challenge, difficulty, setback, and disappointment. Think about gratitude. We cultivate it more deeply and authentically when we have experienced being without something. God can help steady us during our own metamorphosis, but we have to be willing to see our circumstance from an eternal perspective, which God will use to change others and to change us.

When we try to see our circumstances in this way, as a sanctifying process, it really helps us lay our realities at His feet. Take, for instance, having to endure a difficult relationship. When we allow God to work through our situation to bring about something better, we might find ourselves praying for the person who has hurt us, recognizing they are not necessarily the enemy we fight. While those prayers sometimes change the person we pray for, they most certainly change us because we remember compassion, mercy, forgiveness, and who we are truly up against, and we let go of doing the work in someone else that only God can do. Simply said, responding in faith to our struggles changes us. This is what Paul meant when he said, "We rejoice in our sufferings, knowing that suffering produces endurance, and endurance produces character, and character produces hope, and hope does not put us to shame, because God's love has been poured into our hearts through the Holy Spirit who has been given to us" (Rom. 5:3–5).

Because we know that God never leaves us, we must be open to how He will use our suffering rather than allowing our feelings to overcome our faith in Him.

Choose to Focus Less on the Why and More on the What

> *For the sake of Christ, then, I am content with weaknesses, insults, hardships, persecutions, and calamities. For when I am weak, then I am strong.* —2 CORINTHIANS 12:10

Life is filled with things we will never understand. From the stress of mild struggle to the wounds of severe trauma, God, in His love and faithfulness, preserves us. "Though I walk in the midst of trouble, you preserve my life; you stretch out your hand against the wrath of my enemies and your right hand delivers me" (Ps. 138:7). And yet, so often when we go through this, we can ask the question, "Why is this happening? Why, God, are you allowing this?" And in the judgment and anger that ensues, we must remember three things.

First, God never promised us that this world would be fair or kind to us. In fact, He said, Don't be blind about this. He tells His disciples in John 16:33 that they will in fact face trials and difficulties. But take courage. Be strong; refocus. For I am with you and have already overcome this world. Second, God doesn't create our pain. We know that nothing but good can come from God, that all of His ways are loving (Ps. 25:10; 145:17). Third, we know that God promises to take whatever pain we face in this life and use it to shape and refine our souls. The Bible says in Romans 5:3–4, "Not only that, but we rejoice in our sufferings, knowing that suffering produces endurance, and endurance produces character, and character produces hope." In another translation it says that our troubles develop virtue in us, keeping us alert for whatever God will do next. And in our own lives, if we were to think about the most defining and important moments that changed us, refined His image in us, and grew us, we would describe our most difficult moments or transformational seasons, not the celebratory ones. And this is how God works. Peter speaks to our transformation in suffering when he says, "In this you rejoice, though now for a little while, if necessary, you have been grieved by various trials, so that the tested genuineness of your faith—more precious than gold that perishes though it is tested by fire—may be found to result in praise and glory and honor at the revelation of Jesus Christ" (I Pet. 1:6–7).

So we can't tie ourselves in knots trying to understand why we're going through a dark time. Dark times happen. Period. We don't always know in the midst of them how they will be used in our life. But God does not cause them, and He is faithful to pull us through them. We must try to focus our energy on drawing near to God and on what He may be working inside us through our pain. Consider questions like: "What am I learning as I contend with this battle? What is God changing within me? How did my last difficulty change me?" and "How might His image in me be changing? Have I learned to listen to God's voice in this?"

The goal of the maturing Christian is to be continually engaged in growth through struggle, knowing we are not yet perfected in His image. When it gets hard, it helps to remember to "trust in the LORD with all your heart, / and do not lean on your own understanding. / In all your ways acknowledge him, / and he will make straight your paths" (Prov. 3:5–6).

We rest in knowing that when our hardships overwhelm our abilities, it is in our weakness when the power of Christ comes alive within us (2 Cor. 12), and we can remember that He's changing us. Saint Paul even writes:

> Not that I have already obtained this or am already perfect, but I press on to make it my own, because

Christ Jesus has made me his own. Brothers, I do not consider that I have made it my own. But one thing I do: forgetting what lies behind and straining forward to what lies ahead, I press on toward the goal for the prize of the upward call of God in Christ Jesus. (Phil. 3:12–14)

So while we may not understand everything in this life, we can be confident in our hardest moments that because God loves us so much, He is helping us become in practice what we already are in spirit; that as we adjust, accept, and allow God to grow us through every difficulty, He transforms us and strengthens us.

Trust in God

But they who wait [hope] for the Lord shall renew their strength; they shall mount up with wings like eagles; they shall run and not be weary; they shall walk and not faint. —ISAIAH 40:31

As faithful believers, we know we are called to trust in God, to turn to Him in the midst of our worries. But truthfully, at times, if we're honest, it's hard not to worry. Our difficulties can make us lose sight of our faith and the things that once made us feel a stable foundation beneath our feet. Our seasons of strife, scary circumstances, and daily worries can feel overwhelming at times; whether it be our children, our health, our finances, our extended family, the state of the world, the conflict we don't seem to handle well, the problems we don't know how to fix, or the special someone we worry we will never meet. During these times we can find ourselves more focused on our worries than on who we are and who Christ is. We forget that in our worries, it is He who promises to sustain us, to replenish us, to fill us with new perspectives, to open new doors, to give us renewed strength for what we feel up against in this world, and to positively convict us to lead a life of purpose.

The key to winning our battles, according to David, is not to rely on our own strength but to put our trust in God. At the end of the day, human strength and power are not enough: "The king is not saved by his great army; a warrior is not delivered by his great strength. / The war horse is a false hope for salvation, and by its great might it cannot rescue" (Ps. 33:16–17). Trust in God is not the absence of fear; it is going forward in the presence and light of God. Jesus said, "I am the light of the world. Whoever follows me will never walk in darkness, but will have the light of life" (John 8:12). In other words, God can bring "light" to our story. The Bible also says that faith is the substance of things hoped for; it is a spiritual attitude, the belief that He is not only willing but able to sustain us. Faith is what paves the way for joy, possibilities, and hope.

Even when we can't see how things could possibly come together, we must remember that "faith is the assurance of things hoped for, the conviction of things not seen" (Heb. 11:1). God sees the whole picture, even while we only see a fragment of it. He sees the growth that is necessary for us to live our lives in the fullness of His will.

God even invites us to call out to Him when we are in need: "Call upon me in the day of trouble; / I will deliver you, and you shall glorify me" (Ps. 50:15). So, let us all set our eyes and our hearts on the one true God who carries us through every hurt of this life so that we may have everlasting lives with Him. And let us never forget that spending time in the presence of God and trusting in Him is the most important thing we can do at all times, but especially in a state of hurt, as it is His presence that we need more than we need anything else.

Listen for His Voice

When we need assurance of things hoped for but not yet seen, we need to incline our ears to hear God's voice. "My sheep hear my voice, and I know them, and they follow me," Jesus says (John 10:27).

The other day, I (Roxanne) could feel the stress of my day settling into my shoulders as it typically does. Unexpected frustrations were pushing in, crowding out my present awareness, filling me with the burden of more demands atop the ones I already had. I felt so much distance from any semblance of the peace I remembered feeling only yesterday. What did I need to hear? I wasn't sure. But I knew I needed to hear God's voice, which always calms, comforts, encourages, leads, reassures, and stills. Yes, stills. When I struggle to hear it, I usually reach for it by reading it. So, I went to one of my favorite Bible apps for a word of encouragement. I opened it up, and there it was: my scripture for today read,

"In my distress I called upon the Lord; to my God I called. From his temple he heard my voice, and my cry came to his ears" (2 Sam. 22:7).

Once again, His voice brought comfort. No matter our situation, when we call on God, He hears us. Father Nicholas and I are always amazed that the guidance we seek most comes to us when we reach for it, even though we couldn't hear it only moments earlier. God's voice comforts and stills, silencing the noise of this world and bringing peace back to our souls. Any other voice is not from Him.

We know that God gives wisdom to all who ask for it (James 1:5). But why is it that sometimes we ask but do not hear? God says that we must approach our asking with belief and not doubt. "But let him ask in faith, with no doubting, for the one who doubts is like a wave of the sea that is driven and tossed by the wind" (James 1:6). And yet, how often do we come to God so caught up in our worries that we are not really caught up in trusting Him to lead our situations? In our worries, we sometimes forget that God has us all in the palm of His loving hand; that He intimately knows us and yearns to teach us, lead us, guide us, open our hearts and minds, and grow us according to His will.

When we come to God, we must listen for His voice with a trusting heart, with a pure heart. We need nothing more, in our stressful times of affliction, than God's wisdom, leadership, and guidance. But when we close our hearts to His help because of doubt, we feel distant from Him at a time when we need Him most. Instead, we must listen for His voice, remembering that God is bigger than our worries. So, if you have been praying for something and can't hear God, try opening your heart more fully, trusting Him more sincerely, and reading His Word more deeply and reflectively. He hears you. "Then you will call on me and come and pray to me, and I will listen to you. You will seek me and find me when you seek me with all your heart" (Jer. 29:12–13). "For the eyes of the Lord are on the righteous and His ears are attentive to their prayer" (I Pet. 3:12).

Consider a worry you are holding today. Sit back, take a renewing breath, and open your worries in conversation with God. Do you feel goodwill? Do you feel pure of heart as you pray about it? Have you asked God for what you need? The Bible tells us that many were healed because they asked, and Jesus had compassion on them (Matt. 8:13; Mark 5:22–24, 7:26). So "do not be anxious about anything, but in everything by prayer and supplication with thanksgiving let your requests be made known to God. And the peace of God, which surpasses all understanding, will guard your hearts and your minds in Christ Jesus" (Phil. 4:6–7).

For Discussion: The Three Rs— Rest, Reflect, and Respond

1. What's your greatest worry in this moment? How are you explaining this situation to yourself?

2. What are your thoughts like when it comes to this worry? Are they life-giving? Do they restore hope? Peace? Resilience? Trust?

3. Do you feel stuck worrying about the same thing over and over again with no new perspective?

4. Have you prayed about it? Truly prayed about it?

5. How are you talking to yourself about this struggle that could be blocking your ability to accept your circumstance, respond adaptively to it, and truly surrender the part you can't change?

6. Are you stuck in blame? Judgment?

7. Are you getting stuck on the question of why?

8. Are you immobilized by fear?

9. Is it starting to change your soul? (Have you stopped trusting God? Are you angry with Him?) Your heart? (Do you feel less pure of heart and led by goodness?)

Your perspectives? (Have you lost sight of who God is in your difficulties?)

10. Are you trying to manage it all by yourself?

11. Have you been in ongoing conversation with God through prayer? Or do you feel distant? When was the last time you truly opened up? Emptied your stream of consciousness to Him? Shared the good and the bad?

12. How could holding on to this be hurting you or making your situation worse?

13. Have you accepted the reality of your difficulty? Or are you stuck in judgment about it?

14. What is one step you could take to release control over your circumstance? To entrust it to God? To lay what you can't control at the feet of Christ?

15. What does God promise that reminds us to release control?

16. What good have you seen in other situations when you entrusted something to Him?

17. What perspective do you struggle to internalize the most? That God is faithful? That He has equipped

you to handle it? That He loves you deeply? That He always wins?

18. What can you remember in the waiting?

19. What good has been developed within you through difficulty?

20. What could God be developing within you through this circumstance?

21. Do you hear God's voice in the way you are managing it? Thinking about it?

22. Have you asked God for healing?

PRAYER

O Heavenly Father, the King of Glory, the Son of Righteousness, I praise You today and every day for the sacrifice that You made on that Friday. I give glory to You, Father, who sent Your Son to deliver us from the darkness of our sins. From the depths of my heart, with every part of my being, I want to say "thank You." Thank You for the gift of today, the blessings to breathe, and the love that You have for me, despite my many offenses. Even with all the daily miracles You shower down upon me, I recognize that throughout my life, I have a tendency to depend more on myself than on You. Sometimes, I find myself even trying to manage You and telling You how a problem should be solved. For this reason, I call upon You to help me remember that You are always with me, fighting for me and working out Your purpose through my circumstances. Remind me that it was out of Your love that You came and saved us. Not only in the dark seasons in my life but also in the bright seasons, remind me that the greatest distance I will travel each day is the twenty-two inches for my knees to hit the ground in prayer to spend time with You. Renew my soul to remember Your words on the Cross and to place my life in Your compassionate arms. For You are the God of strength, wisdom, and comfort, and I commit my soul to You, the Father, Son, and Holy Spirit, now and forever. Amen.

CONCLUSION

A S WE COME to a close and you begin to put into practice these lessons from the Cross, we want to encourage you with some final thoughts. Take one last journey with us back to the moments after the death of Christ. On that Friday, the disciples and followers of Christ were filled with tremendous pain as well as great fear. Not only had they witnessed the One who had shown them the love of God and declared the promised Kingdom being brutally tortured and murdered, but they also knew that they could be arrested and suffer the same fate. The day we call Great and Holy Friday was the worst day of their lives. They retreated to their lodgings that night, overwhelmed with emotional, spiritual, and physical darkness. We can imagine they struggled with confusion about their faith. Had they been wrong about Jesus, or had God not fulfilled His promise?

We wrote this book for all of you who feel these desperate Friday feelings, for the times when you are scared, angry, distressed, overwhelmed, hurt—and wondering where God is in it all. We know Sunday mornings feel like times to be cheerful, hopeful, and worshipful, but the fact is, we do not always feel cheerful, hopeful, or worshipful. Sometimes we come to church on a Sunday morning with Friday evening feelings in our hearts. We want you to know that the disciples themselves felt the same way. They had walked with Jesus, broken bread with Him, and learned at His feet—and still they felt desperate and abandoned by God when Jesus was killed. Not only that, but this book is premised on the idea that Jesus Himself felt these things—and He was on intimate terms with the Father! In other words, there is no darkness so dark that Jesus hasn't also been through it, so deep that He can't carry you through it.

No doubt the forces of death and darkness were jubilant on that Friday, for they thought they had fulfilled their mission. Death thought that he had prevailed over the Giver of life. Neither earthly nor spiritual beings knew what we all know today: that Sunday was coming. They didn't understand on that Friday that the world would soon change forever. They were unaware on Friday that on Sunday, their fear and pain would be replaced with freedom and joy, that "Why have you forsaken me?" would be replaced with "He is risen!" He turned the symbol of death into a symbol of victory. This is why St. Paul writes, adapting Hosea, " 'O death, where is your victory? / O death, where is your sting?' The sting of death is sin, and the power of sin is the law. But thanks be to God, who gives us the victory through our Lord Jesus Christ" (I Cor. 15:55–57).

The author of death thought that he had put a period at the end of the life of Christ, but we know that Christ allowed it to be a comma, a pause on the way to the promise of eternal life. One of the most triumphant hymns in Christianity proclaims, "Christ is risen from the dead, trampling down death by death, and upon those in the tomb bestowing life." Christ has given us a new life. Saint Paul writes, "Just as Christ was raised from the dead by the glory of the Father, we too might walk in newness of life. For if we have been united with him in a death like his, we shall certainly be united with him in a resurrection like his" (Rom. 6:4–5). Because He died and rose, we will rise and live. His pain gave us a new purpose.

Our prayer is that this book will be a tool for you on the Fridays of life, not only to remember these seven lessons, but to recognize that no matter what comes against you, it is not greater than the amazing God who has risen from the dead for you. The Bible says that the same Spirit that raised Christ from the dead is in you (Rom. 8:11). This doesn't mean that things are always going to work out the way we had hoped or imagined. As we have shared in this book, Christ never promises that earth is supposed to be heaven. It's not. In fact, your Fridays may end up being longer than you thought. For some of you, the hurt and pain will persist, and you may not experience the true comfort, peace, and healing of God on this side of life. But make no mistake: Easter Sunday changes everything. Our job is to activate that spirit within us by trusting in God, surrendering to His will, and recognizing that God has a purpose and plan for us to share His resurrected light, even during the Fridays of life. Constantly seek to become the person that Christ has created you to be so that you can work to fulfill His dream for your life. Challenge yourself each day to inscribe the words of St. Paul on your heart: "I have been crucified with Christ. It is no longer I who live, but Christ who lives in me" (Gal. 2:20).

We hope that this book has left you feeling more equipped and empowered through Christ to deal with the Fridays of life. Don't be discouraged when you find yourself in a Friday time of life. That will happen to us all. Stay encouraged, knowing that you are not alone. Christ is there walking with you, step by step: "Even though I walk through the valley of the shadow of death, / I will fear no evil, / for you are with me" (Ps. 23:4).

Thank you for allowing us to join you on this journey. And now, with renewed strength and conviction, let's take up our cross and follow Him!

ALSO FROM THE LOUHS:

RENEWING YOU

A PRIEST, A PSYCHOLOGIST, AND A PLAN

Are you struggling in your walk with Christ? Do you want to rediscover your reason for living, the person you were created to be? *Renewing You: A Priest, a Psychologist, and a Plan* gives you the keys to unlock areas of your life that hold you back from fully experiencing the renewal and transformation God has in mind for you.

Scan this QR code to find it at store.ancientfaith.com.

We hope you have enjoyed and benefited from this book. Your financial support makes it possible to continue our nonprofit ministry both in print and online. Because the proceeds from our book sales only partially cover the costs of operating **Ancient Faith Publishing** and **Ancient Faith Radio**, we greatly appreciate the generosity of our readers and listeners. Donations are tax deductible and can be made at **www.ancientfaith.com**.

To view our other publications,
please visit our website: **store.ancientfaith.com**

Bringing you Orthodox Christian music, readings, prayers, teaching, and podcasts 24 hours a day since 2004 at **www.ancientfaith.com**